THE
PALESTINIAN
TABLE

THE
PALESTINIAN
TABLE

Reem Kassis

INTRODUCTION

Journey from Jerusalem

I was born to parents from two very different parts of the country. My mother is a Palestinian Muslim from Jaljulya, a rural village in the center of the country famous for its orchards and hearty cooking. My father is a Palestinian Christian from Rameh, a mountain village in the very north, famous for its olive groves and distinctive oil.

I grew up in Jerusalem, a melting pot of foods, religion, and cultures. In a society where marriage was still considered one of a woman's greatest achievements, my parents wanted to ensure my path was different. They always hammered home the importance of education: the great equalizer, key to locked doors, ticket to a larger life.

While I relished the hours my mother was not home and I could sneak into the kitchen to experiment with cooking, mostly, I focused on my schooling. So it came as no surprise when at the age of seventeen I brought home acceptance letters from multiple top US universities.

Soon after, someone we knew quipped to my father, "Why bother paying for such an expensive education? Don't you know, like all Arab women, she is going to end up in the kitchen?"

When I heard this, I was furious. Disheartened even. Indeed, I had seen my grandmothers, my mother, and many aunts, despite their education, spend their days kneading, stirring, stuffing, frying, and feeding. Some part of me must have wondered with anxiety if that would be my destiny too, but I was determined it would not.

So I left for the United States, promising myself that, unlike the great women in my family, I would never return to the kitchen.

Of course I loved my country and my family, but I had other dreams. I wanted to discover something outside the confines of a strong and beautiful, albeit traditional, culture. Little did I know that my journey would take me back to the place where I started, to the kitchen, as a changed person, with a newfound appreciation for the very things I sought to avoid.

For ten years before getting to that point, I worked hard to prove myself, to advance professionally, to succeed. And I did...Professional degrees, glamorous jobs, long hours, and a hectic lifestyle. Along the way, I also fell in love. He was a Palestinian, we shared the same love of food, culture, and a relentless ambition to move forward. After a courtship impeded by political constraints, we moved to London, got married, and a year later I was pregnant with our first daughter, Yasmeen.

I had, by almost any measure, succeeded. I had made my point. While I was happy with how things had turned out,

I had a nagging feeling something was missing. In those moments, I reflected most on the events, coincidences, and ambitions that had led me to this point.

A Change of Direction

My journey with cooking had started years before, when I first left Jerusalem. Back then, I would cook to take me back to my family's kitchen, to the warmth and love I missed. I treasured my family's recipes, and being far away, I found comfort in recreating them when I needed a reminder of home the most. For many years, I continued to cook to recreate the flavors of my childhood, but I also experimented with different ingredients when the ones I wanted weren't available. I shortened and simplified. I tried new recipes and techniques, and I fell back on trusted classics. I cooked for my own family and everyone from acquaintances to closest friends. But I would always return to the "real" professional life I had created for myself.

Still, as much as I tried to avoid it, food infiltrated every aspect of my life. When I went out to eat or heard recommendations from friends about "Arabic" food I should try, I was always disappointed and surprised. Standard mezze and grills had become synonymous with Middle Eastern food, and more recently, chefs simply sprinkled dishes with pomegranates and za'atar and dubbed them Middle Eastern. This oversimplification deeply frustrated me, because our Palestinian food was too unique to be lumped under a single umbrella. It was vaster than a few generic plates, and it was deeper than a sprinkling of spices.

I didn't want the dishes that had survived generations and were still revered to be marred or forgotten. I wanted people to know what real Palestinian food was, to experience it the way I did growing up, the way mothers and grandmothers cooked it to nourish their families' bodies and souls, and to feel the same sense of joy I did through food.

Most of all, I wanted my future children to grow up knowing real Palestinian home cooking and to have a way to preserve our family recipes. They had been such an integral part of my life and I wanted to pass that along.

When my first daughter, Yasmeen, was born, I took some time off from work. It was the first time my motivation for doing things was someone else's happiness, not mine. So with very little sleep, I found myself spending more and more time in the kitchen thinking about our food, and what it meant to me.

As I was contemplating going back to work, my husband asked me, "If you could do anything in the world, what would it be?"

"I would write," I replied. "I would write, and talk to people, and I would also cook. I like cooking."

"So why aren't you doing that then?" he asked in the most matter-of-fact way only he could muster.

There are many reasons not to, I thought. I had worked too hard on a different path. I had no classical training as a chef. I came up with a million other reasons. But deep down, I knew he had a point.

I thought about all the years I had been calling my mother to ask cooking questions. I had heard stories, learned recipes, and spoken to people inside my family and out. Here I was, now, with recipes from my mother, grandmothers, aunts, neighbors, friends, and relatives. Recipes from neighborhoods, villages, and cities, and with every recipe there was a story, a snapshot of life, history, and family. In my mind, they came together to tell the often overlooked narrative of a country and its people.

I concluded that those recipes did not belong to my family alone. They were foods tied to different seasons and events, to sadness and joy, to times of peace and times of war. They were a Palestinian chronicle—a tale of identity—and I wanted to give them back by sharing them with the world and using them as a bridge to better understand Palestinian culture, food, and way of life.

The Women in My Family Who Inspired My Cooking

Teta Asma
"Where is Teta Asma?" I remember asking one day when I didn't see my paternal grandmother in her usual spot at the breakfast table. "She's gone down to the village hall to taste the food for tonight's wedding," I was told.

I must have been no more than four years old at the time, but I remember feeling frustrated that my grandmother wasn't there for breakfast and not understanding why wedding food needed tasting, let alone why she had to do it.

Years later, I understood.

The town people would call my grandmother to sample the food for any big gathering because they considered her the best cook in their village, Rameh—with the most refined taste.

Teta Fatima
"Fatima *akeed* has a secret she doesn't share," I had heard the gossipy village women scoffing at my uncle's henna, so I kept nagging my mother to explain what these women meant about my maternal grandmother. She instructed me to leave the kitchen that night because everyone was busy preparing the food for the henna. The following day though, she explained what they were talking about: Teta Fatima was considered the best cook in their town, Jaljulya, and she really did have a secret. Wide-eyed at seven-years-old and anticipating a riveting fairy-tale like revelation, I was somewhat disappointed to hear my mother explain, "it's love, Reem. Teta Fatima just loves cooking."

Mama

"Nisreen is cooking!" I often heard this in eager tones from cousins, classmates, teachers, neighbors, and friends. I could not understand why the prospect of eating my mother's food evoked delight in people. I ate her food every day and it certainly didn't thrill me or my brother or father in the same way. When I finally left home for the US at seventeen and had to eat in dining halls, restaurants, and other people's kitchens, I began to realize why the fact that "Nisreen is cooking" was so special.

Throughout my life, I have been fortunate to eat at these remarkable women's tables. At times I took them for granted. Other times, I cooked with them, learned from them, or simply enjoyed their company and food. While I may not have seen it happening at the time, looking back, it is clear to me how much of who I am and what I have done with my life has been shaped by these remarkable women.

The Palestinian Table

Growing up, there was the food we ate at our kitchen table in Jerusalem, and the food we ate at my grandmothers' tables in their villages. It was delicious, it was made with love, and it was *our* food. But the thought of these foods making up a Palestinian Table was an elusive notion at the time. Not until I left home for another country did I grasp the undeniable importance of food to national identity and the intricacies associated with defining it.

On my journey to bring these pages to your hands, I came to a quiet clarity: there is no single Palestinian Table. The Palestinian Table spans our entire geography from the mountains of the Galilee to the valleys of the south, from the coast of Yaffa all the way to the West Bank. It is scattered across the globe and built from memories of a time when most of us lived in the same land. In spite of our political circumstances and global dispersion, what ties all Palestinian tables together is more than just good food; it is the notion of "home", the spirit of generosity, the importance of family, and the value of bringing people together.

One of the few things I regret about living abroad is that my own daughters won't get to enjoy that same kind of slow lifestyle with a bevy of aunts, grandmothers, and family cooks coming together around a Palestinian family table, laden with food, steeped in laughter and conversation, and boasting the stories and knowledge of generations. Through the recipes and stories in this book, however, I hope that they can carry our history, our food, our culture, and our home wherever they go in the world and never be too far away from a Palestinian Table.

Left
Coffee pots in a market in the
Old City of Jerusalem.

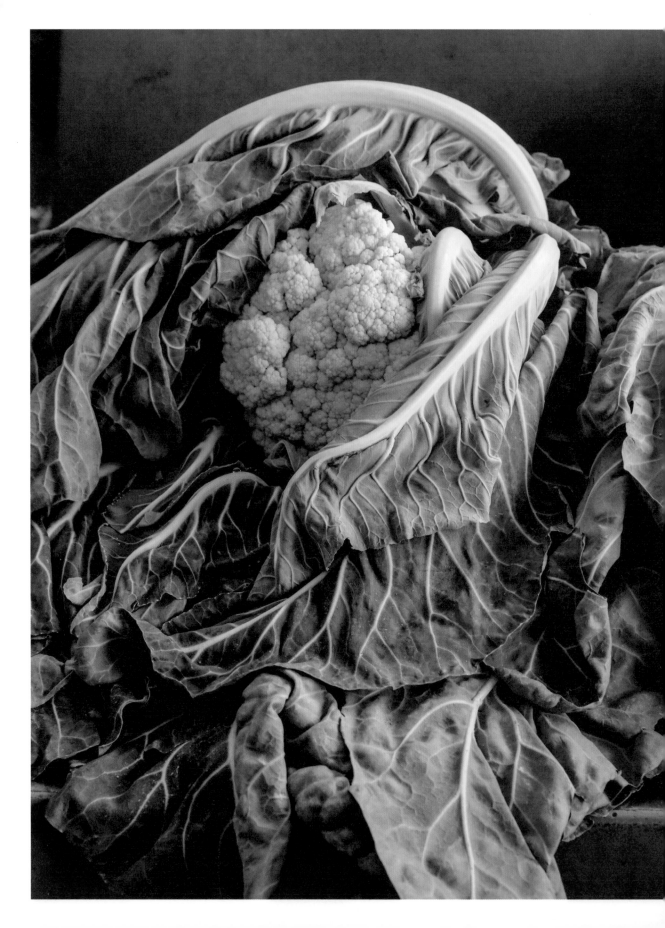

HOW WE COOK

If you've ever tried to get a recipe from a Palestinian mother or grandmother, you'll know the agony that is trying to obtain exact measurements. Often, when I would get together with my mother to test recipes, she would lecture me on why exact measurements don't work.

"But mama, it's a cookbook!" I would try to explain. "I cannot tell people to 'add flour until it's soft like your earlobe' or 'cook until the bottom of pot sizzles' or 'use a tea cup not a coffee mug.'" So for the first runs of many recipes, I measured dry ingredients out exactly, poured them into her hands, and watched what she used, then measured again. She had to do things by touch, by sight, by smell and sound.

Almost everyone I know back home cooks this way. My mother and grandmothers all insisted that recipes could only get you so far.

With that said, Palestinian food is very forgiving, and a little more or less of something in a recipe is not going to alter it dramatically. Spicing and seasoning really do come down to preference. While one cook might prefer a salad so sour it makes your lips tingle, another might like it with barely a squeeze of lemon.

I want to help you recreate dishes that are as close as possible to the ones I enjoy at home, so I have meticulously and painstakingly measured out the ingredients to make the recipes easy to follow. I have also explained the flavor profile to look for; how salty or sour or crunchy or soft something needs to be, and what kind of result you want. Where possible, I have also explained what substitutions and adjustments work well. Once you've followed the main points of a recipe, trust your instincts with the rest. The more you cook, the better you will get to know the recipes as well as your own preferences for their flavor.

Left
Cauliflower from a vegetable market in Jerusalem.

HOW WE EAT

Tighmees

Roughly translating as "dipping," *tighmees* refers to one
of the most common methods of eating in the entire Arab
world. But it is much more than dipping a piece of bread in
hummus. It is a way of life for Palestinians. Bread is like
a utensil to scoop up food—everything from eggs and meat
and stews to dips and fresh salads. We do not dip the bread
in the food though, rather, we shape it into a scoop and use
the bread itself to pick up food. So for many of the recipes
in this book you will need bread as an accompaniment.

The Composition of a Meal

Palestinian meals can be simple or elaborate affairs, and you
can serve one dish or fifteen at the same time, depending
on occasion. Even a very simple meal is never a singular dish,
however. There is almost always a plate of olives or pickles
on the table, many times fresh yogurt or fresh vegetables,
and often accompaniments to the main meal include salads
or spreads. Bread is also readily available.

   Meals comprise one or more dishes intended to be
shared and eaten family style. These dishes, when taken as
a whole, usually strike a fine balance of flavors, textures,
and spices. *Maqlubeh* (page 198), for example, is almost
always served alongside fresh yogurt and Palestinian Salad
(page 104). *Kafta* dishes (pages 147–153) are frequently
served alongside rice and pickles. Grain dishes like freekeh
(page 162), taste best with sharp flavors like the Tomato,
Garlic, and Sumac Salad (page 99).

   ·The choice can vary from family to family and even
from day to day within a family. When Palestinians have
guests over or a large gathering, the number and variety
of dishes also increases dramatically. For the purposes
of this book, every recipe includes serving and
accompaniment suggestions so that the dish can be
served as a stand-alone meal.

Serving Quantities

Because Palestinians eat family style, and because a meal
often comprises multiple dishes, it's difficult to specify
exact serving sizes. My recipes tend to be quite generous,
feeding a minimum of four people, especially when served
with rice, bread, or sides. The serving sizes are for guidance
only and can vary depending on what else you are serving.

   Most recipes can also easily be halved or doubled.
Moreover, many of the dishes taste just as good, if not
better, the following day. So even if you are cooking for
only two, you can make the full quantity to consume
the rest the next day, or freeze for a later time.

<u>Left</u>
Diners in a restaurant
in Jerusalem.

THE IMPORTANCE OF GOOD INGREDIENTS

My best piece of advice to you as you cook from this book is to use the best ingredients you can find.

Good ingredients are the key to good food, but nowhere is this more evident than in simple dishes made up of only a few items, where the flavor of ingredients truly stands out.

Whenever possible, keep these principles in mind for the freshest and best tasting dishes:

— Buy your spices whole, then roast and grind them at home. Not only is it more economical (spice grinders are very affordable and whole spices are cheaper than ready ground), it also ensures you know what is going into your food. Moreover, freshly ground spices guarantee a fresher and deeper flavor to your cooking.

— Make your own stock (chicken, beef, or lamb) in bulk and freeze it. Good quality stock makes a huge difference. It can also be boiled down and concentrated, to take up less space, then diluted with water for cooking. If you are pressed for time, use a good quality store-bought kind (usually it will be refrigerated) and ensure there are no additives or "flavors" in the ingredients list.

— Choose local, fresh produce in season whenever possible. When not available, good quality frozen (okra, mlukhiyeh, beans, and peas), dried (mint, za'atar, mlukhiyeh) and jarred (tomatoes) substitutes are also a good option.

— Buy fresh meat and fish directly from your butcher or fishmonger if possible. For ground meat, ask to have it freshly ground in front of you from cuts of meat you have chosen. The less meats are handled, stored, and processed, the fresher and better the end result.

— Finally, and most importantly, invest in a good bottle of olive oil and use it for everything, except deep frying. You may be tempted to purchase a more affordable bottle because it also says extra virgin, but oils are not created equal and price is often a good indicator. My family produces our own olive oil, so I have rarely had to purchase it. When I do, I choose an oil that is darker in color, packaged in darker bottles or tins, has a date of harvest or pressing on it, is not mass marketed, and is either Palestinian or has a Protected Designation of Origin (PDO).

Left
Vegetables in a market
in Jerusalem.

Overleaf
Goat farm in the mountains around
Rameh village in the Galilee;
shepherd Aref tending to one of
the goats on his farm.

THE BASICS

There is a certain magic to Jerusalem, the city where I grew up, that has to be experienced in all its sights, sounds, and smells to grasp the full depth of its life, from the thawb-clad women carrying baskets of fresh produce on their heads to the sounds of *ka'ak* (bread) carts on cobblestone streets; from the cries of the vendors touting their goods to the tune of the muezzin and the ring of church bells. But it is the smells and flavors that really bring the city to life for me: freshly ground spices, brewed mint tea, and taboon bread straight from the oven.

Just like these many aspects make Jerusalem the city that it is, Palestinian cooking is also about the layering of flavors to produce dishes that are greater than the sum of their parts. So it's very important to understand the basics of our cuisine before you embark on a culinary journey with this book, and this chapter will help you do just that by providing the foundational recipes on which many of the dishes are built. These recipes might seem humble and unassuming—a spice mix, a broth, and some fried nuts, for example—but it is these very elements that will give many dishes in this book an immense depth of flavor.

Much of what I learned about these nuances of Palestinian cooking came from observing the women in my family "in action". In three kitchens, from Jerusalem to Galilee, I picked up many tips and secrets to the best Palestinian home cooking from snippets of conversation: "never stop stirring the yogurt you're cooking or it will curdle," "rice dishes always have to rest before plating," "add yogurt to tahini sauces to break their richness," and so on. But if I've learned one thing from cooking with the women in my family, the real secret to good cooking is love: love for what you're doing, for the ingredients, for the process, and most of all, love for the people you are feeding.

So think of the following recipes as a way to give the other dishes in this book more love. Lamb with Onion and Spices (page 30), for example, is called for in many recipes throughout as a stuffing. The sweetness from the onions combined with the heat from the spices and the crunch from the nuts gives the resulting dishes added texture and aromatic notes. Nine Spice Mix (page 24) is also akin to a magic ingredient that gives most cooked dishes in this book their uniquely Palestinian flavor. The Spiced Cooking Broth (page 34) is so versatile, adding depth to stews, pilafs, and many bakes, while the Flavoured Sugar Syrup (page 35) is the way we sweeten most of our desserts and subtly add hints of flavor.

Become comfortable with these recipes and they will make many of the dishes in this book a breeze to prepare.

Left
Street-side vendor in the Old City of Jerusalem.

23

NINE SPICE MIX

تسع بهارات

Preparation time: 5 minutes
Cooking time: 15 minutes
Makes about 3½ oz/100 g

6 tablespoons allspice berries
6 cassia bark or cinnamon sticks
3 tablespoons coriander seeds
1 tablespoon black peppercorns
1 teaspoon cardamom seeds
½ teaspoon cumin seeds
10 cloves
2 blades of mace
½ nutmeg, crushed

I can still remember walking through Jerusalem's old city as a child with my mother, going from vendor to vendor and buying different whole spices in bulk. My mother would roast the spices when we got home and the house would be drunken on the fresh, earthy aromas. For years after I left home, she continued doing this, always sending me a jar of freshly roasted and ground spices. Today I roast my own, but when I do, the smell always transports me back to that time.

Place all the ingredients in a large skillet (frying pan) over medium-low heat. Stir with a wooden spoon periodically to ensure the spices do not burn, until you begin to smell the aroma of the spices, about 10 minutes.

Remove the pan from heat and set aside to cool completely, about 1 hour. This step is crucial because if the spices are not cooled properly, they will form a paste when ground rather than a powder.

Place all the roasted spices into a heavy-duty spice grinder and grind until you achieve a fine powder consistency. Store the spice mix in an airtight container. It will keep for several months although the aroma will fade with time.

Note: This spice mix is featured in many of the dishes in this book, lending them a uniquely Palestinian flavor. It is my mother's own blend but feel free to adjust to suit your taste, or you can substitute with store-bought *baharat* or Lebanese seven spice mix for an equally tasty, albeit slightly different, flavor profile.

LABANEH

لبنه

Preparation time: 5 minutes
Cooking time: 12 hours, including
straining
Makes 2¼—3¼ lb/1—1.5 kg

8 cups (4½ lb/2 kg) plain yogurt (goat is
    the most traditional but any regular
    yogurt will do as long as it has no
    additives like cornstarch/cornflour)
1 tablespoon fine salt
olive oil, to cover (optional)

A tangy, salty, and smooth cheese, labaneh is the most basic and versatile spread in the Palestinian kitchen. In fact, for sixty-five years now, my father has been eating this strained salted yogurt for breakfast every single day. Even when he travels, he looks for a spreadable soft white cheese, drenches it in olive oil, and has it with fresh vegetables and olives. The ways to enjoy labaneh, however, are endless. You can start by trying it as a spread on a sandwich sprinkled with za'atar and olive oil, as a dip for crisp vegetables, or rolled into small balls and submerged in olive oil (pickled labaneh), where it will last for months.

Put the yogurt and salt into a bowl and mix until fully combined, then pour into a colander lined with a cheesecloth or white muslin cloth. Fold the sides over to cover the yogurt. Place a heavy item like a plate or a brick (gravity is your friend) over the yogurt and place the colander over a bowl to catch the liquid. Alternatively, you can pour the yogurt into a muslin cloth, tie together the opposite corners, then tie this to the kitchen tap or to a wooden spoon suspended over a large bowl or pot—similar to a bindle.

Drain overnight (see Note). Once thickened, scrape the labaneh from the cloth and put into a bowl. Taste and adjust the salt if you prefer it saltier. Mix well with a spoon to smooth out.

Store in an airtight container in the refrigerator for up to 2 weeks or 4 weeks if covered in a thin layer of olive oil.

Note: The consistency of labaneh will depend on how long you drain it; the longer you drain it, the firmer and drier it will become. If using it as a spread, you don't need it to be very dry, but if you are pickling it then you want to remove as much moisture as possible so you can roll it into balls that will retain their shape in the oil.

TAHINI SAUCE

صلصة طحينه

Preparation time: 5 minutes
Cooking time: 5 minutes
Makes about 1¼ cups (10 fl oz/300 ml)

½ cup (4 oz/120 g) tahini
4 tablespoons lemon juice
¼ cup (2 oz/50 g) plain yogurt
½ teaspoon salt

This versatile sauce can be used on its own or as a base for different salads and spreads. The most basic version of it uses only tahini, lemon juice, and water, but I like to add some yogurt to mine—I find it cuts through the richness of the tahini and helps to round out the overall flavor. On its own, it can be used as a dip for Fried Kubbeh (page 90), drizzled on top of Falafel (page 68), or even in sandwiches. It's equally delicious as a spread with parsley or cilantro (coriander) (page 76) and as a salad with tomatoes and cucumber (page 104). Or, if you're me, then by itself with a spoon under the pretence that you are testing the flavor.

Put all the ingredients in a bowl with 4 tablespoons of water and mix until smooth and evenly incorporated. If you prefer it less thick, add 1 tablespoon of water at a time and mix until you reach your desired consistency.

The sauce will keep in the refrigerator, covered, for at least 3 days.

COOKED YOGURT SAUCE

لبن مطبوخ

Preparation time: 5 minutes
Cooking time: 25 minutes
Makes about 6 cups (2½ pints/1.5 liters)

2–2¼ lb/900 g–1 kg goat or sheep milk
  yogurt (see Note)
1–2 teaspoons salt
1 tablespoon olive oil
7–10 cloves garlic, crushed

This sauce—which is more like a soup—is a versatile base for many dishes such as Lamb and Yogurt Rice Stew (page 206). Traditionally, it is made from *kishek*, or *jameed* as we call it at home, which are round blocks of dried fermented sheep yogurt. The drying and salting process intensifies and concentrates the flavors, lending a uniquely sour and salty taste. It is worth hunting down this unique product in Middle Eastern grocers or specialty online stores, although if you cannot find it, goat or sheep milk yogurt will achieve a similar—albeit less intense—flavor. This recipe assumes you are using yogurt, not *kishek*, but see the note below if you do have *kishek*.

Whisk together the yogurt, 1 cup (8 fl oz/250 ml) water, and 1 teaspoon of salt and pour into a heavy pan. Place over medium-high heat and stir with a whisk until the yogurt boils. It is very important to whisk continuously to prevent the yogurt from curdling.

Heat the olive oil in a small skillet (frying pan), add the garlic and fry over medium heat for 1–2 minutes, or until fragrant but still white. Pour the garlic into the yogurt, stir, and remove from heat. The sauce should be quite salty and sour, so taste and adjust seasoning as necessary.

Note: It makes a big difference to use goat or sheep yogurt for this sauce, not only because it is closest in flavor to the traditional *jameed*, but also because it is much less likely to curdle if you forget to stir it for a few minutes. If you can only find plain yogurt, then stir 1 tablespoon of cornstarch (cornflour) into it before cooking and add a squeeze of lemon juice when you are done. Depending on what brand you buy, goat yogurt comes in tubs of either 1 lb/450 g or 1 lb 2 oz/500 g, so use two of them. If you do find *jameed*, blend one disc of it with 2 cups (16 fl oz/475 ml) water in a powerful food processor and use in place of one of the yogurt tubs.

Troubleshoot: If the yogurt does curdle, take off the heat and blend with a handheld immersion blender until it comes together into a smooth sauce.

LAMB WITH ONION
AND SPICES

حوسه

Preparation time: 10 minutes
Cooking time: 15 minutes
Makes about 1 lb 2 oz/500 g

4 tablespoons olive oil
1 quantity Toasted Pine Nuts
(optional, page 31)
2 onions, finely diced
1 lb 2 oz (500 g) ground (minced) lamb
or beef, or a combination of both
1 teaspoon Nine Spice Mix (page 24)
1 teaspoon salt

Although *hosseh* is mostly used to stuff a variety of vegetables and pastries, whenever I smell my mother preparing this in the morning, I insist on eating a plate of it with toasted pita bread. The crunch from the nuts, the richness from the olive oil and meat, and the warmth from the onions and spices all come together in a magical way. This basic version is made with ground (minced) meat, onions, and spices but I almost always add pine nuts, and sometimes walnuts as well. If you do use nuts, it's easiest to fry them first, remove with a slotted spoon and set aside, and then continue with the dish using the same pan.

Heat the olive oil in a skillet (frying pan) over medium-high heat and fry the nuts, if using. Remove from the pan with a slotted spoon and set aside.

Add the onions to the same pan and fry over medium-high heat for 3—5 minutes, stirring, until translucent and starting to brown. Add the meat, spice mix, and salt and cook for 6—8 minutes, or until the water has evaporated and the meat is nicely browned, breaking up any lumps with a wooden spoon.

Remove from heat and mix in the nuts, if using. At this point, the mixture can be used as called for in a recipe, or cooled and stored in the refrigerator for up to 3 days, or the freezer for up to 1 month.

TOASTED PINE NUTS
OR ALMONDS

لوز أو صنوبر مقلي

Preparation time: 5 minutes
Cooking time: 5 minutes
Makes 1 cup (4 oz/120 g)

1 cup (4 oz/120 g) pine nuts or flaked
    almonds (do not fry both together
    as timing is different)
vegetable oil or butter, for frying

Toasted nuts are one of my guilty pleasures. They add so much texture to food and there are very few dishes that aren't enhanced by their presence. You can use them to decorate any rice dish or casserole, you can mix them with stuffings, you can sprinkle them on salads, you can even eat them alone. I generally fry them in olive oil, although any vegetable oil, and even butter, will do. Make sure you remove the pan from the stove when they are one shade lighter than you need because they will continue to cook and darken for a short while after.

Place a small skillet (frying pan) over medium-high heat and pour in enough oil to coat the bottom, around 1 tablespoon. Add the nuts and stir to coat evenly with the oil. Lower the heat and continue to stir until the nuts are a very light golden color.

Remove the pan from heat and drain the nuts onto a plate lined with paper towels. You can use immediately or, once cooled, store in an airtight container in the refrigerator for up to 2 weeks.

Note: Pine nuts are perfect when mixed with foods such as Spiced Lamb and Rice Pilaf (page 166), Freekeh Pilaf with Lamb and Pine Nuts (page 162), and Lamb with Onion and Spices (page 30) as they retain their crunch. Almonds, however, tend to lose their crunch when mixed so it's best to sprinkle them on top of dishes before serving.

VERMICELLI RICE

رز بشعريه

Preparation time: 10 minutes + soaking
Cooking time: 15—20 minutes
Serves 4—6

2 cups (14 oz/400 g) rice (jasmine
  or short grain)
2 tablespoons olive oil
1 tablespoon butter or ghee
3½ oz/100 g vermicelli noodles, broken
  into 1—2-inch/3—5-cm lengths
1 teaspoon salt

Most stews and casseroles in the Palestinian kitchen are served alongside vermicelli rice. Rumor has it that if a woman used vermicelli it was because she was not a good cook as it was a surefire way to ensure the rice grains did not clump together. Truth is, it simply tastes better and richer this way. The proportion of rice to vermicelli noodles is discretionary; I normally do one part vermicelli to four parts rice, but you could easily double or halve that. As for the way I cook the rice, it is a trick I learned while living in France—it requires less work and allows the rice to steam, creating perfectly cooked and fluffy rice every time.

Rinse the rice under running water until the water runs clear. Soak for 15—30 minutes, then drain and set aside.

Melt the oil and butter or ghee in a pan over medium heat, add the vermicelli noodles, and stir continuously until the noodles are a golden brown color, about 5 minutes. Add the drained rice and toss to fully coat in the oil.

Pour 2½ cups (18 fl oz/550 ml) water into the pan, add the salt and bring to a boil. Boil for 2—3 minutes, give it one more stir, and then place a dish towel over the pan, close the lid tightly, and remove from the heat. Let it sit for 10—15 minutes. Remove the lid, fluff with a fork, and serve.

Variation: In the old days, rice was not as abundant in Palestine so most people would cook bulgur to be served alongside stews. It's an equally delicious alternative and even easier to make. Simply use the same amount of coarse grain bulgur in place of the rice (no need to soak or rinse) and add to the fried vermicelli noodles. The bulgur, however, will take more water than the rice so instead of doing the steaming method, add 4 cups (1¾ pints/1 liter) water and salt and bring to a boil, then lower heat and simmer. Check on the bulgur after 3—5 minutes; if the water has completely evaporated but the grains are still hard to the bite, add more water and continue to cook until done, checking and adding more water as necessary while cooking. The amount of water will vary based on the grain itself and the strength of heat; mine normally needs 5—6 cups (2—2½ pints/1.25—1.5 liters). Once the grains are fluffy and no longer hard to bite, they are done. This will take 15—20 minutes.

SPICED COOKING BROTH (STOCK)

مرقه

Preparation time: 5 minutes
Cooking time: 1 hour 30 minutes
Makes 8½ cups (3½ pints/2 liters)

2 tablespoons olive oil
2—3 pieces of mastic
3 bay leaves
2 cinnamon sticks
10 allspice berries
10 black peppercorns
5 cloves
4—5 cardamom pods
1 stewing chicken, jointed
    into 8 pieces
1 onion
2 cloves garlic
2 tablespoons salt

Every couple of months, my father buys a whole lamb and spends the entire afternoon trimming and organizing the meat for different uses; my mother then boils the bones to make a rich, spicy broth (stock), which serves as the base for many of our non-vegetarian meals. The recipe here is for chicken broth, but it can be substituted with beef or lamb. I've used a boiling chicken but you could use a chicken carcass (or lamb or beef bones without meat) and skip the searing step; if using lamb shanks, beef short ribs, or anything else where the meat will be eaten afterwards, searing it before adding the seasonings and water gives another layer of flavor. You can replace the whole spices with 2 tablespoons of Nine Spice Mix (page 24), to be added after the water has boiled and scum has been removed.

Heat the olive oil in a heavy stockpot over high heat. When hot, add the mastic pieces (this helps eliminate any unpleasant meat odour) and the whole spices. Add the chicken pieces, skin side down, and sear until a golden brown color, about 3 minutes each side. Add the onion and garlic and toss everything together. Add 10 cups (4¼ pints/2.5 liters) water and the salt and bring to a boil.

Boil for 5 minutes, skimming off any scum that rises to the surface, then reduce the heat to medium-low and simmer for 1—1½ hours, or until the chicken is cooked through but not falling apart. Take out the chicken pieces and set aside. They can either be broiled (grilled) or refrigerated to use later in salad or soup.

Allow the broth (stock) to cool slightly before straining through a fine-mesh strainer to discard the aromatics. Cool completely before storing in airtight containers. This stock will keep for up to 4 days in the refrigerator, or can be frozen for up to 6 months.

FLAVORED SUGAR SYRUP

قطر

Preparation time: 5 minutes
Cooking time: 5 minutes
Makes 2 cups (16 fl oz/475 ml)

2 cups (14 oz/400 g) superfine
    (caster) sugar
squeeze of lemon juice
½ teaspoon orange blossom water
½ teaspoon rosewater

Most traditional Arabic sweets are sweetened with syrup, which is generally flavored with rosewater or orange blossom water. The strength of these flavorings varies from brand to brand so always add them gradually and taste to avoid ending up with something too strong. Another key point to remember when using syrup in desserts is that unless stated otherwise only one of the two should be hot: either pour hot syrup onto cooled pastry or cooled syrup onto hot pastry.

In a small heavy pan, combine the sugar, 1½ cups (12 fl oz/ 350 ml) water, and the lemon juice and bring to a boil over medium-high heat. Simmer until slightly thickened, about 5 minutes.

Remove from the heat and add the flavorings. Allow to cool before storing in a container in the refrigerator for up to 2 months.

Note: For a runnier consistency use 1 part sugar to 1 part water; for a thicker syrup use 2 parts sugar to 1 part water.

BREAD AND PASTRIES

It wasn't until my first trip back to visit my parents from university in the United States that I realized just how much my idea of "home" was tied to food. When I woke that very first morning back, I smelled the aroma of freshly baked bread wafting up the stairs. Instinctively I knew my mother was baking taboon bread. Jet-lagged and famished, I stumbled into the kitchen to find my mother at her bread oven. My father was squeezing oranges on the counter. Behind him on the breakfast table sat a small bowl of shimmering green olive oil. In that simple breakfast of homemade bread, olive oil, seasonal vegetables, and freshly squeezed orange juice, my parents told me how much they missed me without saying a single word. That meal was like a warm blanket that was saying "welcome home."

As time went on and I spent more and more time away from home, food was the tie that brought me back. On those days I missed home the most, I would take a few leaves of za'atar my mother had packed off with me and rub them in my hand; the scent would take me straight back to her kitchen again. When I yearn for home now, or when my daughters say *ajeen* (dough), because it's what they see my mother make every time she visits, I bake a batch of fresh pita bread and feel my mother's presence around us. I've come to realize now that no matter where life takes us, food is the tie that binds us together. It's an integral part of our lives, not only for nourishment but also for the lessons that it allows us to share from one generation to the next.

Nowhere is this more obvious than in the following recipes of baked goods, generations old, which I grew up on. At their most basic are Pita (page 38) and Taboon (page 42) breads, the cornerstones of many meals and a great side for dips, salads, and stews. More elaborate pastries such as spinach (page 49) or za'atar and cheese turnovers (page 48) are the perfect packed lunch while *mana'eesh* (page 44) and *sfeeha* (page 52) can be served as meals on their own with a simple dip or salad on the side. Whatever recipes you choose to try from this chapter, you can be sure the aromas and flavors will transport you to a simpler time and allow you to experience the true warmth of a Palestinian family kitchen.

Left
Jerusalem sesame bagel cart
in the Old City.

PITA BREAD

خبز

Preparation time: 30 minutes + resting
Cooking time: 5–10 minutes
Makes 8 large round breads

2¼ cups (9 oz/250 g) all-purpose
  (plain) flour, plus extra for dusting
2¼ cups (9 oz/250 g) finely milled
  grade "00" pasta flour (if
  unavailable, substitute with
  plain/all-purpose flour)
2¼ cups (9 oz/250 g) fine whole wheat
  (wholemeal) flour
¼ cup powdered milk (optional)
2 teaspoons salt
1 teaspoon sugar
2 tablespoons olive oil, plus extra
  for oiling
1 tablespoon active dry (fast-action)
  yeast
2–2½ cups (18–20 fl oz/500–600 ml)
  warm water

I don't recall a single time while growing up that we, or anyone we knew, sat down to eat without bread at the table. If it wasn't used to eat the meal itself, then you would have a small piece of bread with olives to round off the meal. To this day, I always have a bag with some bread on my kitchen counter—to scoop up some labaneh, to mop up sauce from my plate, to make a quick sandwich for one of my girls, or to enjoy with a bit of olive oil or cheese at the end of a meal.

Put the flours, powdered milk, salt, and sugar into a large bowl and mix together. Make a well in the middle and add the oil, yeast, and half the water. Mix through with your fingers, gradually adding more water and kneading until the dough comes together. If the mixture feels sticky, leave for 5 minutes then come back and knead again. Repeat this once or twice until you have a soft but fairly robust ball of dough. Alternatively, combine all the dough ingredients, but only half the water, in the bowl of a freestanding mixer fitted with the dough hook and mix on medium speed, gradually adding water as necessary, until the dough comes together.

Rub the dough with some oil, cover the bowl with a damp dish towel or plastic wrap (clingfilm), and set aside until it doubles in size. Once the dough has risen, gently punch down to release the air bubbles. Divide into 8 equal-sized portions and place on a lightly floured work surface. Cover with a dish towel or small tablecloth so the dough doesn't dry out as you roll.

Preheat the oven to 475°F/240°C/Gas Mark 9 (or the hottest it will go). Take one piece of dough and roll into a ball between your palms, then flatten and coat in flour. Roll the dough out with a rolling pin to about 4 inches/10 cm in diameter. Sprinkle with some flour, flip over, and continue to roll out further until you have a circle approximately 8 inches/20 cm in diameter.

Once all the balls are rolled out, you can place two or three at a time on a baking sheet and bake for 5–10 minutes, or until they puff up and develop a very light golden top. If you have a pizza stone, place each rolled pita bread one at a time on the stone until they puff up and develop a light golden color, about 5 minutes.

Place on paper towels or a wire rack to cool. You can store any leftover bread in plastic bags in the freezer for up to 1 month. In fact, they freeze so well that I often triple this recipe when I make it so I have enough bread for a few weeks in the freezer.

JERUSALEM SESAME BAGELS

كعك القدس

Preparation time: 30 minutes + resting
Cooking time: 15–20 minutes
Makes 6 bagels

For the pastry
4½ cups (1 lb 2 oz/500 g) all-purpose
    (plain) or white bread flour
2 tablespoons sugar
2 teaspoons salt
1½ cups (12 fl oz/350 ml) whole (full-fat)
    milk, warm
1 tablespoon active dry (fast-action)
    yeast
1 teaspoon baking powder
olive oil

For the sesame coating
1 cup (5 oz/150 g) hulled sesame seeds
1–2 tablespoons grape molasses
    (see Note, page 70)

It may be a myth, or it may be fact, but all Palestinians agree that the oblong sesame bagels made in Jerusalem taste better than those made anywhere else in the country. We even call them 'Jerusalem' bagels. Perhaps it's the old traditional wood-fired ovens, or the aura of Old City where they are baked, or their ubiquitous presence in the daily life of Jerusalemites. The men push their *ka'ak*-laden wooden carts through the streets shouting "kaaaaaaa'aaaaaak" and everyone, from schoolchildren to workers to store owners— even tourists—gathers round for these delicious and filling breads. No, this recipe will not taste the same as the ones sold on the streets, but they are a delicious and fantastic place holder until one finally visits the Old City.

Put all the dough ingredients except the olive oil into the bowl of a freestanding mixer fitted with the dough hook. Mix on medium speed until the dough comes together in a soft and pliable ball. Alternatively, mix in a large bowl and knead by hand until smooth and pliable. If the mixture appears too stiff, add a little milk and continue to knead. You are looking for a soft, elastic but robust dough. Rub with oil, cover the bowl with a damp dish towel or plastic wrap (clingfilm), and set aside to rise until doubled in size, about 1 hour.

Meanwhile, prepare the sesame coating. In a large shallow bowl, combine the sesame seeds and grape molasses with 1 tablespoon of water. Mix, adding more as neccessary, until you have a wet mixture that is neither too sticky and thick that it clumps up, nor too thin. You just want to be able to coat the dough in the seeds and have them stick.

Once the dough has risen, gently punch down to release the air bubbles. Divide into 6 equal-sized portions and place on a lightly floured work surface. Roll and stretch each piece into a log about 8–12 inches/20–30 cm long, then attach the ends together to form a circle. Set aside to rest for 15 minutes.

Preheat the oven to 450°F/230°C/Gas Mark 8. Take each dough ring, dip it in the sesame mixture, and gently roll and stretch the ring until you have a long oval shape, similar to a stretched out "0". Repeat with each ring, then set aside on a baking sheet to rest a final time, about 10 minutes.

Place the baking sheet or sheets into the oven and bake for 15–20 minutes, or until a deep golden color and cooked through. Set aside on a wire rack to cool.

Serve warm with za'atar (page 244), or white cheese and vegetables, and sweet tea (page 236–237). Freeze leftovers for up to 1 month and reheat in the oven before serving.

Right
Clockwise from top left: olives; pickled turnips (page 241); Duqqa (page 244); Falafel (page 68); pickled cucumbers; Za'atar (page 244); Sesame Bagels (page 40).

TABOON BREAD

خبز طابون

Preparation time: 30 minutes + resting
Cooking time: 5–10 minutes
Serves 8

4½ cups (1 lb 2 oz/500 g) all-purpose
  (plain) flour, plus extra for dusting
2¼ cups (9 oz/250 g) fine whole wheat
  (wholemeal) flour
2 teaspoons salt
1 teaspoon sugar
2 tablespoons olive oil
1 tablespoon active dry (fast-action)
  yeast
2–3¾ cups (18–30 fl oz/500–900 ml)
  warm water

The taboon is a clay oven that has been used for cooking and baking bread in the Middle East since pre-biblical times. Many people use a bread oven or a good oven tray with pebbles at the bottom of it to give the bread its traditional shape, but you can place the bread directly in an oven tray and make indentations in the dough with your fingers before baking. This is used for Chicken, Onion, and Sumac Flatbreads (page 194), one of Palestine's national dishes.

Put the flours, salt, and sugar into a large bowl and mix together. Make a well in the middle and add the oil, yeast, and 2 cups (18 fl oz/500 ml) of the warm water. Mix through with your fingers, gradually adding more water and kneading until the dough comes together. If the mixture feels sticky, leave for 5 minutes then come back and knead again. Repeat this once or twice until you have a very soft ball of dough. Alternatively, combine ingredients, starting with 2 cups (18 fl oz/500 ml) of water, in the bowl of a freestanding mixer fitted with the dough hook and mix on medium speed. Gradually add more water as necessary, until the dough comes together in a very soft ball. The dough should be a bit sticky, so use plenty of flour when shaping.

Shape the dough into a ball, rub all over with oil, cover the bowl with a damp dish towel or plastic wrap (clingfilm), and set aside until it doubles in size, about 1 hour. Once the dough has risen, gently punch down to release the air bubbles. Divide into 8 portions, shaping into a ball and place on a floured work surface. Set aside to rest for 15 minutes.

Meanwhile, preheat the oven to 475°F/240°C/Gas Mark 9 (or the hottest it will go) with the oven tray and bone-dry pebbles, if using. Take one piece of dough, flatten it out on the floured work surface, and coat in more flour. Use your hands to flatten and stretch it out to 4–6 inches/10–15 cm in diameter. Sprinkle with flour, flip, and continue to flatten out until you have a circle 8–12 inches/20–30 cm in diameter.

If using pebbles, open the oven and pull the oven tray out halfway. Carry the dough between your hands to the oven and lay it over the pebbles, stretching it out slightly into a circular shape. If placing directly on the tray, do not stretch out but use your fingers to make indentations. This will give it a similar shape to having pebbles under it.

Bake for 5–10 minutes, or until the bread develops a light golden top. Remove from the oven and place on a paper-towel lined tray to cool. Repeat with the remaining dough.

Store covered for up to 1 day or freeze for several weeks.

VEGETARIAN FLATBREADS

مناقيش

Mana'eesh to a Palestinian is like pizza to an Italian and a little more, even. These freshly baked breads are enjoyed all over the Middle East for breakfast, lunch, or dinner. There are three different toppings here, but the recipe assumes you will only use one, so reduce if trying a mixture.

Preparation time: 1 hour + resting
Cooking time: 10 minutes
Makes 10 (more if you make them smaller)

For the dough
6¾ cups (1 lb 11 oz/750 g) all-purpose (plain) flour
2¼ cups (9 oz/250 g) whole wheat (wholemeal) flour
1½ teaspoons salt
1 teaspoon sugar
½ cup (4 fl oz/120 ml) vegetable oil, plus more for oiling
1 tablespoon active dry (fast-action) yeast
3 cups (25 fl oz/750 ml) warm water

Topping 1: za'atar
1 cup (2 oz/50 g) Za'atar (page 244)
⅔ cup (5 fl oz/150 ml) olive oil

Topping 2: cheese
2 cups (9 oz/250 g) halloumi cheese, grated
1 tablespoon Greek yogurt
1 teaspoon nigella seeds (optional)
1 teaspoon dried za'atar, oregano, or marjoram leaves (optional)

Topping 3: pepper
½ cup (4 fl oz/120 ml) olive oil, plus extra as needed
2 onions, finely chopped
5–6 red bell peppers, deseeded and finely chopped
1 red chilli pepper, deseeded and finely chopped (optional)
1 tablespoon tomato paste (purée)
½ teaspoon salt
1 tablespoon nigella seeds (optional)

Put the flours, salt, and sugar into a large bowl and mix together. Make a well in the middle; add the oil, yeast, and half the water. Mix through with your fingers, adding more water and kneading until the dough comes together. If the mixture feels sticky, leave for 5 minutes then knead again. Repeat once or twice until you have a soft but robust dough. Rub with oil, cover with a damp dish towel or plastic wrap (clingfilm), and set aside until doubled in size, about 1 hour.

Meanwhile, prepare the toppings. To make the za'atar and cheese toppings, simply combine the ingredients in a bowl and mix well to combine. To make the pepper topping, heat the olive oil in a skillet (frying pan) over medium heat. Add the onions and cook, stirring occasionally, until softened, about 5 minutes. Add the bell and chilli peppers and continue to cook, stirring, until the peppers have softened and the mixture has started to thicken, about 10 minutes. Stir in the tomato paste (purée) and salt and cook for 2–3 minutes. Remove from heat and add the nigella seeds. If the mixture appears dry, mix in 1–2 tablespoons of olive oil.

Once the dough has risen, gently punch down to release the air bubbles. Divide into 10 portions, and place on a lightly floured work surface. Cover with a dish towel so the dough doesn't dry out as you roll.

Preheat the oven to 475°F/240°C/Gas Mark 9 (or the hottest it will go). Take a piece of dough and roll into a ball between your palms, then flatten and coat in flour. Roll the dough out with a rolling pin to about 4 inches/10 cm in diameter. Sprinkle with some flour, flip over, and continue to roll out further until you have a circle approximately 8 inches/20 cm in diameter. Return the dough to the work surface to rest and cover while you roll out the remaining dough pieces.

Once all the balls are rolled out, take the first piece you rolled and place either on a baking sheet or preheated pizza stone. With your fingers make some gentle indentations, so the dough does not puff up when baked, and spread the topping using the back of the spoon. Bake until golden around the edges and the topping is cooked, 5–10 minutes.

Transfer to a wire rack to cool. You can store any leftovers in the freezer for up to 1 month.

ZA'ATAR FILLED FLATBREADS

أقراص زعتر

Preparation time: 40 minutes
+ resting time
Cooking time: 7–12 minutes
Makes 10

For the pastry
4½ cups (1 lb 2 oz/500 g) all-purpose
(plain) flour, plus extra for dusting
2¼ cups (9 oz/250 g) fine whole wheat
(wholemeal) flour
2 teaspoons salt
1 teaspoon sugar
2 tablespoons olive oil, plus extra
for oiling
1 tablespoon active dry (fast-action)
yeast
2–2½ cups (18–20 fl oz/500–600 ml)
warm water

For the filling
2 cups (3½ oz/100 g) firmly packed fresh
za'atar leaves (or substitute with
fresh oregano and/or marjoram
and thyme leaves)
8 scallions (spring onions), green and
white parts finely chopped
1 teaspoon salt
½ cup (4 fl oz/120 ml) olive oil
¼ teaspoon black pepper

One of the oldest and most traditional Palestinian pastries, these flatbreads, as well as being delicious, have an emotional significance for my family. My mother's uncle, Yousef, was forced into political exile at twenty. The next time he saw anyone from his family was two decades later when my mother traveled to the United States. He had one request—to bring him some of his mother's *akras za'atar*.

Put the flours, salt, and sugar into a bowl and mix together. Make a well in the middle; add the oil, yeast, and half the water. Mix through with your fingers, adding more water and kneading until the dough comes together. If the mixture feels sticky, leave for 5 minutes then knead again. Repeat until you have a soft ball of dough. Alternatively, combine all the ingredients, but only half the water, in the bowl of a freestanding mixer fitted with the dough hook and mix on medium speed, adding water as necessary, until it comes together in a soft but robust ball. Rub with oil, cover the bowl with a damp dish towel, and set aside to rise for 1 hour.

Meanwhile, prepare the stuffing by placing all the filling ingredients into a large bowl and tossing to combine. Set aside until ready to use.

Once the dough has risen, divide into 10 equal-sized portions. Line a large tray with oiled plastic wrap (clingfilm). Place the dough on the tray. Let rest for 5–10 minutes.

Take one portion of dough and, with your hands, flatten it into a rough circle. Take about a tenth of the filling and spread it evenly over the pastry. Starting at the top use both hands to fold the pastry into thirds, oiling each layer as you fold. You should now have a long rectangle. Take one of the short sides and fold into thirds again, this time horizontally, oiling each layer as you go. You should now have a square shape. Oil the pastry again and set aside on an oiled surface and cover with oiled plastic wrap. Repeat with remaining pastry. Set aside to rest for 15 minutes while you preheat the oven to 475°F/240°C/Gas Mark 9.

Flatten it out with well oiled hands into a 8-inch/20-cm square, then place on a baking sheet. Repeat with the rest of the pastry. Bake for 7–12 minutes, or until a light golden color. Check the underside, if it has not browned, you may need to flip it and bake for 2 minutes to brown the bottom.

Remove from the oven and transfer to a wire rack to cool. Serve warm with halloumi cheese or Labaneh (page 26), a side of fresh vegetables, and a cup of sweet mint tea (page 237).

ZA'ATAR AND CHEESE TURNOVERS

فطاير زعتر وجبنه

Preparation time: 40 minutes + resting
Cooking time: 5–10 minutes
Makes about 25

For the pastry

2½ cups (11 oz/300 g) white bread flour
1¾ cups (7 oz/200 g) whole wheat
    (wholemeal) bread flour
1 tablespoon nigella seeds
1 teaspoon salt
1 teaspoon sugar
¼ teaspoon turmeric
½ cup (4 fl oz/120 ml) olive oil, plus extra
    for greasing
1 teaspoon active dry (fast-action) yeast
1 teaspoon baking powder
½ cup (½ oz/15 g) dried za'atar leaves
    (see Note)
⅔ cup (5 oz/150 g) plain yogurt

For the filling

9 oz/250 g halloumi cheese, finely grated

Turnovers are very common in all Levantine kitchens.
A variety of doughs filled with different stuffings, they make
the perfect snack, quick lunch, or nibble to serve a last-
minute guest. These particular ones are my favorite; I love
eating them with fresh tomatoes sprinkled with sea salt.

Put the flours, nigella seeds, salt, sugar, turmeric, and the
olive oil into a large bowl and work with your hands until
fully combined. Add the yeast, baking powder, za'atar leaves,
yogurt, and ⅔ cup (5 fl oz/150 ml) water and work with your
hands until the dough comes together. It will be quite sticky
at this point. Leave it for about 5 minutes then knead again.

Continue to knead until the dough comes together without
sticking to your hands. You may need to let it rest for a few
minutes a couple of times while kneading. If you've done this
a few times and it's still too sticky you can adjust by adding
more flour—how much will depend on many things, from
the weather to flour variety. Similarly, if the dough feels
tough, add some water and knead again. You are looking for
a soft consistency that isn't sticky.

At this point shape the dough into a ball and oil it all over
with about 1 tablespoon of olive oil. Cover the bowl with
a wet dish towel or plastic wrap (clingfilm) and leave to rise
for 1–2 hours, or until it has nearly doubled in size.

Once risen, knock the air out with your hands and shape
into roughly 25 portions the size of a golf ball. Place on a
large oiled work surface.

One by one, take each ball and flatten out with your hand
into a circle about 3–4 inches/8–10 cm in diameter. Place
a teaspoon of the finely grated halloumi cheese in the
middle of each circle then take two sides and pinch together
to make a triangle. Lift the bottom of the circle toward the
center and pinch all three edges firmly together.

Preheat the oven to 475°F/240°C/Gas Mark 9. Place the filled
turnovers on a parchment lined cookie sheet and bake
for about 5 minutes or until edges are a light golden brown.
Remove from oven and transfer to a wire rack to cool.

Note: We normally use dried or fresh za'atar leaves but these
can be hard to find outside the Middle East. The closest
I've come to replicating the flavor is by using fresh young
oregano leaves. Simply pick the smallest leaves from your
bunch of oregano, or if the leaves are too large, chop them
coarsely. It is also possible to mix some fresh marjoram
and/or fresh thyme leaves with the oregano.

SPINACH TURNOVERS

فطاير سبانخ

Preparation time: 1 hour + resting
Cooking time: 10 minutes
Makes about 20

For the stuffing
9 oz/250 g fresh spinach
1 tablespoon salt
4–5 scallions (spring onions),
    finely chopped
4 tablespoons olive oil
1 tablespoon sumac
1 tablespoon freshly squeezed
    lemon juice
1 teaspoon red chilli flakes or powder
    (optional)

For the pastry
2½ cups (11 oz/300 g) all purpose (plain)
    flour (substitute some for
    whole wheat/wholemeal, if desired)
scant 1 cup (7 oz/200 g) yogurt
scant ½ cup (3½ fl oz/100 ml) olive oil,
    plus extra for oiling
1 teaspoon active dry (fast-action) yeast
½ teaspoon salt
½ teaspoon sugar
¼ teaspoon turmeric (optional)

These turnovers remind me of my childhood school lunches because, like most kids who grew up in the Middle East, my mother always had a stash of them in the freezer, ready to put into our packed lunches. Not only are they easy to transport, but the tangy stuffing inside soft fluffy dough is as delicious as it is healthy. The spinach stuffing can be made a day in advance and stored in the refrigerator, while the baked turnovers freeze quite well for a couple of months. A delicious non-vegetarian alternative can be made using Lamb with Onion and Spices (page 39) as a stuffing.

Chop the spinach into small pieces, put into a colander over a sink, and sprinkle with the salt. Toss to combine then allow to sit for at least 1–2 hours. Squeeze the spinach as much as possible to release all the water then lay on paper towels to absorb any additional liquid.

Combine the remaining stuffing ingredients in a large bowl, add the spinach, and mix well. At this point the stuffing can be used immediately or stored in the refrigerator, tightly wrapped, for up to 1 day.

To prepare the pastry, combine all the ingredients in a large bowl and knead by hand for 15 minutes until you have a smooth and pliable dough. Alternatively, put all the ingredients into the bowl of a freestanding mixer fitted with the dough hook and mix on medium speed until the dough comes together. Shape into a large ball and rub oil all over it to prevent it sticking to the bowl. Cover with a damp dish towel or plastic wrap (clingfilm) and set aside to rise for 1–2 hours, or until doubled in size.

Once risen, divide the dough into roughly 20 equal-sized portions the size of a small egg; lay on an oiled work surface. Allow to rest for 5 minutes.

Preheat the oven to 475°F/240°C/Gas Mark 9 and line two baking sheets with baking paper.

Flatten each piece of dough into a circle, about 3–4 inches/ 8–10 cm in diameter. Place 1 tablespoon of the spinach stuffing in the middle, then take two sides and pinch together to make a triangle. Lift the bottom of the circle toward the center and pinch all three edges firmly together.

Place each completed turnover on the lined baking sheets, leaving some space between them. Bake for about 5 minutes, or until the tops are a light golden brown. Transfer to a wire rack to cool.

Overleaf
From left: Za'atar and Cheese
Turnovers (page 48); Mini Lamb
Flatbreads (page 52); Spinach
Turnovers (above).

MINI LAMB FLATBREADS

صفيحه

Preparation time: 1 hour + resting
Cooking time: 10 minutes
Makes about 30

For the dough
4½ cups (1 lb 2 oz/500 g) all-purpose
     (plain) flour
1 teaspoon salt
1 teaspoon sugar
1 tablespoon active dry (fast-action)
     yeast
½ cup (4 fl oz/120 ml) olive oil
1½ cups (12 oz/350 g) plain yogurt

For the topping
1 quantity Lamb with Onion and Spices
     (page 30)
2 tablespoons Toasted Pine Nuts
     (page 31)
2 tablespoons Labaneh, homemade
     (page 26) or store-bought
2 teaspoons pomegranate molasses
1 tablespoon tahini
1 tablespoon sumac
1 tablespoon fresh oregano or mint,
     very finely chopped (optional)
1 teaspoon red chilli powder (or to taste)

Sfeeha is eaten in various forms all over the Middle East and even parts of Europe. It is, in essence, dough with meat. Sounds simple enough, yet the flavors are anything but. The spicing of the meat makes it both sharp and smooth, which when combined with fluffy pastry and crispy pine nuts is a real flavor triumph. The recipe below is the one my Teta Asma and her sister Teta Salma always made and the one my mother continues to make today as well. If you can resist finishing them, they freeze quite well for up to one month.

Mix the flour, salt, and sugar together in a large bowl. Add the yeast, oil, and yogurt and knead by hand until it is smooth and pliable. If necessary, gradually add some water to help achieve a smooth, pliable dough. Alternatively, combine all the dough ingredients in the bowl of a freestanding mixer fitted with the dough hook and mix on medium speed, adding water as necessary, until the dough comes together. Shape into a large circle, oil all over to prevent it sticking to the bowl, and cover with a damp dish towel or plastic wrap (clingfilm). Set aside to rise, about 1 hour.

Meanwhile, prepare the topping by making the Lamb with Onion and Spices. Set aside to cool slightly. Once cooled, combine with all the other topping ingredients and mix until well incorporated, it should come together and have a spreadable consistency.

Preheat the oven to 475°F/240°C/Gas Mark 9. Once the dough has risen, divide it into roughly 30 small portions the size of a golf ball, and set on an oiled work surface to rest for 5–10 minutes.

Take one piece at a time and, on a lined baking sheet, flatten out with your fingers into a circle roughly ¼ inch (5 mm) thick. Place 1 tablespoon of the topping mixture in the middle and flatten it with your hands to ensure it doesn't come off. You will end up with a very small pizza shape about 3-inches (8 cm) in diameter.

Bake in the oven until the dough on the edges turns golden, about 10 minutes. Remove from the oven and set on a wire rack to cool.

Variation: If you are pressed for time, store-bought all-butter puff pastry is a good substitute for the homemade dough. Simply slice into roughly 2½-inch (6-cm) squares or cut out 3-inch (8 cm) and press a tablespoon of the topping into the middle. Bake according to the package instructions until the pastry is a light golden brown.

ANISEED BREADS

كعك أصفر

Preparation time: 40 minutes + resting
Cooking time: 15–20 minutes
Makes 8

4½ cups (1 lb 2 oz/500 g) all purpose
(plain) flour
½ cup (3 oz/80 g) unhulled sesame seeds,
toasted
4 tablespoons sugar
3 tablespoons ground aniseed
2 tablespoons nigella seeds
2 teaspoons salt
1½ teaspoons turmeric
1 teaspoon mahlab (optional)
½ cup (4 fl oz/120 ml) olive oil, plus extra
for greasing and rolling
1 tablespoon active dry (fast-action)
yeast
2 teaspoons baking powder
1¼–1⅔ cups (10–14 fl oz/300–400 ml)
warm water

This very typical Palestinian bread is generally made for certain holidays—by Christians and Muslims alike—and passed out to the town people. The recipe here comes from a lady in my father's village called Nuha, who is known across town (and many neighboring towns) as the pastry expert. Before the holidays, her kitchen becomes a factory as she makes pastries on order for the town people.

Put the flour, sesame seeds, sugar, aniseed, nigella seeds, salt, turmeric, and mahlab into a large bowl and mix to combine. Pour in the olive oil and work very well with your hands until fully combined; the mixture will be crumbly.

Add the yeast, baking powder, and 1 cup (8 fl oz/250 ml) of the warm water and knead, adding more water as necessary, until the dough comes together in a soft ball. The dough will be a little sticky because of the sugar and oil, you simply want to be able to able to manage it. Grease the dough with some more oil, cover the bowl with a dish towel or plastic wrap (clingfilm), and set aside to rise, about 1 hour.

Once risen, divide the dough into 8 equal balls and place on a greased work surface—I most often use a large tray covered with plastic wrap that I have greased with oil, as this makes cleaning up easier. Grease each ball with some more oil, cover, and let rest for about 15 minutes.

Roll each ball into a circle approximately ½ inch/1 cm thick. Traditionally, we roll the dough onto a wooden mold, which we then invert to reveal a very nicely designed bread. This also serves to prevent the breads from rising. As these molds are difficult to come by, use the prongs of a fork to make a design all over each bread. Alternatively, mooncake molds are easier to purchase online or in Asian markets and can be used to stamp shapes into the dough. Set aside on a baking sheet to rest for approximately 15 minutes.

Preheat the oven to 400°F/200°C/Gas Mark 6. Put the baking sheet into the oven and bake until the breads are lightly browned, about 10–15 minutes. Remove from the oven and brush the top of each bread with some olive oil. Set aside to cool slightly.

Serve alone or, as is traditional, with boiled eggs, halloumi cheese, and Sweet Mint Tea (page 237). Can be eaten warm or at room temperature. They will freeze well for up to 3 months.

SPICED SEEDED CRACKERS

ملاتيت

Preparation time: 15 minutes + resting
Cooking time: 20–25 minutes
Makes about 1 lb 8½ oz/700 g

½ cup (11 oz/300 g) all purpose
    (plain) flour
1¾ cups (7 oz/200 g) whole wheat
    (wholemeal) flour (substitute with
    all purpose/plain flour
    if unavailable)
1 cup (6 oz/175 g) unhulled sesame
    seeds
2 tablespoons ground aniseed
2 tablespoons nigella seeds
2 teaspoons salt
1 teaspoon mahlab (optional)
1 teaspoon baking powder
½ cup (4 fl oz/120 ml) olive oil
½ cup (4 fl oz/120 ml) vegetable oil
1–1¼ cups (7–10 fl oz/200–300 ml) water

I can't recall a single time when I visited Teta Asma and she did not have these little crackers at hand. Whether she'd made the sweet or salty version, she always offered us some with the afternoon coffee. Her youngest daughter, my aunt Lamees, has kept up with this tradition and it is always a treat to have afternoon coffee at her house. Normally made as thin rounds, I find the process much easier if I roll the entire pastry out once then cut into squares or diamonds. Other than this simplification, the recipe here is the same one that has been used in my father's family for generations.

Combine all the dry ingredients in a large bowl and mix well. Add in the olive oil and vegetable oil and mix with your hands until the mixture resembles wet sand.

Gradually add in the water, kneading with your hands, until the dough comes together. Avoid over-kneading and over-watering, you simply want all the ingredients to come together into a pliable dough. Set aside to rest for 15–20 minutes.

Preheat the oven to 350°F/180°C/Gas Mark 4. Divide the dough into 2 equal portions (it's easier to handle smaller portions) and set one aside, covered, as you roll the other. To roll, place the dough between 2 sheets of parchment paper and roll into a large square or rectangle roughly ⅛ inch (3 mm) thick.

Remove the top sheet of parchment paper and transfer the bottom sheet, with the dough on it, to a large baking sheet. Use a knife or pizza cutter to cut the dough into small square or diamond shapes or even strips—it's just a matter of preference. If you have 2 baking sheets you can repeat the process and bake both trays together, swapping the sheets over halfway through baking and turning them round to ensure even baking. Otherwise, the crackers can be baked consecutively.

Bake in the oven until the crackers are a light golden brown, about 20–25 minutes. Remove from the oven and let cool for about 10 minutes before transferring to a wire rack to cool completely. The crackers can be stored in an airtight container at room temperature for up to 3 weeks—if you can resist finishing them off before then!

BREAKFAST

When I left Jerusalem to go to university in the U.S., I didn't think about what I was leaving behind, so focused was I on what lay ahead. I knew I would miss my parents, my family, my home, the spring smells, the humid air, and the food, but I did not really know what that would feel like until my first morning on my own in the university dorms.

You see, for the first time in my life, I found myself eating breakfast alone. The scenario hadn't crossed my mind because I had never experienced it: eating together was simply a way of life. So in that moment, I was overcome with excitement for this new beginning but also with extreme longing for the familiarity of what I had left behind.

More than a decade since, whether surrounded by family or grabbing a quick bite on my own, breakfast remains my favorite meal. Not only because of the vibrancy of its dishes, but because, like those same sentiments I experienced my first time living away from home, breakfast holds the promise of a fresh start while simultaneously reminding me of my roots and what I cherish most.

I can still picture our old family kitchen with the breakfast table: a bowl of labaneh with a well of olive oil in the middle, a plate of sliced cucumbers and tomatoes, a ramekin of za'atar, a small plate of olives, and a pile of freshly baked pita bread. Throughout my childhood, this is what we ate, with alternating additions depending on the season. Home-cooked tomato spread, oil-pickled eggplants (aubergines), apricot jam, mulberry preserve, hummus, avocados, hard-boiled eggs, cheese, and tahini spreads also made the rounds. Weekend breakfasts were, of course, a more elaborate affair with Falafel (page 68), Palestinian Frittata (page 60), or Jerusalem Sesame Bagels (page 40), all served with sweet tea—mint in summer and sage in winter.

When I visit my parents' home in Jerusalem now with my husband and daughters, my mother relishes her pre-dawn rousing to bake us fresh bread. We then all gather around a large straw-tray lined with different plates to enjoy a breakfast that is as delicious as it is nutritious. With a small selection of foods from protein and carbs to vegetables and healthy fats, you really set yourself up for the best start to the day. So I urge you to try your own combinations from this chapter because there truly is nothing like savoring one of these breakfasts: nourishing, generous, and packed with Palestinian flavor.

Left
A lemon tree in the Kassis
family garden.

FRIED EGGS WITH ZA'ATAR AND SUMAC

بيض مقلي مع زعتر وسماق

Preparation time: 2 minutes
Cooking time: 5 minutes
Serves 1

2 tablespoons olive oil
2 eggs
1 teaspoon Za'atar (page 244)
1 teaspoon sumac

To serve
— Labaneh, homemade (page 26)
  or store-bought
— Pita bread, homemade (page 38)
  or store-bought

This is the breakfast my father loves to make us at home. Fried eggs without za'atar and sumac is unacceptable to him so if he's frying the eggs, you can bet there will be plenty of flavor and plenty of olive oil. You can use as little or as much za'atar and sumac as you like; you can also add or substitute Duqqa (page 244) in this recipe. I like to pan-fry the eggs in a lot of olive oil so I can mop up the flavored oil with a piece of fresh bread, but you can use less oil or skip pouring the cooked oil over the eggs as I suggest. If you want the eggs to have crispy edges, cook each one separately.

In a small, non-stick skillet (frying pan), heat the oil over medium heat until hot but not smoking. Crack the eggs into the oil and sprinkle with the za'atar and sumac. When the outer edges start turning opaque, after about 1 minute, cover the pan with a lid and reduce the heat.

Lift the lid every 20 seconds or so, tilt the pan, and spoon some of the oil over the eggs, taking care not to burn yourself with the sputtering oil. This will help the top of the whites to crisp, the yolk to cook faster, and the oil to gain more flavor.

Cook until the egg is your desired level of doneness, about 5 minutes for fully cooked and 3 minutes for runny yolks. Transfer the eggs to a plate and pour the oil over the top. Enjoy with pita bread and labaneh.

PALESTINIAN FRITTATA

عجه فلسطينيه

Preparation time: 15 minutes
Cooking time: 5 minutes
Serves 4

8 eggs
4 scallions (spring onions),
    finely chopped
½ cup (1 oz/25 g) flat-leaf parsley,
    finely chopped
½ cup (1 oz/25 g) fresh mint leaves,
    finely chopped
1 large clove garlic, crushed
1 green chilli, seeded and finely
    chopped (optional)
1 scant teaspoon salt
½ teaspoon ground cumin
¼ teaspoon black pepper
1 tablespoon all-purpose (plain) flour
olive oil, for frying

To serve
— olives, scallions (spring onion),
    mint and tomato
— Labaneh, homemade (page 26)
    or store-bought
— Pita bread, homemade (page 38)
    or store-bought

Palestinians often make frittatas for weekend breakfasts or as a weekend supper dish. It's basically eggs mixed with herbs and spices and some flour, but the result can vary tremendously from one cook to the next. My uncle's wife, Ameera, is famous for her *ijjeh*—the perfect mix of crispy and fluffy, spicy and smooth—and she would never let us leave after a weekend visit without making them for us. She would sit in the kitchen turning out one round disc after the another, until we had a plate piled high with these fragrant and filling frittatas. This is her recipe—it's quite generous with the herbs, but you can add more or less, as you like. A dish definitely worth a try instead of your standard weekend eggs.

Break the eggs into a large bowl and whisk until the mixture is pale yellow and starting to froth. Add the chopped herbs, garlic, chilli, salt, and spices and mix until evenly combined. Sprinkle the flour over the eggs and whisk until incorporated.

Heat a generous amount of olive oil in a skillet (frying pan) over medium-high heat. You can use one very large pan or a small one and work in batches. I prefer using a smaller pan and making several really thin omelets as they come out crispier this way, adding more oil to the pan after each frittata.

Once the oil is hot, pour the mixture into the pan, tilting it around to get an even layer of eggs. Cook until the edges start to curl and the top is starting to solidify, periodically lifting with a spatula to make sure the bottom is not burning. When the frittata is no longer runny on the top, flip it over to brown the other side. Continue to cook for another minute or two until done, then slide the frittata onto a plate. If using a small pan, repeat, adding more olive oil, until the egg mixture is all used up. Serve immediately with fresh pita bread and a side of labaneh.

EGG AND POTATO HASH

بطاطا وبيض

Preparation time: 20 minutes
Cooking time: 20–30 minutes
Serves 4

3 tablespoons olive oil
1 lb 11 oz/750 g potatoes (about 5 small
    or 3 large), chopped into ½ inch/
    1 cm cubes
¼ teaspoon Nine Spice Mix (page 24,
    or use ground allspice)
½ teaspoon salt
¼ teaspoon black pepper (optional)
4 eggs, lightly beaten
fresh herbs and chilli flakes, to garnish

To serve
— Pita bread, homemade (page 38)
    or store-bought

This is traditionally a breakfast dish but it was also one of my mother's go-to dishes for lunch or dinner on busy days when she didn't have time to cook a proper meal. When served with some Labaneh (page 26) and a plate of fresh vegetables, it includes everything you could possibly want in a meal—carbs, protein, dairy, and vegetables—and is ready to eat in about 30 minutes. You do, however, have the option to add other vegetables like onions, garlic, and bell peppers. In that case, just make sure to sauté the vegetables, cooking those with the longest cooking time first.

Heat the olive oil in a large lidded nonstick or cast-iron skillet (frying pan) over medium-high heat. Add the potatoes and cook for 20–25 minutes, tossing frequently, until golden brown and crisp all over.

Add the Nine Spice Mix, salt, and pepper and give it one more toss. If the potatoes are still not soft (a fork should slip into a piece easily if ready), add 1–2 teaspoons of water, cover the pan, and let cook for another 5 minutes, tossing once or twice during that time.

Pour the beaten egg over the potatoes and use a rubber spatula to mix the eggs in until the potatoes are fully coated. Continue to move around the pan with the spatula until the eggs are cooked and evenly dispersed throughout the potatoes, about 2–3 minutes.

Remove from the heat, garnish with fresh herbs and chilli flakes and serve with warm pita bread.

SHAKSHUKA

شكشوكه

Preparation time: 5 minutes
Cooking time: 15–30 minutes
Serves 4–6

3 tablespoons olive oil
8–10 cloves garlic, very finely chopped
3 green chillies, thinly sliced
1 teaspoon crushed red chilli flakes
¼ teaspoon cumin seeds (or use
    ground cumin)
2¼ lb/1 kg fresh tomatoes, diced or
    2 x 14 oz/400 g cans peeled whole
    plum tomatoes
6 eggs
salt and black pepper
fresh mint or flat-leaf parsley leaves,
    to garnish

To serve
— fresh bread

Allthough this dish is of Tunisian origin, it has found its
place in the Palestinian kitchen. For Eid al-Fitr, the holiday
that celebrates the end of Ramadan, we would all gather
with my mother's family for a huge breakfast—although it
was more akin to dinner in terms of the quantity and type
of food served. Everything from braised variety meats (offal),
fried mackerel, grilled cheese, and—of course—shakshuka
would be on the table. Although most versions of this recipe
available today feature onions, peppers, and other additions
like eggplant (aubergine) and feta, my favorite remains this
simple version, flavored only with garlic and chilies.

Heat the olive oil in a shallow Dutch oven (casserole) or cast-
iron skillet (frying pan) over medium heat. Add the garlic,
chillies, red chilli flakes, and cumin seeds and cook until
fragrant, about 2 minutes.

Add the tomatoes and ½ teaspoon salt and stir to combine.
Reduce the heat, cover, and simmer for about 10 minutes, or
until the sauce thickens. (If using fresh tomatoes this could
take up to 30 minutes.)

Remove the lid and crack the eggs on top of the tomatoes.
Sprinkle with salt and pepper then re-cover. Cook until
the eggs are your desired level of doneness, about 5 minutes
for fully cooked, 3 minutes for runny yolks. Remove from
the heat, sprinkle with fresh mint or parsley leaves and
serve with bread.

Note: You can prepare this dish ahead by making the
tomato sauce and refrigerating until you are ready to serve.
Simply reheat the sauce until gently bubbling, then crack
in the eggs and cook as above for a delicious meal that is
ready in minutes.

EGG AND LAMB FRY-UP

لحمه وبيض

Preparation time: 20 minutes
Cooking time: 10–15 minutes
Serves 4–6

1 tablespoon butter
1 tablespoon olive oil
1 lb 2 oz/500 g lamb meat from the leg,
    cut into ½-inch/1-cm cubes
½ teaspoon Nine Spice Mix (page 24)
½ teaspoon salt
6 eggs, whisked with a pinch of salt
    and black pepper
½ teaspoon sumac

To serve
— Pita bread, homemade (page 38)
    or store-bought
— fresh vegetables and pickles

My father always told me this dish tastes best when he eats it at the butchers where he buys his meat because the butcher uses such fresh ingredients, fried simply in olive oil, that it really needs very little else. Humble yet hearty, this dish is quick and easy to make and can be eaten for breakfast, lunch, or dinner. The recipe here is slightly modified from the basic one my father enjoyed, but I have kept it as true to the original as possible.

Put the butter and olive oil into a skillet (frying pan) and place over high heat until hot but not smoking. Add the meat, sprinkle with Nine Spice Mix and salt, and cook for 5–10 minutes, stirring occasionally, until browned on all sides and cooked through. If the meat releases water, cook until all water has evaporated and the meat is brown.

Pour the eggs evenly over the meat and stir with a spoon until the meat and eggs are fully incorporated and the egg starts to set. Cook until the eggs reach the desired consistency, about 2 minutes for softly scrambled and 4 minutes for firmer texture.

Transfer to a plate, sprinkle the sumac over the top, and serve with pita bread, fresh vegetables, and pickles.

CHICKPEAS IN TAHINI SAUCE

مسبحه

Preparation time: 20 minutes
Cooking time: 5–10 minutes
Serves 4–6

2 x 14-oz/400-g cans chickpeas,
    rinsed and drained
1 teaspoon ground cumin
1 cup (8 oz/225 g) tahini
1 large clove garlic, crushed
1 teaspoon salt
½ cup (4 oz/120 g) yogurt
4 tablespoons freshly squeezed
    lemon juice

For the dressing
1 large clove garlic, finely diced
1 green chilli, finely diced
2 tablespoons olive oil
2 tablespoons freshly squeezed
    lemon juice

To serve
— 2 tablespoons finely chopped
    flat-leaf parsley
— ground cumin
— paprika
— fresh bread

I wouldn't be surprised if this dish was the invention of some lazy soul who didn't want to make hummus. After all, it is simply cooked chickpeas dressed in tahini sauce. Lucky for us, it turned out to be a triumph, with the whole chickpeas softening the flavor of the sharp tahini for a truly spectacular combination. The word *msabaha* means "swimming" or "floating" in something and refers to the chickpeas swimming in the tahini sauce. Best served warm, you can prepare the tahini sauce and boiled chickpeas ahead of time then simply rewarm the chickpeas and mix everything together right before you eat.

Put the drained chickpeas and cumin into a pan and cover with water. Bring to a boil, then reduce the heat and simmer, covered, to keep warm as you prepare the rest of the dish.

Meanwhile, put the tahini, garlic, salt, yogurt, and lemon juice into a large bowl and stir to combine; the sauce will be thick and sticky at this point. Set aside.

To prepare the dressing, put the diced garlic and chilli into a small bowl with the olive oil and lemon juice and stir to combine.

To assemble the dish, add half a cup of the hot chickpea cooking water to the tahini sauce and mix well. Scoop out roughly a quarter of the chickpeas, add to the tahini sauce and mix well, using the back of the spoon to mash the chickpeas. Drain the rest of the chickpeas, add to the tahini sauce and mix with a spoon to evenly combine. Transfer to a shallow serving bowl.

Spoon the lemon and garlic mixture over the chickpeas, then sprinkle with the parsley, cumin, and paprika. Serve with bread.

CAULIFLOWER FRITTERS

عجة قرنبيط

Preparation time: 20 minutes
Cooking time: 5–10 minutes
Makes about 15

11 oz/300 g cauliflower (about 1 small
or ½ large)
5 scallions (spring onions), finely
chopped
large handful (1 oz/25 g) flat-leaf
parsley, finely chopped
1 tablespoon finely chopped mint
leaves
2 cloves garlic, very finely chopped
½ teaspoon salt
½ teaspoon ground cumin
½ teaspoon Nine Spice Mix (page 24)
¼ teaspoon turmeric
1 cup (4 oz/120 g) all-purpose (plain)
flour (or use a mixture of
all-purpose/plain and whole
wheat/wholemeal)
4 eggs, beaten
olive oil, for frying

When I make these fritters, I'm reminded of my great-aunt frying them at her kerosene stove many years ago as we all waited around a straw floor mat lined with plates of food. Even in today's busy family life, I still adore these fritters for a weekend brunch with a dollop of labaneh and Palestinian Salad (page 104).

Chop the cauliflower into large chunks and steam or boil until fork-tender but not too soft, about 5 minutes. Remove from the heat, allow to dry for a few minutes then chop into small pieces.

Put the cauliflower into a large mixing bowl and add the scallions (spring onions), parsley, mint, garlic, salt, and spices. Gently toss to combine without mashing the cauliflower. Add the flour and eggs and mix well. At this point the mixture can be used immediately or set aside in the refrigerator for several hours until ready to use.

To pan-fry, pour enough oil into a large skillet (frying pan) to reach at least ¾ inch/2 cm up the sides. Place over medium heat until a drop of the mixture bubbles up right away. Scoop about 4 tablespoons of the mixture into the pan, pressing it gently with the back of a spatula to flatten. Add several more scoops, leaving enough room between them to make flipping easier. Cook for 3–4 minutes on each side, or until golden brown. Drain the cooked fritters on paper towels while you cook the remainder (the fritters can be kept warm in a low oven until you are done frying).

Note: The cauliflower can be steamed and chopped up to one day in advance and left, uncovered, in the fridge until you are ready to prepare the fritters.

FALAFEL

فلافل

Preparation time: 30 minutes
Cooking time: 5 minutes
Makes 30–40, depending on size

1 onion
2 small cloves garlic
2 tablespoons chopped flat-leaf
    parsley
2 tablespoons chopped cilantro
    (coriander)
1 red or green chilli (optional)
9 oz/250 g dried chickpeas, soaked
    overnight in water and drained
    (see Note)
1 teaspoon ground cumin
1 teaspoon ground coriander
1 teaspoon salt
1 teaspoon baking powde
Vegetable oil, for deep frying

To serve
— Pita bread, homemade (page 38)
    or store-bought
— Tahini Sauce (page 28)
— mixed vegetables and pickles

Falafel can be found on every street corner back home, so they are more convenient to buy than to make. I used to love going to the Old City of Jerusalem with my mother as we purchased our way to breakfast: the bakery for *ka'ak*, the hummus store, and finally the falafel stand, where you just tell the vendor how many shekels you want to spend and he gives you the appropriate-sized paper bag filled with these crunchy spheres. Since I've been living abroad, however, the only falafel that can compare are the ones made at home; this is my go-to recipe for those weekend mornings when I'm feeling nostalgic for an Old City breakfast.

Put the onion, garlic, parsley, cilantro (coriander), and chilli into the bowl of a food processor and process until finely chopped. Add the drained chickpeas and continue to process, stopping and scraping down the sides of the bowl occasionally, until everything comes together in a coarse paste. You want it a bit grainier than hummus texture to keep the falafel light and fluffy.

Transfer the paste to a bowl, add the spices and salt, and mix until well incorporated. At this point, if not frying immediately, the mixture can be stored in the refrigerator for a couple of days or in the freezer for a couple of months.

When you are ready to cook the falafel, fill a large wok or skillet (frying pan) with 2–3 inches/5–7 cm vegetable oil and place over medium-high heat until it reaches 350°F/180°C.

Meanwhile sprinkle the falafel mixture with the baking powder and mix well. Using a falafel scoop, drop the falafel balls one by one into the hot oil, taking care not to overcrowd the pan, and pan-fry until a deep golden brown, about 5 minutes. If you do not have a falafel scoop, you can use your hands to roll the dough into walnut-sized balls then very slightly flatten with your palms. Remove from the oil with a slotted spoon and drain on paper towels.

Serve with pita bread, tahini sauce, and mixed vegetables and pickles.

Note: Falafel can also be made with a combination of dried chickpeas and split fava (broad) beans. Dried split fava beans are difficult to find outside Middle Eastern grocery stores, so the recipe I have set down here uses only chickpeas. If you do have fava beans, you can substitute up to half the quantity of chickpeas with them.

<u>Right</u>
Stairs leading down from Damascus
Gate into the Old City of Jerusalem.

TAHINI AND GRAPE MOLASSES SPREAD

دبس وطحينه

Preparation time: 2 minutes
Serves 1–2

2 tablespoons tahini
2 tablespoons grape or date molasses

To serve
— Pita bread, homemade (page 38)
    or store-bought

Pita bread with tahini and molasses is basically the Middle Eastern version of a peanut butter and jelly sandwich. Whenever my father had to go to Hebron for a work meeting in the summer, my mother would insist he bring back the grape molasses the town is so famous for. While it can be used the same way you would use honey or maple syrup, we use it mostly for making this rich flavored *dibs wa tahini* spread. Palestinians tend to use grape molasses; in Egypt treacle is more common, and in the Gulf States date molasses tends to be the preference. The flavor, reminiscent of *halaweh* (halva), is an intense and earthy combination of sweet and salty.

Pour the tahini into a small, shallow bowl. Drizzle the molasses in a nice pattern over the tahini.

Serve with warm pita bread; mix together right before eating or use your bread to mix as you eat.

Note: While I use a tahini-molasses ratio of 1:1, you can adjust to suit your tastes with more or less molasses. If you cannot find grape or date molasses, honey is also an excellent alternative. This spread will keep well at room temperature, covered in plastic wrap (clingfilm), for a day or two.

DIPS AND SMALL BITES

My friends tell me I have a problem with portion control. Whenever I invite them over, we rarely have an appetizer, main dish with side, then dessert—I find that way of eating too rigid. When I entertain, the table has to be so full you can't even see it beneath all the plates of food.

On one such evening, about six years ago while still in college, I invited a couple of friends over for dinner. I'm not quite sure how word spread, but I received several phone calls throughout the day from others who had heard I was cooking and wanted to join. So, out of my tiny kitchen, I put on a feast—in true Palestinian spirit—for the over twenty people who gathered for dinner in my very small apartment.

I find this generosity and hospitality to be one of the most appealing things about Palestinian culture. Our food, after all, is about sharing and enjoying different dishes together. From dips like Garlic and Cucumber Labaneh (page 80) and Hummus (page 82) to small snacks like Deep Fried Cheese and Za'atar Parcels (page 84) and Chicken, Sumac, and Pine Nut Rolls (page 86), eating is all about making the most of what you have and finding flavors that complement each other.

With a few legumes, some fresh vegetables, and staple pantry items, you can make an assortment of dips and snacks that could constitute a full meal or complement a basic one. A practice originally born out poverty— Palestinians were mostly farmers who needed to feed large families, and vegetables was readily available while meat was expensive—this way of eating has seeped into today's life as well. You will notice that a Palestinian meal is rarely made of a single dish or pieces of meat portioned out into exact serving sizes. Instead, meals often have several components and are eaten family style ensuring an unannounced guest is always welcome with enough food to go around. Through this way of eating, it becomes clear why Palestinians are known for their abundant hospitality.

The beauty of the recipes in this chapter is that they are versatile and adaptable. The dishes work equally well for breakfast as for a side during lunch or dinner, or as part of a large spread for a special occasion. Combine a few small plates and you have lunch ready. Prepare some in advance and entertaining friends becomes a breeze. Choose a couple of items to serve with dinner and a simple meal becomes luxurious. The best thing about these recipes is they bring people together and compel you to share.

I hope you enjoy the flavors as much as much as the spirit of these recipes because they can serve as your springboard into a warm, generous, and very Palestinian way of cooking and eating.

<u>Left</u>
Olives and pickles vendor in the Old City of Jerusalem.

MUHAMARRA

محمره

Preparation time: 10 minutes
Serves 6–8

5 oz/150 g (about 1 large) roasted
    red bell pepper (see Notes)
4 tablespoons olive oil, plus extra
    for drizzling
4 tablespoons pomegranate molasses
1 tablespoon honey
1 tablespoon tahini
2 teaspoons chilli powder (see Notes)
1 teaspoon paprika
¼ teaspoon ground cumin
½ teaspoon salt
¼ teaspoon finely ground coffee
    (optional, see Notes)
2 cups (7 oz/200 g) walnut pieces,
    plus extra for garnish
1 cup (2 oz/50 g) breadcrumbs

When Bilad Al Sham (The Levant) was a single territory, there was not a clear delineation between Syria, Palestine, and Lebanon and people moved about and inter-married freely. So in the late 1800s, my Teta Asma's grandmother moved to Palestine from Syria as a bride. Along with her beautiful bridal trunk, she also brought many of her family's recipes. *Muhamarra* was one of them. And although Syrian in origin, it has found its way into the food of certain regions in Palestine. Sweet and tart, crunchy and smooth, this recipe is perfect on its own, with bread, and even as a sauce with grilled meats.

Put all the ingredients, except the walnuts and breadcrumbs, into the bowl of a food processor and process until smooth. Add the walnuts and breadcrumbs and pulse until the walnuts are coarsely chopped. You want this dip to retain some texture and not be smooth, so do not overpulse.

Transfer the dip to a bowl and mix with a spoon to combine. To serve, spread in a platter, drizzle with olive oil, and garnish with walnuts.

Notes: You can roast your own bell peppers at home but I tend to use the jarred variety for convenience. Just make sure there are no flavorings or additives and that they are preserved in vinegar and water, not oil.

The dip is supposed to be spicy, but you can adjust the level of spiciness to your taste. If you reduce the amount of chilli, then increase the paprika by the same amount to retain the nice red color. As for the coffee, my great-great grandmother used to say that it helped bring all the flavors together, but it is an addition that can easily be left out.

AVOCADO, LABANEH, AND PRESERVED LEMON SPREAD

أفوكادو بلبنه وحامض مكبوس

Preparation time: 10 minutes
Serves: 4–6

4 small preserved lemons, pith and
    seeds removed
3 tablespoons lemon juice
3 avocados (about 11 oz/300 g flesh)
3 tablespoons Labaneh, homemade
    (page 26) or store-bought (see Note)
¼ teaspoon salt

Teta Fatima's neighbor and good friend had many avocado trees at home. When it was the season, she would send her, and us, giant bags of avocados every couple of weeks. When you've given all your neighbors and friends avocados, what do you do with the endless bags of this delicious creamy fruit? You get creative. We used to make all kinds of dips with it: with tahini, with labaneh, with cream cheese, with vegetables, and so on. The contrast between the sweet, creamy avocados and the sharp, salty lemons and labaneh is heavenly. But more than that, the ensuing bright green color is so beautiful and stays vivid in the refrigerator for a couple of days, making it an excellent dip to entertain with.

Put all the ingredients, except the salt, into the bowl of a food processor and process until fully incorporated and creamy. Taste and season with salt accordingly. This will depend on how salty the labaneh you are using is.

Note: You can make your own labaneh at home or you can easily buy it from good supermarkets. If, however, you do not have labaneh, you could substitute with a combination of 1¼ oz/30 g feta cheese and 1½ tablespoons of Greek yogurt.

PARSLEY OR CILANTRO (CORIANDER) TAHINI SPREAD

بقدونسيه

Preparation time: 15 minutes
Serves 4–8, depending on use

1 quantity Tahini Sauce (page 28)
1 cup (2 oz/50 g) finely chopped flat-leaf
    parsley or cilantro (coriander)
1 clove garlic, crushed

When you eat out at Arabic restaurants back home, you generally don't look at a menu. The restaurant fills your table with small mezze platters and, if there is still space afterwards, some grilled meat or fish. Whenever we went out, *ba'adounsiyeh* was the dish I sat as far away from as possible—I absolutely hated it as a child. Funny enough, I absolutely love it now and find it to be the perfect condiment alongside fish and meats and even great on its own with bread.

Prepare the Tahini Sauce in a bowl. Add the parsley or cilantro (coriander) and garlic and mix until combined.

If using as a spread, keep the consistency thick like this recipe; if using as a sauce, add a tablespoon of water at a time until you reach the desired consistency.

If you want to make this ahead, omit the garlic and stir in just before serving.

WALNUT AND GARLIC LABANEH

لبنه بجوز

Preparation time: 15 minutes
Serves 6–8

1 lb 2 oz/500 g Labaneh, homemade
(page 26) or store-bought
3 cloves garlic
2 green chillies, seeded and
very finely diced
2 red chillies, seeded and
very finely diced
½ cup (2 oz/50 g) coarsely ground
walnuts
olive oil, for drizzling
small handful of walnuts, to garnish
salt

Rumor has it that my great-great grandmother, who came from Syria as a bride, would on a weekly basis prepare her husband a huge mezze spread; he would consequently spend the evening entertaining his friends, playing backgammon, and singing and drinking into the wee hours of the morning. Unfortunately, rumor also has it that too much of this fun is how he ended up selling much of his land. Stories, I am sure, get embellished while passing from one generation to the next, but the best recipes stand the test of time. This is one of those recipes. Originally made with dried chilli flakes, the only adjustment I have made is to use fresh chillies, but both options deliver a delicious result.

Put the labaneh, garlic, chillies, and ground walnuts into a bowl and mix until evenly incorporated. Taste and add salt as necessary; this will depend on the kind of labaneh you have used.

To serve, spread the mixture onto a serving platter and use the back of a spoon to make a well in the middle, leaving a small mound in the center. Drizzle the olive oil around the mound and garnish with whole walnut pieces.

Overleaf
Clockwise from left: Taboon Bread
(page 42); Parsley or Cilantro
(coriander) Tahini Spread (page 76);
Walnut and Garlic Labaneh (page
77); Deep-Fried Cheese and Za'atar
parcels (page 84); Garlic and Cucumber
Labaneh (page 80); Avocado, Labaneh,
and Preserved Lemon Spread (page 76);
labaneh and bulgur spread (page 81).

GARLIC AND CUCUMBER LABANEH

لبنه وخيار

Preparation time: 10 minutes
Serves 4–6

2 Persian or Lebanese cucumbers
    (5–6 oz/150–180 g)
9 oz/250 g Labaneh, homemade
    (page 26) or store-bought
1 small clove garlic, crushed
½ teaspoon crushed dried mint or
    leaves from 3–4 fresh sprigs,
    very finely chopped
salt
olive oil, to serve

Most Mediterranean, Middle Eastern, and South Asian cultures have their own version of cucumber and yogurt: *raita* for Indians, *tzatziki* for Greeks, *mast wa khiyar* for Persians, and *cacik* for Turks, to name just a few. Palestinians have their version as well, but this recipe, made with garlic and labaneh instead of yogurt, takes things up a notch with more intense flavors that give a real kick. It's delicious on its own with crispy toasted pita bread, or if you're like me, as a side to Spiced Beef Pitas (page 88) or Spiced Leg of Lamb (page 156).

Chop the cucumbers into a very fine dice and put into a large bowl. Alternatively, grate the cucumbers and put into a colander set over a sink to drain some of the liquid.

Mix the labaneh, garlic, and mint with the cucumber until combined. Taste and season with salt as desired. Store-bought labaneh tends to be less salty than the traditional homemade variety, so you may need to add some salt. Spoon into a shallow serving bowl and drizzle with olive oil.

Serve as a dip with bread or alongside grilled meats.

LABANEH AND BULGUR SPREAD

سلطة كشك خضرا

Preparation time: 15 minutes + soaking
Serves 6–8

For the spread
½ cup (3 oz/80 g) fine bulgur wheat,
    washed and drained (see Note)
14 oz/450 g whole (full-fat) plain yogurt
2–3 tablespoons Labaneh, homemade
    (page 26) or store-bought
1 tablespoon dried herbs (or use
    a mixture of mint, za'atar, oregano,
    and marjoram)
1 teaspoon chilli powder (optional)
salt

To serve
4–5 scallions (spring onions),
    finely chopped
½ cup (2 oz/50 g) coarsely chopped
    walnuts, toasted
olive oil, for drizzling

Before refrigeration, people ate seasonally and found ways to preserve certain supplies from one year to the next. *Kishk* was one of those staple items that originated as a pantry ingredient. Right after the wheat harvest at the end of the summer, people would make bulgur from the wheat and mix it with yogurt until it absorbed all the liquid. The ensuing *kishk* was then spread on cloths and left to dry in the sun, after which it was rubbed into a powder and stored. This spread, which literally translates as "green kishk salad", is made from the *kishk* before it is dried. It's the way my Teta Asma always made it; we would eat it with a fork, with bread, or use it as a *mana'eesh* flatbread (page 44) topping.

Combine the bulgur, yogurt, and 1 teaspoon salt in a large bowl and leave at room temperature for several hours, or overnight.

Add the labaneh, a tablespoon at a time, until you achieve a consistency similar to hummus. You may need to add more salt depending on how salty the labaneh you are using is, so taste and adjust the seasoning. Mix in the herbs and chilli powder, if using. At this point, you can transfer the mixture to the refrigerator and keep for up to 1 week, taking out as much of it as you want to eat.

To serve, mix in the scallions (spring onions) and chopped walnuts. Put into a serving dish and, using the back of a spoon, spread the mixture so there is a well in the center. Drizzle generously with olive oil.

Note: If you can only find coarse bulgur wheat, then you will need to soak it in warm water for about 15 minutes before draining and mixing it with the yogurt. If you do this, you may need to adjust the quantity of yogurt and labaneh. This recipe is quite forgiving, so you won't go wrong. If the bulgur seems to have absorbed all the yogurt and is very dry, simply add more. If it seems too liquid, thicken with more labaneh.

HUMMUS

حمص

Preparation time: 10 minutes
Makes about 1 lb 2 oz/500 g

11 oz/350 g cooked and peeled chickpeas
(see Note), reserving a few to garnish
½ cup (4 fl oz/125 ml) tahini, stirred well
before measuring
½ cup (4 fl oz/125 ml) cold water
(or chickpea cooking liquid)
1 tablespoon lemon juice
¾ teaspoon salt
olive oil, for drizzling
paprika, ground cumin, chopped
parsley, to garnish

Probably the most recognizable—and most controversial—Middle Eastern dish. I think there is actually no right or wrong way to make it; there are simply preferences, and there are as many ways to make hummus as there are Middle Eastern families. As a child, we regularly ate it, but I never thought much of it; it was just something that was always around, like labaneh, and I didn't care much for it. It was only when I left Jerusalem to start university in the U.S. that I realized what a big "thing" hummus was. I have since experimented with it: dried and canned chickpeas, peeled and unpeeled, just tahini or tahini and olive oil, with and without garlic and spices—the list goes on. The recipe here is how I like hummus, smooth (peeled chickpeas), rich (lots of tahini), and not too sharp (a little lemon juice but no garlic or spices). Use this as a starting point but experiment and taste as you go along to find your own perfect plate of hummus.

Put all the ingredients into a food processor or blender and process until smooth. If using a powerful blender, you could throw in a few ice cubes while blending to make it even smoother. Bear in mind that once refrigerated, hummus will thicken slightly, so adjust the consistency with water and lemon juice, tasting along the way.

To serve, ladle the hummus into a serving plate and use the back of a spoon to make a well in the center. Place some chickpeas in the middle and drizzle olive oil all over. Garnish with paprika, cumin, or parsley—or all three.

Note: I have tried boiling dried chickpeas and using canned or jarred chickpeas. The result is variable and really depends on the brand and quality of the beans themselves. Depending on what you have access to, you may need to try a few different batches of hummus before you settle on a trusted brand or method. Peeled chickpeas simply mean the hummus will be smoother, but the flavor is not changed much. If using dried chickpeas, my mother would always soak the beans overnight with plenty of water and some baking soda (bicarbonate of soda), then cook until very soft, at which point the skins can easily be rubbed by hand. I personally use jarred (not canned) chickpeas because I find their skins tend to come off more easily. Nowadays, it is possible to find ready peeled chickpeas in some Middle Eastern grocery stores and from specialty online suppliers.

FRIED BABA GHANOUJ

متبل باذنجان مقلي

Preparation time: 10 minutes
Cooking time: 30 minutes
Serves 6–8

2¼ lb/1 kg (about 4 medium or 2 large)
    eggplants (aubergines)
vegetable oil, for frying
4 tablespoons tahini
½ cup (4 oz/120 g) plain yogurt
4 tablespoons lemon juice
1 large clove garlic, crushed
salt

To serve
— finely chopped parsley
— finely diced tomatoes or
    pomegranate seeds
— Pita bread, homemade (page 38)
    or store-bought

Try as I might, I've never been a big fan of traditional *baba ghanouj*—chargrilled eggplants (aubergines) mixed with a tahini sauce—because I've always found it lacking in depth of flavor. The reason, I assume, is because I grew up eating a different version of it at my Teta Fatima's house, which she made on Fridays with the leftover fried eggplants from the *maqlubeh* (page 198). Now, that dip is one I cannot get enough of. Whenever I make it for friends and tell them it's *baba ghanouj*, they stare in disbelief, wondering why it tastes so much better than any other they've had before. Little do they know that the only difference is using fried, instead of chargrilled, eggplants. It may be less friendly to the waistline and require more active work, but the flavor makes it absolutely worthwhile.

Chop the eggplants (aubergines) into small even-sized pieces. Place in a large colander, sprinkle generously with salt, and let stand for about 1 hour. This step helps to release the water from the eggplants so they absorb less oil and are crisper when fried. Rinse the eggplants, then pat dry with paper towels.

To pan-fry the eggplants, heat the oil in a deep fryer or heavy casserole to 350°F/180°C, or until a morsel of bread immediately rises to the surface when dropped in. Working in batches, fry the eggplants until a nice golden brown. Remove with a slotted spoon and drain on paper towels.

Once lightly cooled, pat dry the eggplants again with paper towels to absorb as much excess oil as possible. Transfer the fried eggplant to a large bowl and add the tahini, yogurt, lemon juice, garlic, and 1 teaspoon of salt. Mix very well with a fork, breaking up any large pieces or lumps as you go, until evenly combined.

Spoon the dip into a shallow serving bowl and sprinkle with parsley and either freshly chopped tomatoes or pomegranate seeds—they will help break through the richness of this deliciously addictive dip. Serve with fresh pita bread.

DEEP-FRIED CHEESE AND ZA'ATAR PARCELS

سمبوسك مقلي

Preparation time: 1 hour 30 minutes
Cooking time: 5 minutes
Makes about 80 mini or 40 small parcels

For the pastry
4½ cups (1 lb 2 oz/500 g) all-purpose
    (plain) flour
2 tablespoons semolina (optional)
½ cup (4 fl oz/120 ml) olive oil
2 tablespoons distilled white vinegar
1 teaspoon salt
1 tablespoon nigella seeds
1 tablespoon dried za'atar (see Note)
1–1½ cups (8–12 oz/225–350 g) plain
    yogurt
9 oz/250 g grated halloumi cheese,
    grated (or use 6 oz/175 g feta
    and 3 oz/75 g dry/low moisture
    mozzarella)
vegetable oil, for deep-frying

In small Palestinian towns, people normally don't plan visits; they simply show up. The spontaneity of it somehow adds to the fun. For the woman of the house, though, this meant a need for an unlimited supply of treats that can be served at a minute's notice. These fried parcels were a favorite with my mother and aunts: straight from the freezer into the deep fryer and all you needed was a bowl of *tabuleh*, labaneh, olives, pickles, and nuts and your coffee table became a feasting table.

Put the flour, semolina, and olive oil into a large bowl and mix together with your hands until you have a crumbly texture. Add the vinegar, salt, nigella seeds, and za'atar and mix until well combined.

Gradually add the yogurt and start kneading. Depending on the flour variety you use, you may not need all the yogurt, or you may need the entire quantity plus 1–2 tablespoons of water. Knead until you arrive at a pliable dough that isn't too soft. Put into a bowl, cover with plastic wrap (clingfilm), and set aside to rest for 15 minutes.

Once rested, divide your dough equally into 2 balls. Leave one covered in the bowl and roll out the other on a floured surface, as thinly as possible. Using a 2½-inch/7-cm cookie cutter (for the mini version), cut out circles from the dough.

Place about a teaspoon of the grated halloumi into each circle, leaving a very small border around the perimeter. Fold over into a half-moon shape and, using a fork, crimp the edges shut to give a nice design and ensure the filling won't fall out. Repeat until all the circles are filled.

Gather up the scraps, knead into a ball, and set aside to rest while you work on the second ball of dough. Repeat until you have used up all the halloumi. At this point, the parcels can be frozen: freeze in a single layer, then transfer to a suitable airtight container and freeze for up to 3 months.

To fry the parcels immediately, heat the oil in a deep fryer or heavy Dutch oven (casserole) to 350°F/180°C, or until a morsel of dough immediately rises to the surface when dropped in. Deep-fry the parcels, in batches to avoid overcrowding the pan, for 5 minutes, or until a deep golden color. Drain on paper towels and serve immediately.

Note: We normally use dried za'atar leaves, rubbed by hand, to flavor this dough. An alternative would be to use dried za'atar or a mixture of dried oregano and thyme.

<u>Right</u>
Bunches of freshly gathered
za'atar leaves at a market
in Jerusalem.

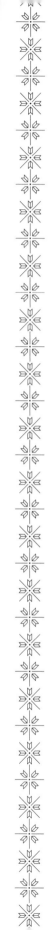

CHICKEN, SUMAC, AND PINE NUT ROLLS

أصابع مسخن

Preparation time: 1 hour
Cooking time: 10–15 minutes
Makes 30–40

For the rolls
½ cup (4 fl oz/120 ml) olive oil, plus
    extra for brushing
3 onions, finely chopped
1 tablespoon sumac
1 teaspoon ground cumin
½ teaspoon Nine Spice Mix (page 24)
1 teaspoon salt
1 lb 2 oz/500 g shredded cooked chicken
    (see Simplification)
1 tablespoon Toasted Pine
    Nuts (page 31)
30 rolling pastry sheets, 5 × 7 inches/
    12 × 18 cm (see Note)
olive oil, for brushing

For the dip
scant 1 cup (7 oz/200 g) plain yogurt
1 clove garlic, crushed
sumac
salt

When I was a child, we visited my maternal grandparents every Friday. On one Friday each month, Teta Fatima would make us *msakhan*: she would be up from the break of dawn baking her own taboon bread, boiling the chickens, and cooking the onions. I often crave those flavors but rarely have the time to make this elaborate dish. On those days, my eternal stash of msakhan rolls in the freezer saves the day—they are especially good served with a yogurt and garlic dip. This recipe assumes you will be freezing some of the rolls, but you can easily make half or double to suit your needs.

Heat the olive oil in a large skillet (frying) pan and cook the onions, spices, and salt over a medium heat, stirring, until softened but not browned, about 15 minutes. Remove from the heat and mix in the shredded chicken and pine nuts.

Unwrap the pastry, cut into the desired shape, if necessary (see *Note*) and cover with a damp dish towel to avoid drying out. Lay one sheet on your work surface and place about 2 teaspoons of filling at the bottom, leaving about ¾ inch/2 cm empty at each side. Fold over the sides and roll up. Continue until you have used up all wrappers and filling. At this point, you can freeze these rolls to use at a later time—they will keep for up to 2 months. If cooking immediately, preheat the oven to 350°F/180°C/Gas Mark 4.

Brush the rolls with olive oil and bake in the oven for 10–15 minutes, or until they are golden brown and crispy.

Meanwhile, prepare the dip by combining the yogurt and crushed garlic together. Season with salt and sprinkle with sumac. Serve with the fresh crispy rolls.

Simplification: You can shred any leftover chicken (roast, boiled, broiled/grilled) to use in this recipe. Leftovers of the Chicken, Onion, and Sumac Casserole (page 144) are ideal. So a good tip is to make that for dinner one night and use the leftovers to have the stuffing for these rolls ready in minutes.

Note: Traditionally, we make these rolls with *shrak* bread, a large, round, paper-thin bread. This very common bread in the Levant region is easily found in Middle Eastern grocery stores. While the taste and look is most traditional with it, alternatives include phyllo (filo) pastry, and spring roll or samosa wrappers. If using any of these, you can freeze without baking and when ready to eat, bake direct from frozen according to pastry package instructions.

SPICED BEEF PITAS

عرايس لحمه

Preparation time: 15 minutes
Cooking time: 10 minutes
Serves 4

4 medium Pita bread, homemade
    (page 38) or store-bought
11 oz/300 g ground (minced) beef or lamb
1 tomato, seeded and very finely diced
1 small onion, very finely diced
1 green chilli, very finely diced
1 tablespoon finely chopped flat-leaf
    parsley
1 tablespoon finely chopped cilantro
    (coriander)
1 tablespoon olive oil
1 teaspoon salt
½ teaspoon Nine Spice Mix (page 24)
½ teaspoon red chilli flakes (optional)
olive oil, for brushing

To serve
— Garlic and Cucumber Labaneh
    (page 80)
— fresh tomatoes

Arayes are basically a Middle Eastern hamburger, a fantastic treat of juicy, spiced meat housed in crunchy pita bread. The best thing about them is you can whip them up in no time and can cook them in so many ways—broiler (grill), oven, or panini press. I find that chopping the ingredients by hand gives a better texture and prevents the meat mixture from releasing too much water, but if you're in a rush, you could pulse everything in a food processor. Try to use thicker pita bread as it cooks more evenly with the meat.

Use a serrated, pointed knife to cut around each pita in half, giving you two flat, round pieces of bread. Set aside.

Put the meat into a large bowl with all the other ingredients, except the olive oil, and mix until well combined. Evenly spread a thin layer of the meat mixture into each half. Gently press together to close.

Generously brush each bread with olive oil on both sides. Place in a panini press and cook on medium heat until the meat is fully cooked and the bread has nicely browned and crisped up, about 5–10 minutes.

Serve with Garlic and Cucumber Labaneh (page 80) and fresh tomatoes.

Note: You could also cook the pitas in the oven or on an outdoor grill. For the oven, preheat to 400°F/200°C/Gas Mark 6 and place on a baking sheet or oven rack and cook for 15–20 minutes, or until the meat is done and the bread is crispy. For an outdoor grill, simply place on the grill until the meat is cooked through, about 5–10 minutes.

KUBBEH: THE GUIDING PRINCIPLES

Everyone who tastes my mother's kubbeh always says there's something different about it, something better. So one morning not too long ago, while sitting together at our kitchen table making *kubbeh*, I asked her to reveal her secret. She looked at me, smiled, and showed me her hands. "Thirty years," she said, "that's my only secret." Not the answer I was hoping for, but one I couldn't argue with either. I have to agree that kubbeh really is a case of practice makes perfect.

But that shouldn't deter anyone from attempting this delicious dish common across the entire Levant. If anything, it should encourage you, because as long as you follow a few basic principles, you are on the road to perfecting your very own kubbeh.

Kubbeh is basically a combination of bulgur and meat that is prepared, cooked, and shaped in many different ways. Syria, where my great-great grandmother is from, is said to have more than 100 varieties of kubbeh. While the possibilities and combinations are endless, the recipes included in this book (pages 90, 92, 170, and 200) are more common in Palestine and particularly common in my family. Keep practicing and you will perfect the art of kubbeh. Until then, here are a few points to keep in mind:

— Make sure the meat is fresh, lean, and finely ground (minced) to a paste, preferably at home. You can do this by running it twice through a fine meat mincer. Otherwise, choose a good cut of meat and ask your butcher to grind (mince) it twice for you.

— Keep a bowl of iced water next to you as you work to ensure your hands remain cold and the meat stays fresh.

— Use only fine bulgur wheat.

— We normally prepare all our kubbeh at a bulgur to meat weight ratio of 1:1. However, it's simply a matter of preference; using less meat will make the kubbeh more crunchy but the mixture will require a bit more kneading.

— Lemon zest and herbs are optional but they do add a subtle hint of fresh flavor.

— If you want to freeze kubbeh, do so after you have prepared it but before cooking it. Freeze on trays until frozen, then transfer to a suitable airtight container. They can then be cooked direct from frozen.

FRIED KUBBEH

كبه مقليه

Preparation time: 1 hour 30 minutes
Cooking time: 5 minutes
Makes about 45

For the kubbeh dough
2¾ cups (1 lb 2 oz/500 g) very fine
   bulgur wheat
1 large onion, quartered
2 small sprigs marjoram, thyme, basil,
   or oregano, leaves only (optional)
¼ teaspoon lemon zest (optional)
1 tablespoon salt
1 teaspoon Nine Spice Mix (page 24)
1 teaspoon ground cumin
1 lb 2 oz/500 g lean goat, lamb, or beef
   meat, finely ground (minced)

For the filling
1 quantity Lamb with Onion and Spices
   (page 30)

vegetable oil, for frying

To serve
— Tahini Sauce (optional, page 28)

A crispy dough encasing a spiced meat and nut filling, these crunchy, meat filled parcels are a go-to dish for any gathering, and no mezze table is complete without them. This recipe yields a large quantity, but if you are already going to the trouble of making them, it's well worth making extra to freeze as they keep well for a couple of months and can be fried directly from frozen.

To make the dough for the shells, put the bulgur into a large bowl and cover with cold water. Soak for 15 minutes, then drain, squeezing out as much excess water as you can.

Put the onion, herbs, lemon zest, salt, and spices into the bowl of a food processor with 2 tablespoons of cold water and process until finely ground (minced). Add the meat and pulse until evenly combined. Finally add the bulgur and continue to process until it resembles a smooth dough.

Tip the mixture into a large bowl and knead briefly to ensure everything is evenly combined. Refrigerate for at least 1 hour, and up to overnight, to make it easier to work with.

Meanwhile, prepare the filling ingredients and mix together; set aside.

Pour some iced water into a shallow bowl and keep nearby to wet your hands as necessary while you shape the kubbeh.

To prepare the kubbeh, tear off a small egg-sized chunk of the dough and roll into a ball. Place in the palm of one hand and with the index finger of the other hand make a hole in the center. Continue pushing into it while rotating, until you have a small cup shape with thin walls.

With a small spoon, fill the kubbeh with the filling, being careful not to overfill so you can close it properly. Once filled, gather the open edges together to seal. With moist hands, gently form the kubbeh into the shape of an egg, using the tips of your fingers to shape the top and bottom into pointed ends. Continue until you have used up all the dough and filling. At this point, the kubbeh can be fried or frozen.

To deep-fry the kubbeh, heat oil in a deep fryer to 350°F/180°C. Working in batches, place several kubbeh in the oil, taking care not to overcrowd the pan. Fry for about 5 minutes until a deep golden brown, then remove with a slotted spoon and drain on paper towels. Serve immediately with a side of Tahini Sauce, if desired.

VEGETARIAN FRIED KUBBEH

كبه نباتيه مقليه

Preparation time: 1 hour 30 minutes
Cooking time: 5 minutes
Makes about 45

For the dough
1 cup (6 oz/175 g) very fine bulgur wheat
¾ cup (6 fl oz/175 ml) boiling water
1 cup (4 oz/120 g) all-purpose (plain)
　flour
½ teaspoon salt
½ teaspoon Nine Spice Mix (page 24)
4 tablespoons vegetable oil

Filling 1: cheese
7 oz/200 g feta cheese, crumbled
3½ oz/100 g dry/low moisture
　mozzarella, shredded
1 tablespoon dried mint

Filling 2: chickpea
1 tablespoon olive oil
1 small onion, finely diced
½ teaspoon salt
¼ teaspoon black pepper
¼ teaspoon ground cumin
1 x 14-oz/400-g can chickpeas,
　drained and rinsed
¼ cup (1 oz/25 g) chopped walnuts,
　lightly toasted

This recipe is a vegetarian take on one of the most prevalent foods in our culture, making it possible for non-meat eaters to enjoy these delicious parcels too. There are many possible vegetarian fillings, but below are two of my favorites.

Put the bulgur into a large mixing bowl, pour over the boiling water and mix. Set aside until the bulgur has absorbed the water and cooled down, about 1 hour, then place in the refrigerator to cool further—for at least 30 minutes and up to 3 days.

Meanwhile, prepare the filling. For the cheese option, simply combine all the ingredients in a bowl and toss to combine. For the chickpea option, heat the olive oil in a skillet (frying pan) over medium heat and add the onion, salt, and spices. Cook, stirring occasionally, until softened and just starting to brown. Add the chickpeas, tossing to combine, then remove from the heat. Add the walnuts and mix well.

When you are ready to make the kubbeh, remove the bulgur from the refrigerator and add the flour, salt, and spices. Gradually add the oil until it comes together as a dough. To test, tear off an egg-sized chunk and squeeze with the palm of one hand—if it stays together and can be easily shaped, then it is ready. If it falls apart, then knead some more, adding oil if it is too dry or sprinkling with flour if too wet.

To shape, tear off a small egg-sized chunk and roll into a ball. Place the ball in the palm of one hand and with the index finger of the other hand make a hole in the center. Continue pushing into it, but not all the way to the other side, rotating until you have a cup shape with thin walls.

With a very small spoon, fill the kubbeh with your chosen filling, being careful not to overfill so you can close it properly. Once filled, gather the open edges together to seal. With moist hands, gently form the kubbeh into the shape of an egg, using the tips of your fingers to shape the top and bottom into pointed ends. Alternatively, you can shape the kubbeh into balls—less traditional but easier to shape. At this point, the kubbeh can be fried or frozen on a tray and transferred later to a suitable airtight container; they will keep in the freezer for up to 3 months.

To deep-fry the kubbeh, heat oil in a deep fryer to 350°F/ 180°C. Working in batches, place several kubbeh balls in the oil, taking care not to overcrowd the pan. Fry for 5 minutes until a deep golden brown, then remove with a slotted spoon and drain on paper towels. Serve immediately.

SALADS, SIDES, AND VEGETABLES

Vegetables and fruits are the basis, and often the lead actors, in many Palestinian dishes. Driving around the country, you see a landscape dotted with olive and fig trees, with grape vines and lemon trees. You see mountains blossoming with za'atar and sage, and fields flowing with dandelions and cauliflowers.

Our people are deeply connected to this landscape, and the land represents their lives and livelihood. Produce is not something Palestinians simply pick up at the supermarket; it is often something we grow or our neighbors and families harvest, it is something we forage for or pick up from a local market. It is something we are familiar with and whose unique properties—like the bitterness of dandelion or prickliness of gundelia (a type of wild vegetable)—we've come to embrace.

This is partly because vegetables were often all Palestinian families had to eat, so we learned how to treat them well. We learned how to create a rich variety of dishes whose origin came out of poverty. These vegetables have repaid us lavishly with an abundant repertoire of dishes from smooth Arugula (Rocket) and Garlic Yogurt (page 112) to cool Gazan Tomato Salsa (page 113), from Dandelions with Caramelized Onions (page 110) to a multitude of fresh salads. Having moved away from this land, though, I've found that that doesn't meant letting go of it. It means finding new ways to connect to it, and that's what writing this book was about—using food to preserve a piece of our culture and identity regardless of our geography.

The best thing you can do is to approach the following dishes with the same flexible mindset. These recipes are some of the most vibrant, creative, and fresh ones in this book. They can work as stand-alone meals or as sides, and they almost all rely on some kind of produce. With fresh eyes, an awareness of the landscape around you, and an attempt to use what is local and seasonal, your food can be magical. Can't find dandelions? Use kale. Eggplants (aubergines) not in season for the yogurt and nut salad? Substitute with cauliflower. Tomatoes not at their best for the Palestinian salad? Try red bell peppers instead. The methods of preparation (e.g. mixing with yogurt or caramelizing onions) and the dressings (such as those with pomegranate molasses or garlic and lemon) are what lend many of these dishes their distinctive flavors. So get creative with the produce and you will not be disappointed.

Left
Freshly picked scallions (spring onions) sold on the streets of the Old City of Jerusalem.

EGGPLANT (AUBERGINE), YOGURT, AND NUT SALAD

سلطة باذنجان ولبن

Preparation time: 15 minutes
Cooking time: 20 minutes
Serves 4–6

2¼ lb/1 kg (about 4 medium)
    eggplants (aubergines)
olive oil, for brushing
salt and black pepper

For the yogurt sauce
1½ cups (14 oz/400 g) Greek yogurt
1 small clove garlic, crushed
½ teaspoon salt
½ teaspoon lemon juice (optional)

For the garnish
2 tablespoons pomegranate seeds
½ cup (2 oz/50 g) lightly toasted mixed
    nuts such as almonds, pistachios,
    hazelnuts
small handful of green leaves such as
    arugula (rocket), dill, or chives

Whenever we invited people over for a big lunch, my mother would usually make a variation of this salad and it would be the highlight for me. Her version was much richer than this one, though, because she fried the eggplants (aubergines), used a very strong garlic labaneh instead of yogurt, and topped it with plenty of fried pine nuts.
Over the years I've adapted it into something that we can eat at home on a weekly basis—just as flavorful, but on the lighter and healthier side. As far as the nuts and garnish go, I often play around with it depending on my mood, so feel free to adjust based on what you have to hand.

Preheat the broiler (grill) to high. Slice the eggplants (aubergines) into ¾-inch/1.5-cm rounds, brush both sides with olive oil, and sprinkle with salt and pepper. Place the eggplants on an oven rack and broil (grill) for about 10 minutes on each side, or until they develop a golden brown exterior.

In the meantime, put all the ingredients for the yogurt sauce into a bowl and whisk together to a smooth consistency. The lemon juice is optional but it helps bring all the flavors together, especially if you are using a mellow yogurt, not a tangy one.

Once the eggplants are done, arrange in overlapping circles on a round platter. Spoon over the yogurt mixture then top with pomegranate seeds, toasted nuts, and green leaves.

Variation: Use zucchini (courgettes), cut in half and sliced lengthwise, instead of the eggplants and use walnuts, pomegranate seeds, and sumac for the garnish.

TETA ASMA'S TABULEH

تبولة تيتا أسمى

Preparation time: 20 minutes
Serves 4 as a main or 8 as an appetizer

1½ cups (9 oz/250 g) coarse bulgur wheat
1½ cups (3 oz/75 g) finely chopped
    flat-leaf parsley
½ cup (1 oz/25 g) finely chopped
    fresh mint
4 medium (about 1 lb 2 oz/500 g)
    tomatoes, finely diced
½ cup (2 oz/50 g) shelled pistachios,
    lightly toasted
⅓ cup (1½ oz/40 g) coarsely chopped
    walnuts, lightly toasted
⅓ cup (2 oz/50 g) raisins or golden
    raisins (sultanas)
4 scallions (spring onions), finely chopped
1 cup (2 oz/50 g) pomegranate seeds

For the dressing
4 tablespoons extra virgin olive oil
4 tablespoons lemon juice (from about
    1 large lemon)
1 tablespoon pomegranate molasses
1 teaspoon salt
½ teaspoon chilli flakes (optional)
¼ teaspoon black pepper
¼ teaspoon ground cumin
¼ teaspoon dried marjoram, rubbed to a
    powder with your fingers (optional)

The name of this dish is a bit misleading as it's not really tabuleh. Its origins are the stuffing that my Teta Asma would use for her vegetarian vine leaves. She preferred it to traditional tabuleh—which is mostly parsley with a bit of fine bulgur—and I couldn't agree more. While traditional tabuleh will always have its place, I find that I make this salad much more at home. The nuts and raisins are my own additions, so feel free to take them out for a more authentic dish.

Put the bulgur into a salad bowl and cover with 1½ cups (12 fl oz/350 ml) very hot or just boiled water. Stir, then set aside until the bulgur has absorbed the liquid and cooled, about 30 minutes.

Meanwhile, prepare all the remaining ingredients and make the dressing by putting all the ingredients into a small bowl and whisking until combined.

To assemble the salad, fluff up the bulgur wheat with a fork until the grains are separated. Add the chopped parsley and mint and toss to combine. Add the tomatoes and give them another gentle toss. Pour the dressing over the salad, then add the nuts and raisins and give one final toss to combine and scatter with pomegranate seeds, if using.

Serve immediately or refrigerate until ready to serve.

ZA'ATAR SALAD

سلطة زعتر

Preparation time: 10 minutes
Serves 4

11 oz/300 g mixed color tomatoes
    (any variety will do)
3 scallions (spring onions)
10 large sprigs fresh za'atar or oregano
3½ oz/100 g halloumi or feta cheese

For the dressing
1 teaspoon lemon juice
1 tablespoon olive oil
1 teaspoon sumac
pinch of salt

To serve
— fresh Pita bread, homemade (page 38)
    or store-bought

Za'atar is a herb, similar to oregano, and can be very strong in flavor—the younger the leaves, the more subtle the taste. Nowadays, with za'atar grown year-round, you can make this salad whenever the mood strikes. Outside the Middle East fresh oregano is the best alternative.

Chop the tomatoes into small cubes and put into a serving dish. Slice the scallions (spring onions) into thin rounds and sprinkle over the tomatoes. Remove the leaves from the za'atar or oregano and sprinkle over the salad. Finally, chop the halloumi into cubes and scatter over the salad.

To make the dressing, mix the lemon juice and olive oil together with a pinch of salt to taste. Drizzle over the salad.

Sprinkle over the sumac before serving with pita bread.

TOMATO, GARLIC, AND SUMAC SALAD

سلطة بندوره وثوم

Preparation time: 15 minutes
Serves 4–6

1 lb 5 oz/600 g seasonal or heirloom
    tomatoes, sliced into ½-inch/1-cm
    rounds
2 green chillies, seeded and finely
    chopped (optional)
3–4 sprigs fresh mint, stems removed
    and leaves coarsely chopped
flaked sea salt
½ teaspoon sumac

For the dressing
2 cloves garlic, crushed
2 tablespoons olive oil
2 tablespoons lemon juice

This salad makes me so happy—a plate of it looks just like summer. Bright red tomatoes topped with fresh mint and green chillies, and not to mention the sharp dressing of lemon and garlic with olive oil and sumac: delicious, fresh, and so cheerful. At home, my mother would peel the tomatoes and cut them into large cubes. This worked because she made it with what we call *bandoora baladiyeh,* or organic tomatoes grown in season so they are all flesh rather than seeds and water like the supermarket variety. When I make it, I use either heirloom or seasonal tomatoes and I love to mix colors like yellow, green, deep red, and orange—it just looks so pretty—and I slice them in rounds without peeling. If you can't find them, then the best alternatives are cherry or plum tomatoes cut in half.

Arrange the tomato slices in a pretty serving platter.

Put all the ingredients for the dressing into a small bowl, whisk until well combined, then spoon over the tomatoes.

Sprinkle the tomatoes with flaked sea salt, then top with the chopped green chillies and mint leaves and sprinkle with sumac. Serve immediately.

Overleaf
From left: Teta Asma's Tabuleh;
Za'atar Salad (both page 98);
Tomato, Garlic and Sumac Salad
(page 99).

CAULIFLOWER, POTATO, AND EGGPLANT (AUBERGINE) SALAD

سلطة مقالي

Preparation time: 15–20 minutes
Cooking time: 30 minutes
Serves 6–8

vegetable oil, for frying
1 head of cauliflower, cut into florets
2 potatoes, cut into bite-size cubes
1 eggplant (aubergine), cut into
    bite-size cubes
salt and black pepper

For the dressing
1½ cups (14 oz/400 g) Greek yogurt
3–4 tablespoons lemon juice
2 tablespoons finely chopped flat-leaf
    parsley
1 clove garlic, crushed
1 teaspoon salt

To serve
— 1 cup (5 oz/150 g) cherry tomatoes,
    quartered
— 2 green chillies, thinly sliced
— ¼ cup (1 oz/25 g) Toasted Pine Nuts
    (page 31)

This inspiration for this salad comes from the sandwiches my mother used to make us as children. She would often have fried cauliflower, eggplants (aubergines), or potatoes on hand for whatever lunch dish she was preparing. If we got hungry before the meal was ready, she would spread some labaneh in a pita bread, put some of the fried vegetables inside and top it with fresh tomatoes or peppers. As simple as it sounds, the flavors were so delicious and satisfying. This salad is my take on those childhood sandwiches. Use just one vegetable or all three, as I do here.

Heat the oil in a deep fryer or heavy Dutch oven (casserole) to 350°F/180°C.

Working in batches, deep-fry first the cauliflower, then the potatoes, then the eggplant (aubergine) until a nice golden brown. Remove each batch with a slotted spoon and drain on paper towels to absorb the excess oil and cool slightly. Sprinkle with salt and freshly ground black pepper.

Meanwhile, combine all the ingredients for the dressing and mix well. Gradually add some water until you reach a drizzling consistency, similar to buttermilk or maple syrup. Taste, and adjust the salt and lemon juice as desired, bearing in mind the dressing should be quite bold in its sour and salty notes.

To serve, arrange the fried vegetables in a serving platter and drizzle with the dressing. Top with the cherry tomatoes and green chillies and sprinkle over the pine nuts.

Note: If you prefer, you could roast the vegetables instead of frying them. Simply toss with olive oil, salt, and pepper and place on a baking sheet in an oven preheated to 400°F/200°C/Gas Mark 6 for 30–40 minutes, until golden.

Variation: A delicious variation on the dressing is to use tahini instead of yogurt. In that case, you will probably need to add a little more water to thin the dressing to a drizzling consistency. Generally I use 4 tablespoons of tahini, 4 tablespoons of water, 1–2 tablespoons of lemon juice and ¼ teaspoon salt, but again, you can adjust as desired. Just remember to check the seasoning before adding to the salad.

PURSLANE SALAD

سلطة بقله

Preparation time: 15 minutes
Serves 4–6

200g purslane or mache (lamb's lettuce)
    or curly endive
4–6 scallions (spring onions), thinly
    sliced
1 whole lemon

For the dressing
2–3 tablespoons lemon juice
2–3 tablespoons olive oil
½ teaspoon salt
½ teaspoon sumac, plus extra
    for garnish

Extremely fresh and sharp, this salad will make your taste buds tingle. If you're like my father-in-law, you can have it on a daily basis alongside every meal or as a meal in itself! Otherwise, it's a perfect complement to spiced rice dishes like Flipped Over Chicken and Vegetable Rice (page 198) or Stuffed Vegetables in Tomato sauce (page 184) because its fresh sharpness really cuts through all those rich flavors. It is also one of those few salads that tastes just as good the following day once all the flavors have melded together.

Tear the purslane into bite-size pieces, put into a large salad bowl, and toss the scallions (spring onions) on top.

Use a sharp knife to peel the yellow rind from the lemon, keeping the pith intact. Dice the lemon into bite-sized cubes then set aside.

In a small bowl, whisk together the dressing ingredients and pour over the purslane and scallions. Very gently toss to combine.

Top with the diced lemons, sprinkle with a little extra sumac and serve.

Variation: For a more substantial dish, you can top the salad with ¼–½ cup (1–2 oz/30–60 g) of grated halloumi cheese.

PALESTINIAN SALAD

سلطة ناعمة

Preparation time: 15 minutes
Serves 4–6

4 large or 8 small (about 2¼ lb/1 kg)
    tomatoes (see Note)
2 small cucumbers (about 7 oz/200 g)
2 green chillies (optional)
1 whole unwaxed lemon
1 onion or 4–6 scallions (spring onions)
4 tablespoons finely chopped fresh
    mint leaves or 1 tablespoon crushed
    dried mint
4 tablespoons olive oil
4 tablespoons lemon juice
1 teaspoon salt

Palestinians know this as "finely diced or farmer's salad"; to everyone else it's Palestinian salad. In its most basic version, it is finely diced tomatoes, onions, and dried mint lightly dressed with olive oil, lemon, and salt. In other variations, however, it can also include cucumbers, bell peppers, chillies, lemons, parsley, or radishes. Mine usually includes whatever produce I have found that is most fresh, as well as a very finely diced whole lemon—a trick I learned from my mother-in-law, which gives this salad a real kick. Feel free to add any other vegetables you like, as the dressing is generous and the salad is quite forgiving. It's an absolute must next to the lentil pilafs (page 164 and 167) and a wonderful accompaniment to most *kafta* and rice dishes.

Chop the tomatoes into very small cubes and put into a large bowl. Dice the cucumbers into similar-sized small cubes and add to the tomatoes. If you are using a traditional large cucumber, make sure to peel and seed it first.

Seed the chillies (if you prefer even less heat, remove all the white membrane as well). Chop very finely, and add to the vegetables. Slice the lemon into thin rounds, discarding the top and bottom rounds and any seeds as well, then chop each round into small cubes. Add to the salad. Dice the onion very finely and add to the salad. Finally throw in the chopped fresh mint leaves or dried mint.

Drizzle with olive oil and lemon juice and sprinkle with salt. Toss very lightly with a large spoon and serve immediately.

Note: Choose a very fleshy variety of tomatoes with little pulp and seeds for this salad. Beefsteak tomatoes are a good option, as are other firm heirloom varieties.

VEGETABLE AND TAHINI SALAD

سلطة طحينه

Preparation time: 15 minutes
Serves: 4–6

1 quantity Tahini Sauce (page 28)
2 tomatoes (7–9 oz/200–250 g), finely
　　diced
2 Persian or Lebanese cucumbers
　　(5–6 oz/150–180 g), finely diced
1–2 green chillies, seeded and finely
　　chopped
1–2 cloves garlic, crushed
3–4 tablespoons finely chopped
　　fresh mint leaves, or 1 tablespoon
　　dried mint

No *shawarma* or falafel sandwich is complete without this health bomb of a salad. The calcium and minerals from the tahini and the vitamins and antioxidants from the vegetables are sure to counteract any negative effects of the fatty and fried foods it's so often served with. That doesn't mean it can't be enjoyed on its own as well with a fresh piece of bread. In fact, it's often my nightly supper at home when I want something fresh and quick to make. With hot bread and a fresh cup of mint tea, it's a wonderfully satisfying end to the day.

Prepare the Tahini Sauce in a large bowl and set aside.

Add all the remaining ingredients to the tahini and mix with a spoon to combine. Serve on its own with fresh bread or as a side to Falafel (page 68) or Shawarma with Onions and Sumac (page 156).

CABBAGE SALAD TWO WAYS

سلطة ملفوف

Preparation time: 10 minutes
Serves 6–8 as a side

For the tomato version
1 head of green or sweetheart cabbage, finely shredded
3 tomatoes, diced into small cubes
small bunch flat-leaf parsley, coarsely chopped
1 green chilli, finely diced (optional)
3 tablespoons lemon juice
1½ tablespoons olive oil
½ teaspoon salt
½ cup (2¼ oz/60 g) flaked almonds, lightly toasted (optional)

For the mint version
1 head of green or sweetheart cabbage, finely shredded
3 tablespoons lemon juice
3 tablespoons olive oil
1 tablespoon dried mint
1 large clove garlic, crushed
1 teaspoon salt

These two salads transform the humble cabbage into something that makes a wonderful side to many of our dishes. The first one with tomatoes is most often eaten alongside pilafs like Spiced Lamb and Rice Pilaf (page 166), while the other one we tend to serve alongside grilled meats and mop it up with bread. Green or sweetheart cabbages are the best varieties to use for these salads as they tend to soften more quickly, and that's exactly what you want. The mint version in particular tastes better the longer it sits, and is best served with bread, even the following day, to mop up all the delicious juices.

Cabbage and tomato salad
Put the shredded cabbage into a large salad bowl and add the tomatoes, parsley, and green chili, if using. Pour the lemon and olive oil over the cabbage, sprinkle with the salt, and toss to combine. Scatter the almonds on top and serve.

Cabbage and mint salad
Put the shredded cabbage into a large salad bowl, add all the other ingredients and toss well to combine. Allow to sit for at least 15 minutes before serving as it tastes best once the cabbage has softened and released some juices. This salad will keep well for 2 days.

CUMIN AND SCALLION (SPRING ONION) POTATO SALAD

سلطة بطاطا

Preparation time: 10 minutes
Cooking time: 10–20 minutes
Serves 6–8

2¼ lb (1 kg) non-waxy potatoes
    such as Russet, Idaho, King Edward,
    or Maris Piper
1 tablespoon salt
4–6 scallions (spring onions), white
    and green parts finely sliced

For the dressing
6 tablespoons olive oil
4 tablespoons lemon juice
½ teaspoon ground cumin
½ teaspoon salt
¼ teaspoon black pepper
2 teaspoons cumin seeds

This is the quintessential Palestinian picnic salad. We take it to the beach, to the mountains, or just eat it at home. Perfect to make ahead and easy to transport, it's the flavors of this salad that deliver the real punch. Don't restrict yourself to making it for picnics, though. It's also a great accompaniment to grilled meats and I almost always serve it with my Spiced Leg of Lamb (page 156). The fried cumin seeds are my own addition, but their crunchy warmth gives the salad a kick and helps the flavors to shine. Although potato salads are generally made with waxy potatoes that don't fall apart during cooking, we Arabs tend to prefer a more starchy or all-purpose variety as it absorbs more flavor. The key is to keep the potatoes al dente and not overcook them—only then will you get the best of both worlds.

Dice the potatoes into 1-inch/2.5-cm cubes and put into a large pan. Cover generously with cold water and add the salt. Bring to a boil, then reduce the heat, and simmer for 10–20 minutes—test the potatoes with the tip of a sharp knife every minute or two and remove from the heat once the potatoes are almost done but still present a bit of resistance to the knife. How long this takes depends on the potatoes, the pan, the heat...hence the continuous testing. You do not want to overcook the potatoes or the salad will become one giant mush.

Meanwhile prepare the dressing: combine 4 tablespoons of the olive oil with the lemon juice, ground cumin, and salt and pepper and mix well. Set aside until the potatoes are done.

When cooked, drain the potatoes and put into a large bowl. Add the scallions (spring onions), then pour the dressing over and very gently toss to combine. Taste and adjust the levels of lemon, salt, and cumin as desired before transferring to a serving bowl or platter.

Heat the remaining 2 tablespoons of olive oil in a small skillet (frying pan) over medium heat. Add the cumin seeds and fry for 1–2 minutes, or until fragrant. Pour the fried cumin seeds and oil over the potatoes. Serve the salad warm, at room temperature, or even cold. Leftovers will keep in the refrigerator for at least 3 days.

DANDELIONS WITH CARAMELIZED ONIONS

هندبا بالبصل

Preparation time: 10 minutes
Cooking time: 30 minutes
Serves 4

4 tablespoons olive oil
1 large onion, sliced into thin half-moons
11–18 oz/300–500 g dandelion greens
(see Note), coarsely chopped into
bite-size pieces
1 large lemon
salt

Long before foraging infiltrated the fine dining scene, it was a way of life for Palestinians. Throughout the year, my family would trek through the surrounding mountains and valleys picking the greens of the season. From leaves for stuffing and herbs for drying to numerous greens for sautéing and cooking, we knew the land and its offerings like the back of our hands. *Hindbeh*, my father's favorite, is a form of chicory (known as dandelion greens in the United States), which is quite bitter but extremely healthy. We normally blanch it before cooking, but the varieties available in supermarkets are more tender, and so can be cooked directly. If you can't find dandelion or chicory, kale leaves are an excellent substitute—just make sure you remove the hard stems.

Heat oil in a large skillet (frying pan) over medium-high heat. Add the onion, sprinkle with salt, and cook, tossing regularly, until golden and starting to crisp up, about 15 minutes. When ready, transfer a large spoonful to a plate lined with paper towels to use as garnish (leave the rest of the onion in the pan).

Add the dandelion greens to the onions and toss to combine. Lower the heat, cover, and cook, tossing occasionally, until the greens have completely wilted and come together with the onion. This could take 15–30 minutes, depending on the variety of leaf.

Meanwhile, peel the lemon, leaving the pith intact, and chop into cubes.

To serve, transfer the dandelion greens to a shallow bowl. Spoon the fried onions into the center, and arrange the lemon cubes around the onions and all over the dandelions. Can be eaten with a fork as a side or scooped up with bread as a meal on its own.

Note: The exact plant foraged in Palestine is difficult to find outside the country. There are, however, many plants from the same family or with a similar flavor profile. These include dandelion greens, puntarelle chicory, curly endive, escarole, and even turnip greens or kale. The cooking time will vary depending on how tender the leaves are, as will the weight of the leaves needed because some greens have thicker stalks and more weight will be lost in trimming stems and stalks.

MIXED VEGETABLE YOGURT

لبن وخضرة

Preparation time: 15 minutes
Serves 4–6

1 lb 2 oz/500 g plain yogurt (not Greek)
4 scallions (spring onions), finely
    chopped
2 small Persian or Lebanese cucumbers
    (about 5–6 oz/150–180 g), finely diced
    (see Note)
2 tomatoes (about 7–9 oz/200–250 g),
    finely diced
1 romaine lettuce heart, thinly sliced
small bunch fresh mint leaves, finely
    chopped
1 teaspoon lemon juice
1 teaspoon salt

The Middle Eastern climate is hot and our food tends to be spicy, so yogurt is a staple at almost every lunch table. From plain and soupy to thick and garlicky, how this yogurt is served varies from family to family and from dish to dish. This recipe, with a variety of vegetables and some fresh mint, is one of my favorites. The proportion and amount of vegetables is a matter of preference, so adjust to your liking and you won't go wrong with this refreshing and light salad.

Tip the yogurt into a large bowl. Add all the vegetables, the mint, lemon juice, and salt and mix to combine. Taste and adjust the salt and lemon juice as desired—it really is a matter of preference. Serve with rice dishes or grilled meats.

Note: Middle Eastern cucumbers tend to be small (about 6 inches/15 cm long) with thin, edible skin and very few seeds. If you are using the standard large supermarket cucumbers, I recommend peeling them and removing the watery centers first.

ARUGULA (ROCKET) AND GARLIC YOGURT

لبن وجرجير

Preparation time: 5 minutes
Serves 4–6

About 5 cups (3½ oz/100 g) arugula
    (rocket), thinly sliced
1 lb 2 oz/500 g plain yogurt (not Greek)
1 clove garlic, crushed
1 teaspoon salt
olive oil, for drizzling

Over the last few years, my parents-in-law have switched to a mostly vegetarian diet, so my mother-in-law is always trying unique twists on traditional Palestinian salads to keep things interesting. This is a variation on a very old Palestinian salad made with plant known as *hwarneh* or hedge mustard, which grows mostly in the Levant region in winter. In its place she uses arugula (rocket), which has a similar sharp, peppery taste. This salad is perfect drizzled with olive oil and eaten with bread, but also as a side to grilled meats.

Put the arugula (rocket), yogurt, garlic, and salt into a bowl and stir together until well combined. Spoon into a bowl and drizzle with olive oil before serving.

Keep in the refrigerator for up to 3 days.

GAZAN TOMATO SALSA

دقه غزاويه

Preparation time: 10–15 minutes
Serves 4

1 tablespoon dill seeds
1 teaspoon coarse sea salt
2–3 green chillies
1 lb 2 oz/500 g tomatoes (see Note)
1 tablespoon olive oil
1 tablespoon lemon juice

One of my mother's best friends is from Gaza; whenever she visited us, she would make us this salsa in a pestle and mortar, the way it has been done in her family for generations. *Dagga* literally means something that has been pounded or ground with a pestle. The dill seeds impart a very distinct flavor to what would otherwise be a simple tomato salsa. One time she made it for breakfast, and my mum had been cooking Lamb and Yogurt Rice Stew (page 206) for lunch, so I mixed the two together and since that day I never looked back—I now never eat anything cooked with Yogurt Sauce (page 29) without this salsa on the side. I also absolutely love it with bread or as a dip for tortilla chips. To make life easier, I only use a pestle and mortar for the dill seeds, then do everything else in a mini chopper or food processor.

Use a pestle and mortar to pound the dill seeds and salt together until coarsely ground.

Put the ground dill seeds and salt, chillies, tomatoes, olive oil, and lemon juice into a food processor and pulse until you reach a salsa consistency.

Note: It is important to use tomatoes that are not very watery and have a lot of flesh. Heirloom and seasonal tomatoes are an excellent choice, but if not available, use either cherry or baby plum tomatoes. You can halve or quarter larger tomatoes to fit into the food processor, but leave the cherry ones whole.

SOUPS AND STEWS

Because my mother's family are Muslim and my father's family are Christian, the holidays that we celebrated, the traditions we observed, and the dishes we ate while growing up, were a real melting pot of food and festivities. There was, however, one constant shared across all these kitchens, the cornerstone of all Palestinian family meals, and that was the humble stew. The cooking methods and ingredients sometimes varied: my mother's family, for instance, cook *mlukhiyeh*, a leafy green vegetable, as a smooth soup (page 122) while my father's family cook it as a whole leaf stew with plenty of sliced garlic (page 124). However it is prepared, a soul-soothing stew enjoyed with rice is a dish you could count on any day of the week at any of these Palestinian family tables.

It would not be an exaggeration to say that eating together at these tables was sacred in our family. To my mother and grandmothers, they were not simply cooking. They were feeding our bodies, our hearts, and our minds. Today I cook for my family and friends in much the same way my mother and grandmothers have done: not only to nourish, but also to soothe, and nothing does that quite as well as a hearty soup or stew.

These recipes for soups and stews are not fancy or complicated. Many of them can be put together in a couple of short steps. The soups tend to constitute full meals on their own, especially when enjoyed with some bread and fresh vegetables on the side. The stews are perfect weekday meals as they are simple to prepare and taste just as good the following day. Almost always eaten alongside rice, the majority of stews feature a single vegetable and can be made in both vegetarian and non-vegetarian variations. Most are tomato based (e.g. peas and carrots, beans, okra) while others are cooked in a stock flavoured with garlic and lemon (e.g. spinach, *mlukhiyeh*). At its most basic, the method for the non-vegetarian version involves choosing a cut of meat (lamb shanks, braising beef, chicken, etc.), boiling the meat until cooked through, then adding the vegetable and various flavourings such as tomato paste or lemon and garlic. The vegetarian version involves sautéing onions and/or garlic then adding the vegetables and chosen liquid.

While different ones were originally made in different seasons based on what produce was available, nowadays, with frozen (okra, spinach) and dried (*mlukhiyeh*) vegetables you can enjoy any of these delicious stews year-round.

<u>Left</u>
An olive tree on the hills of Rameh Village in the Galilee.

SPLIT LENTIL SOUP

شوربة عدس مجروش

Preparation time: 5 minutes
Cooking time: 30 minutes
Serves 4

4 tablespoons olive oil
1 onion, finely diced
1 small carrot, finely grated
1 teaspoon ground cumin
½ teaspoon turmeric
½ teaspoon Nine Spice Mix (page 24)
1 cup (8 oz/225 g) red split lentils,
    picked over and rinsed
1 teaspoon salt

To serve
— pita croutons
— lemon wedges

I've always wondered how one humble ingredient cooked so simply can result in such a delicious dish. Naturally, I experimented with all kinds of additions and spices, only to find myself returning to this original version. In spite of its simplicity, this perfect winter dish is very hearty and makes a great stand-alone meal. Because of its nutritional value, this soup is for many people the default or official Ramadan soup, giving them a nutritional boost after a day of fasting without being too heavy. Try topping it with pita croutons and a squeeze of lemon juice and, if you really want to do it the Palestinian way, take bites of radish, scallion (spring onion), and green chilli in between sips.

Heat the oil in a large pan over medium-high heat. Add the onion and carrot and cook for 3–5 minutes, stirring occasionally, until starting to soften. Sprinkle in the spices and continue to toss until aromatic and the onions are starting to brown around the edges, another 2–3 minutes. Add the lentils and mix to evenly combine.

Pour in 6 cups (48 fl oz/1.5 liters) hot water and bring to a boil, then reduce the heat to low and simmer for 20–30 minutes, or until the lentils are cooked and have fallen apart. The lentils will turn a yellow color when cooked and easily mash against the side of the pan. Once done, stir in the salt.

Using an immersion blender, puree the soup, if desired. I find that pureeing it improves its color and allows the flavors to really come together, but you can easily forgo this step. If you prefer the soup thicker, boil it a little longer until it reaches the desired consistency, bearing in mind that the soup will thicken the longer it sits. If you find it too thick, gradually add more water until you reach the desired consistency.

To serve, ladle the soup into bowls and top with pita croutons and a squeeze of lemon.

LENTIL, GARLIC, AND PASTA SOUP
رشتايه

Preparation time: 5 minutes
Cooking time: 45–50 minutes
Serves 4

½ cup (4 fl oz/120 ml) olive oil
1 onion, finely diced
1 cup (8 oz/225 g) lentils (green or
    brown), picked over and rinsed
1 teaspoon ground cumin
¼ teaspoon black pepper
1 teaspoon salt
200g tagliatelle or linguini, broken into
    1–2-inch/3–5-cm lengths (see Note)
5–6 cloves garlic, crushed

To serve (optional)
— chopped flat-leaf parsley
— sumac or lemon juice

Just like lentil pilafs (pages 164 and 167), this is a peasant dish that dates back to a time when people needed to create hearty, yet affordable meals. In the Middle East, beans and legumes were often the protein of choice over more expensive and harder to source meat. Inevitably, these vegetarian and vegan dishes made up for the lack of meat with ample flavor, and the flavors in this dish—earthy lentils, fiery garlic, and smooth pasta—are indeed very satisfying. To make it even more flavorful, top with parsley and sumac or lemon juice.

Pour half the olive oil into a Dutch oven (casserole), add the onion and cook over medium-high heat, stirring regularly, for 6–8 minutes, or until the onions have softened and started to crisp around the edges.

Add the lentils, cumin, and pepper and toss to combine. Pour in 6 cups (48 fl oz/1.5 liters) water, add the salt and bring the mixture to a boil, then partially cover the pan and reduce the heat to maintain a gentle simmer. Cook until the lentils are tender but still hold their shape, 20–30 minutes depending on variety.

Once the lentils are cooked, add the pasta, increasing the heat to a vigorous simmer, and cook, covered, for 10–15 minutes, or until the pasta is done.

Meanwhile, heat the remaining olive oil in a small skillet (frying pan) and add the garlic. Cook until fragrant and light gold in color, about 3 minutes. Take care not to burn the garlic as it can quickly go from gold to burnt. Once ready, pour the garlic and oil over the lentils and pasta and stir.

If the consistency is too thick, add 1 cup (8 fl oz/250 ml) water and bring to a boil. If it's too thin, cook the soup for another couple of minutes until some liquid evaporates. You want a consistency similar to bean soup—not so thin it falls off the spoon but not so thick it feels like pudding.

To serve, ladle into individual bowls and sprinkle with toppings, if desired.

Note: Traditionally, this dish is made with a dough of flour, water, and salt that is rolled out thinly then rolled onto itself and sliced into short fettuccine or linguini-like strips. I substitute with dried linguini, which I break into short pieces but I often use fresh pasta for an almost identical result to the original version, so if you find fresh tagliatelle, linguini or fettuccine, simply chop into strips and throw in, keeping in mind it will require less cooking, about 3 minutes. For an easier version, you can also use any small dry pasta shape.

KALE AND DUMPLING SOUP

جعجوله

Preparation time: 15 minutes
Cooking time: 20–30 minutes
Serves 4–6

3 tablespoons olive oil
1 onion, finely chopped
½ teaspoon Nine Spice Mix (page 24)
½ teaspoon salt
3½–4 oz/100–120g kale or cavolo nero,
    stalks removed and leaves finely
    chopped
6 cups (48 fl oz/1.5 liters) chicken broth
    (stock), homemade (page 34) or
    store-bought, or water
1 teaspoon tomato paste (purée)

For the dumplings
2 eggs, lightly beaten
5 tablespoons all-purpose (plain) flour
5 tablespoons whole wheat (wholemeal)
    flour (or use all-purpose/plain flour)

This is a rather obscure Palestinian soup; the original is not even made with kale, but with the leaves of the arum lily, a plant thought to be poisonous. Nonetheless, people use it in small quantities and tout it as a panacea for many ailments, most notably cancer. What part of that is true and what part urban legend, I cannot say. What I do know, however, is that this soup is absolutely delicious and when made with kale or cavolo nero, the way I make it now, it tastes just as good, but with the added bonus that I don't have to worry about using too much of the greens and numbing my mouth. A Middle Eastern version of the classic chicken dumpling soup, this is the recipe to try for a warming meal on a cold day.

Heat the oil in a large pan over medium-high heat and add the onion. Cook for about 5 minutes, stirring occasionally, until softened but not browned.

Sprinkle the spices and salt, tossing to coat evenly, then add the chopped kale leaves. Cook, stirring at regular intervals, until wilted and darker in color, about 10 minutes. Scoop out 4 tablespoons of this cooked mixture and set aside in a large bowl to cool.

Pour the broth (stock) into the pan and add the tomato paste (purée). Bring to a boil while you prepare the dumpling mixture.

Put the eggs and flour into the bowl with the kale and onion mixture and mix well. You will end up with a sticky, thick batter. Coat a teaspoon in some olive oil (this will help the batter to slide off the spoon more easily) and scoop out a teaspoon of the batter; dip it into the pan of boiling soup, and let it fall off the spoon. Repeat the process with the remaining batter. This will make around 20 dumplings.

When the dumplings float to the top of the soup they are almost ready; simmer for another minute. Taste and adjust the seasoning (if you have used water instead of broth, you will likely need to add more salt). Ladle the soup into bowls and serve immediately.

FREEKEH SOUP

شوربة فريكه

Preparation time: 5 minutes
Cooking time: 15–20 minutes
Serves 6–8

1 tablespoon olive oil
1 teaspoon clarified butter
1 onion, very finely chopped
1 cup (5 oz/150 g) freekeh
½ tablespoon Nine Spice Mix (page 24)
¼ teaspoon ground cumin
1 tablespoon sumac, plus extra to serve
8 cups (3½ pints/2 litres chicken broth
    (stock), homemade (page 34)
    or store-bought
salt
chopped flat-leaf parsley, to serve

Freekeh—a cracked, roasted green wheat which can be cooked in a similar way to rice and bulgur—has a very distinct taste because of the burning process when roasting it. Growing up, this was either the soup my grandmother made on the days she made Chicken, Sumac, and Pine Nut Rolls (page 86) because she had broth (stock) from the boiled chicken; or it was the soup my mother made the day after cooking a huge pot of Freekeh Pilaf (page 162) and wanted to change up the leftovers. The sumac is not the most traditional spicing of this soup, but since we often had this soup with Chicken, Onion, and Sumac Flatbreads (page 194) there would always be a plate of sumac on the table; my father would sprinkle a big spoon over his plate and in my family the tradition was born to eat freekeh soup with sumac. Feel free to omit if you do not like the sour flavor.

Heat the oil and butter in a large pan. Add the onion and cook over medium heat for about 5 minutes, stirring occasionally, until the onions are soft and translucent.

Add the freekeh and spices to the onions and stir for 2–3 minutes until the grains are fragrant.

Pour the broth (stock) over the freekeh and bring to a boil. Cook for 10 minutes then reduce the heat, cover, and simmer until the freekeh is cooked but a little al dente, 10–15 minutes. Season to taste with salt (the amount will depend on the kind of broth you have used).

Ladle into bowls and sprinkle with sumac and chopped parsley to serve.

JUTE MALLOW SOUP

ملوخيه ناعمه

Preparation time: 5–10 minutes
Cooking time: 2 hours
Serves 6–8

1 whole chicken (about 4–5 lb/1.8–2.2 kg)
2 bay leaves
1 onion
1 teaspoon Nine Spice Mix (page 24)
about 2 cups (11 oz/300 g) finely crushed
    dry *mlukhiyeh* (jute mallow) leaves
1 tablespoon tomato paste (purée)
4 tablespoons olive oil
8–10 cloves garlic, crushed
salt

To serve
— lemon wedges
— green chillies
— Vermicelli Rice (page 32) or bread

Mlukhiyeh (jute mallow) season in the summer was a fascinating time for me as I saw the women in my mother's family sitting on Teta Fatima's veranda, huge bowls of fresh leaves in their laps, using one hand to hold a bunch of leaves and the other to hold a knife with which they'd chop the leaves against their own hands. I remember marveling at how they transformed the leaves into a paste without a single cut. The finely chopped leaves would then be frozen for use throughout the year. When not in Palestine I tend to use the dried variety, as it's easier to find. You can serve this with rice, or you can also scoop it up with bread like you would a thick, hearty soup. Lemon is often served alongside *mlukhiyeh* to be squeezed into individual bowls and bites of green chilli are often taken between spoonfuls for a harmony of flavors like no other.

Put the chicken into a large stockpot and cover with water. Bring to a boil, skimming away the scum that rises to the surface, then add the bay leaves, onion, 1 tablespoon of salt, and the Nine Spice Mix and reduce the heat to a simmer. Cook, covered, until the chicken is cooked through, about 1–1½ hours (20–25 minutes in a pressure cooker). When done, remove the chicken from the broth (stock). When cool enough to handle, remove the meat from the bones and shred; set aside.

Strain the broth (approximately 6½ cups (51 fl oz/1 ½ liters) into a large pan and place back over medium heat. Gradually pour in the dried *mlukhiyeh* leaves, whisking continuously to avoid any lumps. Continue to whisk until evenly combined. Add the tomato paste (purée), which helps prevent the jute mallow from becoming slimy during cooking, and whisk again to combine. Simmer, covered, for 15–20 minutes.

Meanwhile, heat the olive oil in a small skillet (frying pan), add the garlic and sprinkle with some salt. Cook for about 2 minutes until the garlic is fragrant and golden in color. Pour the garlic and its oil over the soup and whisk to combine. If the leaves seem to separate from the liquid, if there are still lumps of dry *mlukhiyeh*, or if the consistency is too coarse, use an immersion blender at this point to achieve the desired consistency.

When the soup is almost done, add the shredded chicken, mixing to combine, and continue to cook for 5 minutes.

To serve, ladle the soup into individual bowls and serve with some lemon wedges and hot green chillies to be enjoyed with each bite. Can be eaten on top of rice or with bread.

SPINACH AND CHICKPEA STEW

يخنة سبانخ

Preparation time: 5 minutes
Cooking time: 30 minutes
Serves 6–8

3 tablespoons olive oil
2 small onions (or 1 large), diced
6–8 cloves garlic, crushed
3 pieces mastic
1 lb 5 oz/600 g lamb or beef, cut into
    ½-inch/1-cm cubes (or use ground/
    minced lamb or beef)
2 teaspoons Nine Spice Mix (page 24)
1½ teaspoons salt
2¼ lb/1 kg fresh spinach, chopped
    (see Note)
2 cups (16 fl oz/475 ml) chicken broth
    (stock), homemade (page 34)
    or store-bought, or use water
1 teaspoon tomato paste (purée)
    (optional)
1 x 14-oz/400-g can chickpeas,
    drained and rinsed

To serve
— Vermicelli Rice (page 32)
— lemon wedges
— yogurt

Growing up, I always knew when summer was around the corner because my mother would start cooking with spinach. She would mostly make this stew and Spinach Turnovers (page 49) and the two couldn't possibly taste more different. Whereas the turnovers are tangy and sharp, this is mellow with earthy flavors—it's therefore complemented very well by lemon juice squeezed directly on your plate before eating.

Heat the oil in a large pan, add the onions, and cook over medium heat, tossing until softened, about 3 minutes. Add the garlic and mastic and cook for another minute. Add the meat, spice mix, and salt and cook for 10–15 minutes, stirring occasionally, until any water has evaporated and the meat is nicely browned.

Add the chopped spinach and broth (stock) to the pan. Cover, reduce the heat and cook for 5–10 minutes, or until the spinach has wilted. Remove the lid and stir in the tomato paste (purée), if using (although optional it does help to concentrate the flavors). If using water instead of broth, taste for salt and adjust the seasoning.

Pour in the chickpeas and cook for another 5 minutes. Remove from the heat and serve with vermicelli rice, lemon wedges to be squeezed over the spinach, and yogurt.

Note: In Palestine, this stew is normally made in late spring and summer when spinach is abundant and in season. We use the large leaf spinach, which has the most flavor, and chop it into short, thin strips. Now, with spinach available year round, you can make it whenever you like. If you cannot find the large leaf kind, you can substitute with baby spinach or even frozen, although frozen spinach will produce more liquid so you may need to use less stock.

JUTE MALLOW STEW

ملوخيه ورق

Preparation time: 5–10 minutes
Cooking time: 2 hours
Serves 6–8

2 oz/50 g ghee or butter
2 tablespoons olive oil
10 cloves garlic, very finely chopped
1 lb 2 oz/500 g *mulukhiyeh* (jute mallow) leaves, very roughly chopped (fresh or frozen and defrosted with the excess water squeezed out)
2 teaspoons Nine Spice Mix (page 24)
4–6 cups (1¾–2½ pints /1–1.5 liters chicken, lamb, or beef broth (stock), homemade (page 34) or store-bought
2 teaspoons salt, or to taste
2 tablespoons lemon juice

For the meat and pine nut topping
1 tablespoon olive oil
1 lb 2 oz/500 g lamb leg meat or beef sirloin/fillet, cut into ½-inch/1-cm cubes
1 teaspoon Nine Spice Mix (page 24)
1 teaspoon salt
½ cup Toasted Pine Nuts (page 31)

To serve
— Vermicelli Rice (page 32)
— lemon wedges

An extremely nutritious green leaf rich in iron, vitamins, and fiber, *mlukhiyeh* (jute mallow) is widely cooked across Palestine. How it's cooked, however, varies from one locale to the next. In the north, it's cooked as a whole leaf stew while in the central and southern regions it is cooked as smooth, thick soup. Used fresh when harvested in the summer, the leaves can also be frozen or dried for use throughout the year. This recipe is for the stew that my Teta Asma used to make and is best made with fresh or frozen leaves, not dried.

Warm the ghee and olive oil in a large Dutch oven (casserole) over medium-high heat and add the garlic. Cook for 1–2 minutes until fragrant but still white. Add the *mlukhiyeh* leaves, tossing continuously with a spoon, until the leaves start to wilt and their water evaporates, about 10 minutes. If using frozen leaves, this step will take longer, 20–30 minutes.

Sprinkle the leaves with the Nine Spice Mix and give them one more toss to coat evenly. Pour in two-thirds of the broth (stock) and the salt (you may need more or less depending on your broth) and bring the mixture to a boil, then partially cover the pan and reduce the heat to maintain a gentle simmer. Cook until the leaves have darkened slightly in color and the stock has thickened, 15–30 minutes. The consistency is supposed to be like a thick soup—not too thin but with enough thick liquid to serve as sauce with the rice. Check the consistency throughout the cooking and if necessary add more stock. If you add too much stock, simply increase the heat and simmer for a little while longer.

While the stew is simmering, make the topping. Heat the olive oil in the same pan over high heat until hot but not smoking. Add the meat, sprinkle with the spice mix and salt and cook, stirring frequently, for 10–15 minutes, or until any released water evaporates and the meat has started to brown. Remove the pan from the heat, add the toasted pine nuts, and stir together.

Remove the stew from the heat and stir in the lemon juice. To serve, place some rice in shallow bowl, ladle the stew over the rice and top with the meat and pine nut mixture and lemon wedges for squeezing.

OKRA AND RED CHILLI STEW

يخنة باميه

Preparation time: 5 minutes
Cooking time: 25–30 minutes
Serves 4–6

4 tablespoons olive oil
1 onion, finely diced
4 cloves garlic, crushed
2 green chillies, finely diced
1 lb 2 oz/500 g okra, fresh or frozen,
    stems trimmed (see Note)
1 lb 2 oz/500 g ripe vine tomatoes,
    chopped (or use a 14-oz/400-g can
    chopped tomatoes)
1 teaspoon salt
½ teaspoon Nine Spice Mix (page 24)
¼ teaspoon ground cumin
1 tablespoon pomegranate molasses
1 tablespoon red chilli paste,
    such as harissa (optional)

To serve
— Vermicelli Rice (page 32) or bread

When I was a little girl, I remember visiting a friend of mine who lived in the Old City of Jerusalem. Her mother sent us down to the market to buy some fresh red chilli paste. I had no idea what she needed it for until we sat down for lunch to eat some okra stew and tears started streaming down my cheeks. I was never a big fan of the traditional stew made with lamb, but when I tasted this ultra spicy vegetarian version, I fell in love with the dish—despite the tears. This recipe is my adaptation of that dish I had over 20 years ago—spicy and sharp, but not so hot it will make you cry. For the more traditional version, see the variation below.

Heat the oil over medium-high heat in a Dutch oven (casserole), add the onion and cook for 3–5 minutes until softened. Add the garlic and chillies and fry for another minute, then add the okra and continue to stir until the okra gets a nice golden color, about 5 minutes.

Add the tomatoes, salt, and spices and stir to combine. Bring to a boil then lower the heat and simmer, covered, until slightly thickened, about 15 minutes. Remove the lid, add the pomegranate molasses and red chilli paste, and stir to combine. Remove from the heat and serve either warm with vermicelli rice or at room temperature with bread.

Note: Okra can be slimy when cooked. In the Middle East we tend to use very small okra and remove only a small part of the stem; this way the seeds are not visible, which helps reduce the sliminess. Frozen baby okra—found in Middle Eastern grocery stores—is also less slimy than the standard large okra found in supermarkets. So if you must use the supermarket variety, try to pick the smallest pieces you can find, remove only the very coarse part of the stem leaving the seeds concealed, and make sure you sauté it very well before adding any liquid.

Variation: For a more hearty stew with meat, you will need to boil 1 lb 2 oz/500 g stewing lamb or beef, 1 onion, 1 teaspoon of Nine Spice Mix and 2 teaspoons of salt in 4 cups (1¾ pints/1 liter) water. Add both the broth and meat to the okra when you add the tomatoes.

CAULIFLOWER AND YOGURT STEW

مطفيه

Preparation time: 10 minutes
Cooking time: 2 hours
Serves 6–8

1 lb 12 oz/800 g stewing lamb or beef,
   cut into 2-inch/5-cm cubes
   (or 1 lb/2.2 kg bone-in stewing cuts
   of lamb or beef)
1 whole onion
15 allspice berries
4 cardamom pods
3 bay leaves
3 pieces mastic, crushed to a powder
   (optional)
1 teaspoon salt
1 large head of cauliflower, cut
   into florets
olive oil, for brushing
1 quantity Cooked Yogurt Sauce
   (page 29)

To serve
— Vermicelli Rice (page 32)
— Toasted Pine Nuts (page 31)

This dish, typical of Hebron, Jerusalem, and the surrounding area, is usually made in winter, when the most delicious cauliflower is in season. Combining the roasted florets with a rich meat and yogurt sauce makes for a very warming dish in the cold weather. Because yogurt sauce is meant to be white, any broth (stock) to be cooked with it often uses whole spices to avoid coloring it. If you do not have these to hand, it is perfectly fine to substitute all the spices in this recipe with one teaspoon of Nine Spice Mix (page 24) or another similar spice blend like *baharat* or Lebanese seven spice mix. The resulting dish will be darker in color but just as delicious.

Preheat the broiler (grill) to high.

Put the meat and onion into a large stockpot, cover with 6 cups (2½ pints/1.5 liters) water and place over high heat. Bring to a boil, skimming away the scum from the surface, then add the whole spices, bay leaves, mastic, and salt. Reduce the heat and simmer for 1½–2 hours, or until the meat is tender.

Meanwhile, arrange the cauliflower florets on a rimmed baking sheet and brush all over with olive oil. Broil for about 15–20 minutes, or until golden brown all around. Check on the cauliflower several times throughout cooking, flipping over and moving around to ensure even browning. When done, remove from the oven, and set aside.

In the meantime, prepare the yogurt sauce in a large pan.

When the meat is tender, strain the broth (stock) through a fine-mesh strainer (sieve) into the yogurt sauce. Add the meat pieces to the sauce, discarding the onion and spices. Add the roasted cauliflower to the meat and yogurt sauce and simmer together over medium heat for another 15 minutes. Taste and adjust the seasoning if necessary. Remove from the heat and serve with vermicelli rice or bulgur. Garnish with toasted pine nuts.

Note: Traditionally, the cauliflower in this dish is deep-fried rather than roasted. I prefer roasting it, however, because it's easier and healthier and given the intense flavor of the yogurt and meat, the difference is hardly noticeable.

EGGPLANT (AUBERGINE), LENTIL, AND POMEGRANATE STEW

رمانيه

Preparation time: 15 minutes
Cooking time: 2 hours
Serves 6–8

about 1 cup (9 oz/250 g) green or
    brown lentils
2¼ lb/1 kg eggplants (aubergines),
    chopped into bite-size pieces
14 oz/400 g tomatoes, roughly chopped
1 large onion, finely chopped
1 green chilli, finely chopped (optional)
½ cup (4 fl oz/120 ml) olive oil, plus
    2 tablespoons
4 tablespoons pomegranate molasses
1 tablespoon tomato paste (purée)
1–2 tablespoons honey
1½ teaspoons salt
½ teaspoon ground cumin
½ teaspoon crushed red chilli flakes
    (optional)
4–6 large cloves garlic, finely chopped
4 tablespoons finely chopped fresh mint
    leaves, or 1 tablespoon crushed
    dried mint
fresh pomegranate seeds, to garnish
    (optional)

To serve
— bread or rice

This famous dish from Gaza is traditionally made by boiling lentils and eggplants (aubergines) together until they form a thick spread (sometimes it is even thickened with flour or tahini) and then finished off with pomegranate molasses and fried garlic. My version, however, is slightly different from the traditional one: the addition of tomatoes came about by chance. I was trying to make two dishes for lunch one day and, with a screaming toddler next to me, accidentally put the tomatoes in the wrong pot. Surprisingly, this addition intensified the flavors of this dish. After several trials, I finally settled on this recipe, made even easier by leaving it to cook on its own for the majority of the time. A perfect make-ahead meal, this dish is as healthy as it is delicious.

Put the lentils into a large, heavy pan and cover with water. Bring to a boil over high heat, then reduce the heat and simmer until cooked, 15–25 minutes depending on variety. Drain and return to the pan.

Add the eggplants (aubergines), tomatoes, onion, and chilli to the lentils and toss to combine.

In a small bowl, mix the ½ cup (4 fl oz/120 ml) olive oil with the pomegranate molasses, tomato paste (purée), honey, salt, cumin, and chilli flakes, if using, and pour over the vegetable mixture, tossing to combine. Bring the stew to a boil over high heat (there is no need to add water as the vegetables will release their own), then reduce the heat and leave to cook, covered, until most of the liquid has evaporated, the color has darkened, and stew has come together, about 1½ hours.

About 15 minutes before the stew is ready, heat the remaining olive oil in a small skillet (frying pan) and add the chopped garlic and mint leaves. Cook until fragrant and the garlic is just starting to take on a golden color, about 1–2 minutes. Pour the contents of the pan over the lentil stew and gently toss to combine. Cover and cook for another 5–10 minutes.

Remove from the heat and allow to cool for a few minutes before serving, garnished with pomegranate seeds. Serve this hot, warm, or at room temperature with bread or rice.

SPICED LAMB IN TOMATO SAUCE

قلاية بندوره

Preparation time: 10 minutes
Cooking time: 45–60 minutes
Serves 4–6

4 tablespoons olive oil
1 lb 2 oz/500 g lamb leg meat or
    beef sirloin/fillet, cut into small
    ½-inch/1-cm cubes
1 teaspoon Nine Spice Mix (page 24)
8–10 cloves garlic, finely chopped
    or sliced
2–3 green chillies, finely chopped
    or sliced
3¼ lb/1.5 kg ripe, fleshy tomatoes, peeled
    and diced (or use 3 x 14-oz/400-g
    cans whole peeled tomatoes)
2 teaspoons salt

To serve
— rice or bread

Very popular in Palestine and Jordan, this dish is normally served for breakfast or supper. A vegetarian version of it, prepared exactly the same way but without the meat, is often served as a side to be scooped up with bread. It is best to use very fleshy tomatoes that have been peeled to give the sauce a thick and more uniform texture. To make things easier, however, you can substitute with canned whole peeled tomatoes. The aroma of this dish while it cooks is irresistible, but do let it cook low and slow; the result will be absolutely worth it.

Heat the oil in a deep-sided skillet (frying pan) over medium-high heat until hot but not smoking. Add the meat to the pan and sprinkle with the Nine Spice Mix. Continue to cook, stirring occasionally, until all the water released by the meat has evaporated and the pieces are nicely browned, about 10 minutes.

Once the water around the meat has evaporated and you see oil again, add the garlic and chillies and cook, stirring regularly, for 2–3 minutes until fragrant.

Add the tomatoes and salt and stir to combine. If using canned tomatoes use a spoon to break up the whole pieces. Bring to a boil, then reduce the heat and simmer, covered, for 30–60 minutes, or until the tomatoes have cooked and deepened in color and the sauce has thickened and come together. The exact time will vary based on the tomatoes you used and how much liquid they have released. If the tomatoes have cooked but the sauce has not thickened enough, uncover and cook over high until the liquid evaporates and the sauce reaches the desired consistency.

Transfer the tomatoes to a shallow serving dish and serve warm with either rice or bread.

SWEET PEA AND MEATBALL STEW
يخنة بازيلا

Preparation time: 15 minutes
Cooking time: 30 minutes
Serves 4–6

For the meat
1 lb 2 oz/500 g ground (minced) beef
1 small onion, finely grated
1 teaspoon Nine Spice Mix (page 24)
1 teaspoon salt
½ cup (1 oz/25 g) coriander leaves, finely
     chopped (optional)

For the stew
5 cups (40 fl oz/1.25 liters) chicken, beef,
     or lamb broth (stock)
3 tablespoons tomato paste (purée)
1 teaspoon Nine Spice Mix (page 24)
1 lb 2 oz/500 g frozen peas
7 oz/200 g carrots (about 3 medium),
     chopped into cubes
salt

To serve
— steamed rice

When cooking, I have a tendency to experiment, to add, to spice up, but this is one dish I think best left alone because its beauty is in its simplicity. So don't expect an explosion of different flavors on your tongue, rather, the smooth and comforting taste of sweet peas and carrots contrasted with rich tomatoes. Simple. Beautiful. It's so easy to make that we rarely serve it as a meal in itself, but as a side to other meals with rice. Teta Fatima most often made it if she was cooking Rice-stuffed Chicken (page 190), Flipped Over Chicken and Vegetable Rice (page 198), or Spiced Lamb and Rice Pilaf (page 166) because she would have good chicken broth (stock) leftover and all she had to do was add some peas, diced carrots, and homemade tomato paste (purée). For a stand-alone meal, I make it with meatballs and serve with rice.

Preheat the oven to 400°F/200°C/Gas Mark 6. Put all the meatball ingredients into a large bowl and mix until well combined. Shape into small balls, about the size of a cherry, and place on a baking sheet. Bake for about 15 minutes until nicely browned. Remove and set aside when done.

Meanwhile, bring the broth (stock) to a boil, add the tomato paste (purée) and Nine Spice Mix, and stir until dissolved. Add the frozen peas and carrots and cook for 5–10 minutes, or until the carrots are tender. Taste and add salt as necessary depending on your broth.

Add the meatballs to the stew and cook together for another 5 minutes. Remove from the heat and serve with steamed rice.

EGGPLANT (AUBERGINE) STEW

يخنة باذنجان

Preparation time: 15 minutes
Cooking time: 2 hours
Serves 4–6

2¼ lb/1 kg eggplants (aubergines)
1–2 tablespoons coarse sea salt
vegetable oil, for frying
1 tablespoon olive oil
1 large onion, sliced into half-moons
1 teaspoon salt
3–5 tablespoons tomato paste (purée)
    (see Note)
½ teaspoon ground pimento
½ teaspoon ground cinnamon
¼ teaspoon black pepper
1 x 14-oz/400-g can chickpeas, rinsed
    and drained (optional)

To serve
— bread or rice

This dish that my Teta Fatima made on days when she was tired of cooking meat—and that's saying something because she absolutely loves meat—was my go-to meal at university. In my tiny room I would cut and salt the eggplants (aubergines) to fry later in the communal kitchen. As crazy as that sounds, to me it was worth it for a dish that is a perfect balance of flavors and so rich and light all at the same time. Because the eggplants are fried, they absorb quite a bit of oil; for a lighter version, you could brush them with oil then broil (grill) instead. Either way, once cooked in the sauce, they become very creamy and absorb plenty of flavour; the only way to do them justice is to mop up every last drop with some good bread.

Cut the eggplants (aubergines) in half and slice each half into 3–4 pieces. Set on a rimmed baking sheet or large colander and sprinkle with the salt. Let stand for 1 hour, then rinse the eggplants and pat dry.

Heat the oil in a deep fryer or heavy Dutch oven (casserole) to 350°F/180°C. Working in batches, carefully place the eggplant pieces into the pan, without crowding them, and fry on both sides, turning occasionally, for about 5 minutes until golden brown. Drain on paper towels and pat with more paper towels to absorb any excess oil. Repeat until all the slices are fried.

Meanwhile, heat the olive oil in a pan over medium heat and add the onion and salt. Stir with a spoon for 10–15 minutes, or until softened and golden at the edges. Add the tomato paste (purée) and spices and toss for another minute. Pour in 4¼ cups (34 fl oz/1 liter) water, stirring well to combine (if you like the stew less thick, you could add more water), then add the fried eggplants and give one final gentle toss, careful not to break up the eggplants. Add the chickpeas, if using, and bring to a boil then lower the heat, cover, and simmer for another 10–15 minutes.

This can be eaten warm or at room temperature, but it does taste even better once it's had time to sit and all the flavors have melded together. Serve with rice or bread.

BAKES AND BRAISES

Growing up, my father's mother, Teta Asma, raised her own chickens and goats and planted many of her own vegetables too. Back then, I didn't appreciate the freshness and quality of what I was eating or the beauty of this simple life. Only when I started my own forays into the world of cooking did I realize the value in eating local and seasonal and the appeal of simple recipes that have stood the test of time.

The following recipes have been in my family for generations, many of them passed down from Teta Asma and her sister Teta Salma. They are mostly tray bakes and braises—things you can toss together and throw in the oven quickly or braise on the stove without much effort. It sounds simple enough, but by using delicate spices like we do in the Chicken, Onion, and Sumac Casserole (page 144), by slow cooking as we do with the Spiced Leg of Lamb (page 156), and by using strong flavors like lemon and garlic, (see Fish in Olive Oil, Lemon, and Cilantro (Coriander) Sauce (page 138)) you always end up with meals that are more than the sum of their parts.

In addition to being a great cook, Teta Asma was also a woman of incomparable curiosity and honesty. She never held back, and this generosity shone through her food. She passed away when I was six years old, and the first thing I asked my mother, with uninhibited honesty, was "so who will cook all the yummy food for us when we come here now?"

The memories and flavors of her food are surprisingly vivid, I still long for them today. Things like her melt-in-the-mouth stuffed eggplant (aubergine) bake (page 154) which always kept me coming back with more bread to mop up every last drop of sauce; or her *kafta* dishes that were delicately spiced and perfectly cooked every time. The list of her culinary triumphs goes on, and you will see many of them throughout this chapter.

Today, when I make many of the recipes she passed down to us, I keep two important things she taught me in mind. First, use the best ingredients you can find, because when dishes are simple, every flavor shines and has nowhere to hide. Second, don't be afraid to generously spice and salt your food, to add all the garlic and lemon recipes call for, or to use plenty of fresh herbs—it is these flavors that will make your dishes magical. More than their magical flavors though, the following recipes are a window into my childhood and the day-to-day life of most Palestinian families: pure, simple food, easy to put together and often made up of few ingredients, but an expression of our generous culture and family love nonetheless.

Left
Old City of Jerusalem.

FISH WITH TAHINI AND ONION SAUCE AND PINE NUTS

سمك بطحينه

Preparation time: 10 minutes
Cooking time: 15 minutes
Serves 6–8

2¼ lb/1 kg firm, skinless fish fillets,
    such as bass, bream, turbot,
    or halibut
3 tablespoons olive oil
2 tablespoons lemon zest
1 teaspoon ground cumin
1 teaspoon ground coriander
½ teaspoon salt
¼ teaspoon black pepper

For the sauce
½ cup (4 fl oz/120 ml) olive oil
3 onions, sliced into half-moons
1 cup (8 oz/225 g) tahini
½ cup (4 oz/120 g) yogurt
4–5 tablespoons freshly squeezed
    lemon juice
1 teaspoon salt

To serve
— 1 tablespoon Toasted Pine Nuts
    (page 31)
— Vermicelli Rice (page 32) or
    Pita Bread, homemade (page 38)
    or store-bought

Most Palestinian fish recipes come from coastal towns like Yaffa or Akka, and Rameh, my father's village, is a neighboring town to Akka. Often made to use up leftover cooked fish, it's so delicious that it's actually worth making from scratch, and I very often do. If you are making it for a quick weeknight dinner, you can halve or quarter this recipe and even skip the final baking part: simply spoon the sauce over pan-fried or baked fish. The flavors are so rich and intense—nutty tahini, sharp lemon, sweet onions, and succulent fish—you just cannot go wrong with this dish.

Put the fish into a roasting pan (this is the same dish it will be served in, so choose accordingly), drizzle with the olive oil, and sprinkle with the lemon zest, spices, salt, and pepper. With your hands, rub the marinade all over the fish and set aside to marinate at room temperature for 15–20 minutes while you preheat the oven to 400°F/200°C/Gas Mark 6.

When ready, bake the fish in the oven until the fish is half way cooked through or is an opaque white color. The exact time will vary according to the fish type and thickness, but rarely will fillets require longer than 10–15 minutes in a preheated oven, thinner ones need less time.

Meanwhile, make the sauce. Pour half the olive oil into a skillet (frying pan) and place over medium heat. Add in the onions and cook, stirring regularly, until the onions have completely softened but are not yet crisp, about 10 minutes. While the onions cook, combine the tahini, yogurt, 2 cups (16 fl oz/475 ml) water, the lemon juice, and salt in a bowl and mix well. When the onions are ready, pour the tahini sauce over them, stir to combine, then remove from the heat and set aside.

To assemble, remove the fish from the oven, pour the sauce over the fish and return to the oven for a further 10–15 minutes, or until the fish is fully cooked through and the tahini starts to bubble and get patches of golden brown on top.

Remove from the oven, sprinkle with pine nuts and serve immediately, with either rice or bread.

FISH IN OLIVE OIL, LEMON, AND CILANTRO (CORIANDER) SAUCE

سمك بحامض وكزبرة

Preparation time: 15 minutes
Cooking time: 10 minutes
Serves 4–6

1¾ lb/800 g firm white fish fillets
    (see Note)
1 teaspoon salt
½ teaspoon ground cumin
½ teaspoon black pepper
½ cup (4 fl oz/120 ml) olive oil
10 large cloves garlic, thinly sliced
3–4 green chillies, thinly sliced
½ cup (4 fl oz/120 ml) freshly squeezed
    lemon juice
1 packed cup (2 oz/50 g) cilantro
    (coriander) leaves, coarsely chopped
1 teaspoon crushed red chilli flakes

To serve
— crusty bread

The inspiration for this dish came from an appetizer I once had at a restaurant by the sea in Akka many years ago: sardines fried in olive oil and plenty of garlic, drizzled with a mixture of cilantro (coriander) and lemon juice. I still remember that burst of flavor in my mouth from the zingy lemon juice and sharp garlic. After experimenting several times with the dish, I finally settled on this version— it has more fire from the chillies and more sauce, making it a perfect meal to serve with rice or couscous or, my personal favorite, plenty of fresh crusty bread.

Season the fish on both sides with the salt, cumin, and black pepper and set aside. Heat the olive oil in a large, lidded skillet (frying pan) over medium heat and add the garlic. Cook for 1–2 minutes until fragrant but not colored, then add the green chillies and fry for another minute.

Turn the heat up and add the fish fillets without crowding the pan. Leave to cook until almost done (this will depend on the fish you are using; you are looking for a white opaque color), then flip over and allow to finish cooking all the way through. If the garlic starts to brown, reduce the heat and continue cooking.

When the fish is done, pour in the lemon juice, sprinkle over the cilantro (coriander) leaves, and cover with the lid. When the sauce starts to simmer again, after about 1 minute, remove from the heat and let stand for 1 minute before serving.

Sprinkle with crushed red chilli flakes and enjoy with crusty bread to mop up the delicious, tangy sauce.

Note: I prefer to use firm, thick, white fish so it can be completely skinned but still retain its shape during cooking. I most often use pollock or halibut, but the best choice is whatever is fresh and in season in your area. I have tried this dish with shrimp (prawns) and scallops and both are excellent alternatives as well, just adjust the cooking time to avoid overcooking the shellfish.

SHRIMP (PRAWNS) IN TOMATO AND CHILLI SAUCE

زبدية

Preparation time: 5 minutes
Cooking time: 40 minutes
Serves 6–8

For the sauce
3 tablespoons olive oil
1 large onion, finely diced
3–4 green chilies, finely chopped
6–8 cloves garlic, crushed
1¾ lb/800 g tomatoes, peeled and diced
    (or use 2 x 14-oz/400-g cans peeled
    whole tomatoes)
1 tablespoon tomato paste (purée)
1 teaspoon Nine Spice Mix (page 24)
1 teaspoon ground coriander
½ teaspoon ground cumin
½ teaspoon hot chilli powder (optional)
1 teaspoon salt
½ teaspoon sugar
1 small bunch fresh dill, finely chopped

For the prawns
2¼ lb/1 kg uncooked jumbo shrimp
    (king prawns), peeled and deveined
1 tablespoon olive oil
squeeze of lemon juice
½ teaspoon ground coriander
½ teaspoon ground cumin
salt and black pepper

To serve
— 1 quantity Toasted Pine Nuts
    (page 31)
— bread

Like some other Palestinian dishes (Lamb, Garlic, and Chickpea Pilaf, page 202), this traditional Gazan dish is also named after the vessel in which it is cooked. A *zibdiyeh* is a glazed terracotta pan, similar to a cazuela in Spain and Latin America, that can be used both on the stovetop and in the oven and transferred sizzling hot from kitchen to dining table. Regardless of whether you cook this dish in one of these pans or not, the result is astounding, with deeply concentrated flavors from the cooked tomatoes and sweet shrimps (prawns) against the fiery heat from the chillies. I personally cook it an enameled cast-iron shallow casserole for the most authentic flavor and rustic presentation.

Preheat the oven to 400°F/200°C/Gas Mark 6.

First make the sauce. Heat the olive oil in a large ovenproof braiser or skillet (frying pan) and add the onion and green chillies. Cook over medium heat for 6–8 minutes, or until the onions are softened and just starting to brown. Add the garlic and cook for another 1–2 minutes. Pour in the chopped tomatoes, tomato paste (purée), spices, salt, sugar, and dill and bring to a boil. Reduce the heat and simmer for 10–15 minutes until the tomatoes thicken and darken in color. If using canned tomatoes, use a spoon to break them up as you cook. Taste and adjust the seasoning if necessary.

Meanwhile, heat a nonstick skillet (frying pan) over high heat while you mix the shrimp (prawns) with the olive oil, lemon juice, and spices. Add the shrimp to the pan and cook, turning once, until the shrimp are opaque and pearly pink, about 1 minute on each side. Avoid overcooking the shrimp as it will cook more in the sauce.

Add the shrimp to the tomato sauce and toss to combine. Transfer the dish to the oven and bake for 5–10 minutes, or until starting to brown around the edges.

Remove from the oven and top with the toasted pine nuts. To serve, bring the pan to the table, ladle portions into each person's plate and enjoy with fresh crusty bread.

HERB-STUFFED WHOLE FISH
ON POTATOES

سمك مشوي على بطاطا

Preparation time: 20 minutes
Cooking time: 20–30 minutes
Serves 4–6

1 large or 2 small whole fish, such as sea
    bream, sea bass, or red snapper
    (about 4½–5½ lb/2–2.5 kg), gutted
    and scaled, head and tail left on
3 potatoes, very thinly sliced (preferably
    on the thicker setting of a mandolin)
olive oil
salt

For the stuffing
6 cloves garlic
5–6 sprigs fresh za'atar, leaves only
    (or use fresh oregano)
4 green chillies (seeded and membranes
removed if you prefer less heat)
1 small bunch (about 2 oz/50 g) flat-leaf
    parsley
1 teaspoon crushed Aleppo pepper
    (or use crushed red chilli flakes)
1 teaspoon salt
1 teaspoon ground cumin
1 teaspoon ground coriander
1 teaspoon lemon zest
¼ teaspoon black pepper
4 tablespoons olive oil
4 tablespoons lemon juice

To serve
— lemon wedges, to serve

Palestinians, particularly those who live in coastal towns like Haifa, Akka, and Gaza, eat fish on a regular basis. The fish is normally cooked very simply—deep-fried, oven-baked, or pan-fried—and served with fresh lemon and sometimes Parsley or Cilantro (Coriander) Tahini Spread (page 76). For special occasions or gatherings, however, you'll find a more elaborate preparation of the fish, where it is stuffed, crusted or cooked in sauce. This particular recipe comes from Yaffa, from the mother of my mother's best friend, Juju. Serve some Tahini Sauce (page 28) on the side for a creamy counterpoint to the sharp, zesty fish.

Sprinkle the fish with salt, wash under cold running water, pat dry and set aside. It is always best to let fish sit at room temperature for 10–15 minutes before baking, so that it cooks more evenly. Meanwhile, preheat the oven to 400°F/200°C/Gas Mark 6. Grease an ovenproof dish, large enough to hold the fish, with olive oil and set aside.

Combine all the stuffing ingredients in a food processor or mini chopper and process to a pesto-like consistency. Set aside.

Drizzle the potatoes with some olive oil, generously sprinkle with salt and toss to coat evenly. Layer the potatoes, slightly overlapping each other, over the base of the ovenproof dish.

With the tip of a sharp knife, score each side of the fish with 3–4 diagonal slits, taking care not to reach the bones. Spoon as much stuffing as possible into the slits and generously stuff the cavity of the fish. Place the fish on top of the potatoes and spoon any remaining stuffing over the potatoes as well.

Cover tightly with aluminum foil and place in the oven. Bake for 20–30 minutes for 1 large fish, or 15–20 minutes for 2 smaller fish, then remove the foil and bake for a further 10–15 minutes, or until the fish is cooked through and the potatoes have started to crisp. To test for doneness, insert the tip of a sharp knife just under the head (the thickest part of the fish) and twist gently. If it flakes easily, the fish is done; if it resists, then continue to cook for 5 minutes and test again.

When done, remove from oven and allow to rest for a couple of minutes. To serve, bring the dish to the table. Carve the fish and serve a portion to each person with some potatoes and lemon wedges.

CHICKEN AND POTATO
IN NINE SPICE

صينية دجاج وبطاطا

Preparation time: 10 minutes
Cooking time: 1 hour 15 minutes
Serves 4–6

2½ lb/1.25 kg chicken pieces (about
    4 whole legs or 6 skin-on breasts)
1 lb 8½ oz/700 g potatoes, quartered
8–10 cloves garlic, unpeeled
1 tablespoon Nine Spice Mix (page 24)
1 tablespoon salt
2–3 tablespoons olive oil
1 teaspoon pomegranate molasses
    (optional)

To serve
— bread

The easiest and quickest of all the *suniyehs* (tray bakes) Palestinians make, this is a wonderful canvas on which you can build many different flavors. It's a fantastic way to use up any vegetables you have in the refrigerator and you can experiment with different herbs as well. This simple version with only chicken, potatoes, and my mother's spice mixture is the closest to my heart because it's how she made it for us growing up.

Preheat the oven to 350°F/180°C/Gas Mark 4.

Put the chicken, potatoes, and garlic into a greased or nonstick deep roasting pan, making sure the chicken pieces are not too crowded.

In a small bowl, mix together the Nine Spice Mix, salt, olive oil, and pomegranate molasses until evenly combined. Pour this mixture over the roasting pan and work into the chicken and potatoes, ensuring everything remains in an even layer with the chicken skin side up.

Pour 1 cup (8 fl oz/250 ml) water into the tray, cover with aluminum foil, and bake in the oven for about 1 hour, or until the chicken is fully cooked. Check once or twice during cooking to make sure the liquid has not entirely evaporated and add more water if necessary. You are looking for a gravy-like sauce to mop up with bread.

Once the chicken is cooked, remove the foil and return to the oven for another 10–15 minutes to allow the chicken skin to crisp up. Remove from the oven and allow to sit for 5 minutes before serving with bread.

Variation: Instead of the chicken, you can use veal or lamb chops or beef chuck steak—just make sure you sear the meat in a pan before placing in the roasting pan. You can also add a variety of vegetables like carrots, fennel, parsnips, onions, and tomatoes, all of which will go really well with red meat.

CHICKEN, ONION, AND SUMAC CASSEROLE

محمر

Preparation time: 15 minutes
Cooking time: 1 hour 15 minutes
Serves 4–6

2½ lb/1.25 kg chicken pieces (about
　4 whole legs or 6 skin-on breasts)
6–7 onions, diced
3–5 potatoes, cut into rounds (optional)
3 tablespoons sweet paprika
2 tablespoons sumac
1 tablespoon ground cumin
1 teaspoon Nine Spice Mix (page 24)
1 tablespoon salt
3–4 tablespoons olive oil
2 tablespoons Toasted Pine Nuts
　(page 31), to serve

To serve
— pita bread (if not using potatoes),
　homemade (page 38) or
　store-bought (optional)

The combination of onions and sumac cooked in olive oil is one of the most traditional and uniquely Palestinian flavors you will ever come across. The combination is sublime: it makes you want to go back for another bite... and another... and another. In this recipe, which is more common in the northern part of Palestine, the onions and spices are cooked with chicken, and sometimes potatoes, in a roasting pan. The word *mhammar* can mean both roasted and red and aptly refers to the use of paprika, which lends the dish a distinct reddish color. It makes a perfect weeknight dinner, as it can be oven-ready in less than 15 minutes; if you have leftovers, you can always use them as stuffing for Chicken, Sumac, and Pine Nut Rolls (page 86).

Preheat the oven to 350°F/180°C/Gas Mark 4.

Put the chicken, onions, and potatoes, if using, into a greased or non-stick, deep roasting dish.

In a small bowl, mix together all the spices, salt, and olive oil until evenly combined. Pour the mixture into the roasting dish and use your hands to work the spice rub evenly into the onions, chicken, and potatoes. Make sure the chicken pieces are not crowding each other and that they are skin side up.

Add ½ cup (4 fl oz/120 ml) water to the tray, cover with aluminum foil, and bake in the oven for 1–1¼ hours until the chicken is fully cooked. Check once or twice during cooking to make sure liquid has not entirely evaporated and top up with more water if necessary. You do not want the dish to be completely dry but you also do not want a soup, more of a gravy sauce coating the onions.

Once the chicken is cooked, remove the foil and increase the oven temperature (or preheat the broiler/grill). Continue to cook for another 5–10 minutes to allow the chicken skin to crisp up. Remove from the oven and allow to sit for 5 minutes before serving. Sprinkle with toasted pine nuts and serve with pita bread, if desired.

SHAWARMA WITH ONIONS AND SUMAC

شاورما

A classic street food, *shawarma* is so prevalent in the Middle East and abroad that you may be wondering if it's even worth making at home. The answer is an unequivocal "yes!" Once you try this homemade flavor bomb, you will seldom, if ever, go back to the street variety again. The recipe is quite generous and can be halved, but then again, it's so delicious you will probably end up eating more than you bargained for. The garnishes are more of a suggestion, but they definitely enhance the flavor and overall experience of making your own shawarma sandwiches at home.

Preparation time: 10 minutes
      + marinating
Cooking time: 10 minutes
Serves 6–8

2¼ lb/1 kg beef, lamb, or chicken meat
      (see Note)
6 tablespoons olive oil
4 tablespoons vinegar (red wine,
      white wine, cider, or distilled)
2 tablespoons freshly squeezed
      lemon juice
2 teaspoons salt
2 teaspoons Nine Spice Mix (page 24)
2 teaspoons curry powder
1 teaspoon chilli powder
1 teaspoon garlic granules
3 pieces mastic, ground to a powder
      (optional)
Pita bread, homemade (page 38)
      or store-bought, to serve

To serve
– 2 onions, sliced into half-moons,
      mixed with 1 tablespoon sumac
      and ½ teaspoon olive oil
– 1 quantity Tahini Sauce (page 28)
– 2 tomatoes, diced
– 2 mini cucumbers, diced
– fresh mint leaves
– pickles of your choice

Chop the meat into large chunks, place on a plate, and freeze until almost completely frozen but not rock hard. You could also defrost previously frozen meat in the refrigerator for a few hours. Timing will vary based on your freezer, the chosen meat, and the size of your chunks. You want the meat to not be so hard you cannot cut through it with a knife, but hard enough so you can cut paper-thin slices with a sharp knife.

Use a sharp knife to cut the frozen meat into very thin slices. Put the sliced meat into a large bowl with 4 tablespoons of the olive oil, the vinegar, lemon juice, salt, and spices and mix until fully coated. Allow to sit for at least 1 hour and preferably overnight.

Heat the remaining olive oil in a large, heavy skillet (frying pan) over high heat until hot but not smoking. Add the meat and pan-fry until fully cooked and nicely browned, about 10 minutes. If your meat releases a lot of water, you will need to wait longer for the water to evaporate before the meat can brown. Remove from the heat and serve with pita bread and a selection of garnishes so each person can make their own sandwich.

Note: Shawarma can be made from beef, lamb, or chicken. If using beef, the tenderest cuts are sirloin or rib-eye cuts. Those, however, tend to be more expensive and since the shawarma is going to be marinated ahead of time, one could very easily get away with cheaper cuts like rump, flank, or even arm chuck. If using lamb, choose a cut from the hind leg and if using chicken then either breast or boneless thigh will work equally well. The main thing is to cut the meat into paper-thin slices, which is why freezing before slicing is very helpful as it allows you much more control of the meat.

MEATBALLS IN LEMON
GARLIC SAUCE

كفتة بحامض وثوم

Preparation time: 30 minutes
Cooking time: 45 minutes
Serves 4–6

For the meat
1 lb 5 oz/600 g coarsely ground
    (minced) meat (beef, lamb, veal,
    or a combination)
1 tomato, quartered
1 small onion, quartered
1 clove garlic
2 tablespoons breadcrumbs
1 tablespoon chopped flat-leaf parsley
1½ teaspoons salt
1½ teaspoons Nine Spice Mix (page 24)
1 teaspoon lemon zest (grated zest
    of 1 lemon)
½ teaspoon sweet paprika
5–6 potatoes (about 2¼ lb/1 kg),
    cut into ¾-inch/2-cm cubes

For the sauce
2 tablespoons butter
8 cloves garlic, finely crushed
1 teaspoon salt
3 tablespoons flour
4 cups (1¾ pints/1 liter) chicken
    or beef broth (stock)
14 oz/400 g white (button) mushrooms,
    thinly sliced (optional)
2 tablespoons freshly squeezed
    lemon juice
½ teaspoon turmeric

To serve
— Vermicelli Rice (page 32)

An affinity to sour flavors is apparently genetic, so it must be from my father's family that I acquired my love for all things lemony, as well as this recipe for *kafta* (meatballs). Although the sauce has a tang, the lemon is quite subtle and not overpowering: the perfect combination of sharp and smooth. The mushrooms are optional, but they do add a layer of depth to the sauce, so use them if you have to hand. If using store-bought broth (stock), taste the sauce before adding the seasoning and adjust accordingly.

Preheat the oven to 425°F/220°C/Gas Mark 7. Put the meat into a large mixing bowl and set aside.

Put the tomato, onion, garlic, breadcrumbs, parsley, salt, spice mix, lemon zest, and paprika into a food processor and process to a coarse paste. Pour this mixture over the meat and mix well with your hands until fully combined.

Shape the meat mixture into small balls, slightly larger than the potato cubes. Place the meat and potatoes in single flat layer on a baking sheet and bake in the oven for 15–20 minutes, or until they have started to brown. If the baking sheet isn't large enough to hold the meat and potatoes in a single layer then you can divide between 2 baking sheets.

In the meantime, prepare the sauce by heating the butter in a large, heavy pan over medium heat until melted. Add the crushed garlic and salt and sauté for 1 minute, then add the flour and whisk for 2–3 minutes until you achieve a very light golden color. Pour in the broth (stock), whisking continuously until the sauce is smooth. Add the mushrooms, lemon juice, and turmeric to the pan and allow the mushrooms to cook fully, about 5 minutes. Taste the broth and adjust the seasoning as necessary.

Add the meatballs and potatoes to the sauce and allow to cook for another 15 minutes until the sauce has thickened slightly. Remove from the heat and serve with vermicelli rice.

KAFTA AND TAHINI BAKE

صينية كفته بطحينه

Preparation time: 30 minutes
Cooking time: 30–40 minutes
Serves 6–8

1¾ lb/800 g coarsely ground (minced)
    meat (beef, lamb, veal, or a
    combination)
3½ oz/100 g pita bread or white bread
    with crust removed, roughly torn
1 tomato, quartered
1 small onion, coarsely chopped
2 cloves garlic
1 green chilli (optional)
2 tablespoons chopped cilantro
    (coriander)
2 tablespoons chopped flat-leaf parsley
1 tablespoon olive oil
1 tablespoon salt
1 tablespoon Nine Spice Mix (page 24)
2¼ lb/1 kg potatoes, sliced into thick
    wedges

For the sauce
1 cup (8 oz/225 g) tahini
½ cup (4 oz/120 g) yogurt
3 cups (25 fl oz/750 ml) water
4–5 tablespoons freshly squeezed
    lemon juice
1 teaspoon salt

To serve
— 1 tablespoon Toasted Pine Nuts
    (page 31)
— chopped flat-leaf parsley and red
    chilli flakes
— Vermicelli Rice (page 32)

Ask any Palestinian woman about this dish and she will likely tell you it's a dish she makes when she's tight on time, has a last minute guest, or needs a simple dish to add to an elaborate spread. After all, it is very easy to make and the sharp tahini sauce, when combined with the rich meat and crispy potatoes, creates a wonderful burst of flavors in your mouth. A favorite in my home out of all the *kafta* dishes, we normally eat it with Vermicelli Rice (page 32) and a side of Palestinian Salad (page 104) for a nutritionally dense and balanced meal. For a vegetarian option, use roasted cauliflower florets in place of the meat.

Preheat the oven to 425°F/220°C/Gas Mark 7. Place about one quarter of the meat in a large mixing bowl and set aside. In a separate bowl, soak the bread in enough water to cover it and set aside.

In a food processor combine the tomato, onion, garlic, chilli, cilantro (coriander), parsley, olive oil, salt, and spice mix, and pulse to a coarse paste. Drain the bread, squeezing any excess moisture with your hands, and add to the food processor, pulsing to evenly combine. Alternatively, very finely chop or grate everything by hand and mix together with the bread, mashing with a spoon as you mix.

Pour the mixture over the quarter of the meat in the bowl and mix very well with your hands until fully combined. Add in the remaining meat and mix very gently with your hands, just until evenly distributed. Avoid mixing any more than necessary.

Shape the meat mixture into about 15 mini sausage shapes. Place the meat and potatoes in a single flat layer on the baking sheet and insert into the oven. Cook until they have started to brown, about 15–20 minutes. If the baking sheet is not large enough to accommodate the meat and potatoes in a single layer then you can divide between two baking sheets or brown them successively.

In the meantime, whisk all the ingredients for the sauce together, taste seasoning and adjust, and set aside.

Remove the baking sheet from the oven and transfer the kafta and potatoes, along with any juices, into a large rectangular or round baking dish. Arrange them upright at an angle, alternating between the potatoes and meat. Pour the sauce over the meat and return to the oven until it starts to get patches of golden brown color, about 10–15 minutes.

Scatter with toasted pine nuts, parsley, and red chilli flakes and serve with vermicelli rice.

BEEF PATTIES IN GRAPE LEAVES

لحمه بورق

Preparation time: 30 minutes
Cooking time: 45–55 minutes
Serves 6–8

2¼ lb/1 kg coarsely ground (minced)
    beef, lamb, veal, or
    a combination)
3½ oz/100 g pita bread or white bread
    with crust removed, roughly torn
1 onion, quartered
1 tomato, quartered
1 small bunch flat-leaf parsley
2 tablespoons olive oil
1 tablespoon Nine Spice Mix (page 24)
2 teaspoons salt
45–50 fresh grape leaves, blanched
    in boiling water for 1 minute
    (if using jarred, soak in cold water
    for 15 minutes then rinse thoroughly
    to remove any brine flavor)
3–4 potatoes, sliced into ¾-inch/2-cm
    rounds
3–4 tomatoes, sliced into ¾-inch/2-cm
    rounds

For the sauce
2½ cups (1 pint/600 ml) broth (stock)
    or water
2–3 tablespoons tomato paste (purée)
1 teaspoon Nine Spice Mix (page 24)
1 tablespoon olive oil, plus extra
    for drizzling
salt and black pepper

To serve
— Vermicelli Rice (page 32), to serve

Long before wrapping meat and fish in grape leaves became popularized in the West, it was a technique used across Palestine and the Levant to add flavor and preserve the moisture of meat during cooking. This particular variation, which wraps minced meat patties in the leaves, is considered one of the signature dishes of Jerusalem. It is often reserved for special gatherings or dinner parties because it looks so impressive.

Preheat the oven to 375°F/190°C/Gas Mark 5. Put about a quarter of the meat into a large mixing bowl and set aside. In a separate bowl, cover the bread in water and leave to soak for a couple of minutes.

Meanwhile, put the onion, tomato, parsley, olive oil, Nine Spice Mix, and salt into a food processor and process to a coarse consistency. Drain the bread, squeezing any excess moisture out with your hands, and add to the food processor, pulsing to evenly combine. Alternatively, very finely chop or grate everything by hand and mix together with the bread, mashing with a spoon as you mix.

Pour the mixture over the set-aside meat in the bowl and mix very well with your hands until fully combined. Add in the remaining meat and mix very gently with your hands, just until evenly distributed. Once you've added in the remaining meat, avoid overmixing in order to retain the coarse texture that will give the patties their fluffy texture.

Divide the mixture into about 15 portions. On a clean work surface, overlap 2–3 of the grape leaves, vein side up, (if the leaves are very large then use only 1) and place one portion of meat in the center. Gently shape into a round patty and fold in the sides of the leaves around it. Repeat with the remaining meat and leaves. Set aside.

In a small mixing pitcher (jug), combine the broth (stock) with the tomato paste (purée), Nine Spice Mix, 1 teaspoon of salt, and the olive oil and set aside.

In a round oven dish, arrange the grape leave parcels upright at a slight angle with potato and tomato slices between them. Pour the sauce mixture over, drizzle with some more olive oil and sprinkle with salt and black pepper.

Cover the dish with aluminum foil and bake in the oven for 40 minutes. Remove the foil and return to the oven for a further 15 minutes, or until the potatoes have started to brown. Remove from the oven and serve with vermicelli rice.

KAFTA AND TOMATO BAKE

صينية كفتة ببندوره

This is probably the most traditional way Palestinians make *kafta*. Each person has their own way of arranging and shaping the ingredients but the ultimate result is a well-spiced meat mixture with crispy potatoes in a rich tomato sauce. This recipe is the way Juju, my mother's best friend, makes it. If you want to give it more of a kick, you could add green chillies and garlic to the sauce, but I love it as is because Juju does it the way her mother and grandmother before her have done it for generations. Tried, tested, and unbelievably tasty, this dish is as perfect for a midweek dinner as it is for a weekend feast.

Preparation time: 20 minutes
Cooking time: 45 minutes
Serves 4

For the meat
1 lb 2 oz/500 g coarsely ground (minced) meat (beef, lamb, veal, or a combination)
small bunch chopped flat-leaf parsley
1 small onion, finely grated
½ teaspoon ground pimento
½ teaspoon ground cinnamon
¼ teaspoon black pepper, plus extra for grinding
1 x 14-oz/400-g can crushed tomatoes
2 cloves garlic, crushed (optional)
4 tablespoons olive oil, plus extra for drizzling
5 potatoes, thinly sliced
5 tomatoes, sliced into rounds
1 green bell pepper, sliced into rounds
salt

To serve
— Vermicelli Rice (page 32) or Pita bread, homemade (page 38) or store-bought, to serve

Preheat the oven to 400°F/200°C/Gas Mark 6. Put the meat, parsley, onion, spices, and 1 teaspoon of salt into a large bowl and mix gently with your hands until just combined, taking care not to over mix the meat.

In a separate bowl, mix together the crushed tomatoes, garlic, olive oil, and ½ teaspoon of salt. Pour into an ovenproof baking dish, about 12×8 inches (30×20 cm).

Shape the meat mixture into mini hamburger shapes. Arrange in rows in the baking dish, alternating with slices of potato, tomato, and green bell pepper. Grind over some black pepper and drizzle with olive oil. Cover the dish with aluminum foil and bake in the oven for 20–30 minutes. Remove the foil and return to the oven for a further 15 minutes, or until the potatoes are golden brown on top.

Remove from the oven, let stand for 5 minutes, then serve with vermicelli rice or pita bread.

LAMB AND NUT STUFFED AUBERGINE BAKE

صينية باذنجان

Preparation time: 45 minutes
Cooking time: 30 minutes
Serves 6

For the filling
1 quantity Toasted Pine Nuts (page 31)
1 quantity Lamb with Onion and Spices
    (page 30)
1 teaspoon sumac (optional)

For the aubergines
6 medium sized or 12 baby eggplants
    (aubergines) (about 3½ lb/1.5 kg)
vegetable oil, for frying (see Note)
12 oz/350 g tomatoes (about 3 medium),
    diced
olive oil, for drizzling
1½ cups (12 fl oz/350 ml) chicken broth
    (stock), homemade (page 34) or
    store-bought, or water
½ teaspoon Nine Spice Mix (page 24)
1 tablespoon pomegranate molasses
salt and black pepper

To serve
— rice or bread

My great-great-grandmother brought this recipe with her from Syria when she moved to Palestine. She then passed it down to my great-grandmother, who passed it on to my Teta Asma, who gave it to my mother, who passed it on to me. There is something to be said of recipes that stand the test of time and continue to please generation after generation. This is a spectacular dish that is definitely worth the effort.

Prepare the filling by frying the pine nuts then making the Lamb with Onion and Spices in the same pan. Combine with the sumac, if using, and set aside. This can be prepared a day or two in advance and refrigerated until ready to use.

Using a vegetable peeler, peel alternating strips from the skin of each eggplant (aubergine) to create a striped effect. Cut the eggplants in half lengthwise, set in a colander, sprinkle generously with salt, and allow to sit for about 1 hour. When ready, rinse and pat dry with paper towel. If you are using baby eggplants, keep them whole, skip the salting, and pierce with a knife before frying.

Pour enough vegetable oil into a large skillet (frying pan) to reach about ¾ inch/2 cm up the sides. When the oil is hot, pan-fry the eggplants in batches, taking care because the oil may splutter from the water, and turn over once until golden brown on both sides, about 10 minutes. Remove from the oil and drain on paper towels. Continue, until all the eggplants are fried.

Preheat the oven to 375°F/190°C/Gas Mark 5. Place the eggplants cut side up in an ovenproof dish, approximately 12 × 16 inches/30 × 40 cm. With a pointed knife, make an incision halfway into the flesh, leaving 1¼ inch/3 cm at each end. Gently push apart at the incision with your fingers to make a large pocket and stuff each eggplant with the filling. If any filling is left, scatter it around in the dish.

Top the eggplants with the diced tomatoes, scattering any extra in the dish as well. Drizzle the tomatoes with olive oil and sprinkle with some salt and black pepper. Combine the broth (stock) or water, Nine Spice Mix, pomegranate molasses, and 2 teaspoons of salt. Stir until combined then pour into the dish. Bake in the oven for 30 minutes.

Remove from oven and allow to sit for at least 5 minutes before serving with rice or bread.

Note: To roast the eggplants instead of frying, brush with oil and cook in a 425°F/220°C/Gas Mark 7 oven for 20–30 minutes.

SPICED LEG OF LAMB

فخدة خروف بالفرن

Preparation time: 10 minutes +
    marinating
Cooking time: 3 hours 30 minutes
Serves 6–8

3 tablespoons pomegranate molasses
2 tablespoons olive oil
1 tablespoon salt
1 tablespoon ground coriander
1 tablespoon ground cumin
2 teaspoons ground dill seeds
2 teaspoons sumac
4 large cloves garlic, crushed
1 teaspoon Nine Spice Mix (page 24)
½ teaspoon red chilli powder
4 large cloves garlic, crushed
2–3 bay leaves
4½ –5½ lb/2.2–2.5 kg leg of lamb
    on the bone

In the old days, meat was expensive so it was generally reserved for holidays. Probably because of this, serving large cuts of meat was seen, and to this day continues to be considered, as a sign of utmost respect to guests. In addition to the traditional meals like Lamb and Yogurt Rice Stew (page 206), Flipped Over Chicken and Vegetable Rice (page 198) and Lamb, Garlic, and Chickpea Pilaf (page 202), which are often topped with large bone-in pieces of lamb, one of the main things my mother made when we had guests was whole roast leg of lamb. It would cook slowly for several hours in the oven on low heat and the meat would be fall-apart and melt-in-the-mouth tender when served. There are many ways to spice the leg of lamb—the key is the low and slow roasting. This version is one of my favorites, but you could also swap out the spices for Za'atar or Duqqa (page 244).

Start by putting all the ingredients, except for the bay leaves and lamb, into a small bowl and mixing until thoroughly combined to make a marinade.

Using a sharp knife, make deep incisions all over the lamb leg to help it absorb as much of the marinade flavor as possible. With your hands, rub the marinade all over the leg, pushing as much of it as possible into the incisions, and tuck the bay leaves in as well. Allow to sit for at least 1 hour, preferably overnight in the refrigerator.

Preheat the oven to 425°F/220°C/Gas Mark 7 and find a large roasting pan, preferably with a rack inside. Put the leg of lamb into the roasting pan, skin side up, and place in the oven for 15 minutes.

Remove the lamb from the oven and reduce the heat to 325°F/160°C/Gas Mark 3. Pour ½ cup (4 fl oz/120 ml) water into the roasting pan, cover the pan with aluminum foil, keeping it high enough so it does not come into direct contact with the lamb, and return to the oven for 3 hours. Check on it halfway through cooking, adding more water if it seems to have dried up.

After 3 hours, remove the foil, increase the heat back to 425°F/220°C/Gas Mark 7, and roast for a further 5–10 minutes until the top has crisped up. Remove from the oven, re-cover loosely with the foil, and let rest for 15 minutes before serving.

Right
Spice vendor in Souk El Attarine
in the Old City of Jerusalem.

RICE, GRAINS, AND FATTEH

Like most children, I couldn't wait to grow up. Now that I have, I wish more than anything I could go back to those days I spent at my Teta Fatima's house listening to her and my grandfather's tales, everything from fiction to family history and anecdotes.

Through all the stories I heard growing up, the importance of land was always highlighted. After all, it was the life and livelihood of most Palestinian families. It gave them wheat and its ensuing grains, like bulgur and freekeh, and by extension bread, all of which were, and continue to be, vital to the Palestinian diet.

It was no surprise to me then to learn that, when the war of 1948 broke out and many people left their homes until situations settled, my great-grandfather refused to leave. The entire family packed themselves up and set off except for him and his oldest son, staying back to safeguard their land. It was also early summer, so their storerooms were filled to the brim with wheat. To them, this was worth more than gold—it was their life's work and sustenance—and they stayed behind to protect it and the land that provided it. My grandmother's family were lucky to eventually come back to their homes and not become refugees, but this story sheds light on how heavily Palestinians relied on essential grains, both as a source of nourishment and of capital.

Many of the following recipes are based on these affordable, nutritious, and satisfying native grains. While at first glance they might seem too simple to be as delicious as I describe, often it is the smallest step, like almost burning the onions for the Lentil and Bulgur Pilaf (page 164), and the most basic technique, like sautéing the the freekeh in ghee or butter before cooking it (page 162), that elevate these humble ingredients into something luxurious. In other recipes like *Hashweh* (page 166), adding minced meat and spices turns modest white rice into a substantial dish. Although rice is not native to Palestine, by the end of the Ottoman rule and start of the British mandate it was being imported in large quantities from Egypt and has since found its place as a staple in the national cuisine.

From the simple to the more elaborate, these rice and grain dishes are steeped in tradition. They may be made with the staple ingredients like wheat, freekeh, bulgur, rice, and bread, but the flavor is amplified with different vegetables, spices, and cooking methods. So relish the taste as well as the simplicity of these dishes, because in so doing you will experience the essence not only of authentic Palestinian home cooking but also our way of life.

Left
A flour mill in Nahef village
in the Galilee.

YOGURT AND GARLIC RISOTTO

لبنيه

Preparation time: 5 minutes
Cooking time: 30 minutes
Serves 4

1 lb 2 oz/500 g plain yogurt (preferably
    goat)
1 teaspoon salt
1 teaspoon cornstarch (cornflour)
    (omit if using goat yogurt)
1 tablespoon olive oil
4 cloves garlic, crushed
1 teaspoon lemon juice (optional)
2 cups (12 oz/350 g) cooked plain
    white rice

To garnish (optional)
olive oil, for frying
2 garlic cloves, thinly sliced
¼ cup (1 oz/25 g) Toasted Pine Nuts
    (page 31)
1 tablespoon crushed dried mint

A fantastic way to use up leftover rice or Cooked Yogurt
Sauce (page 29), this is one of my all-time favorite comfort
meals. The sharp yogurt and strong notes of garlic running
through the dish symbolize Palestinian comfort food at
its best. For a slightly more elaborate presentation, I top it
with either fried pine nuts or fried garlic slices.

Put the yogurt, 2 cups (16 fl oz/475 ml) water, salt, and
cornstarch (cornflour), if using, into a heavy pan and bring
to a boil, whisking continuously, over medium-high heat.
It is very important to whisk continuously to prevent
the yogurt from curdling. Once it boils, reduce the heat to
a bare simmer while you prepare the garlic.

Heat the olive oil in a small skillet (frying pan), add the
garlic, and sauté over medium heat for 1–2 minutes until
fragrant but still white. Pour the garlic into the yogurt
and stir. The sauce should be quite salty and sour, but will
vary based on the yogurt used, so taste and adjust the
seasoning with salt and lemon juice, as needed.

Add the rice to the yogurt, and stir to combine. Increase
heat slightly and bring to a simmer, cooking until you reach
a consistency similar to a thin risotto. You may need to
add more water depending on the rice you are using. Keep
in mind that the consistency will thicken considerably as
it cools.

Just before serving, heat the olive oil in a small frying pan
and add in the garlic slices. Fry until a very light golden
color, remove from the oil and drain on kitchen paper.

To serve, ladle the rice into shallow bowls, and top with the
fried garlic slices. Alternatively sprinkle each bowl with
toasted pine nuts and some dried mint.

Note: This recipe assumes you are making the yogurt sauce
from scratch, but you can also use leftover yogurt from
any of the recipes in this book that call for it such as Lamb
and Yogurt Rice Stew (page 206) or Lamb Dumplings in
Yogurt Sauce (page 204). In that case, you can skip the
frying garlic step, as the yogurt sauce will already have fried
garlic in it; simply heat the leftover yogurt, add the cooked
rice, and simmer for a couple minutes, adding water and
salt as necessary.

FREEKEH PILAF WITH LAMB AND PINE NUTS

فريكه مفلفله

Preparation time: 15 minutes
Cooking time: 1 hour
Serves 6–8

2 tablespoons butter
2 tablespoons olive oil
2 onions, finely diced
1 teaspoon salt
1 teaspoon Nine Spice Mix (page 24)
½ teaspoon ground cumin
1 lb /450 g freekeh
4 cups (1¾ pints/1 liter) chicken broth
    (stock), homemade (page 34) or
    store-bought

For the lamb and pine nut topping
1 quantity Toasted Pine Nuts (page 31)
3 tablespoons olive oil
1 lb 2 oz/500 g lamb leg meat or beef
    sirloin/fillet, cut into ½-inch/1-cm
    cubes
1 teaspoon Nine Spice Mix (page 24)
1 teaspoon salt

There's something about the smokiness of freekeh that lends it a taste unlike any other grain. When combined with the richness of butter and olive oil, sautéed onions, and the warmth of spices, it produces a flavor combination that is a feast for the taste buds. The dish also looks quite impressive in a platter topped with toasted pine nuts and lamb, making it a good choice for entertaining. You could also use lamb cutlets, chicken legs, or even a whole chicken.

Heat the butter and oil in a large pan over medium heat until hot but not smoking. Add the onions, salt, and spices, reduce the heat, and cook, stirring occasionally, for 6–8 minutes until the onions have softened and started to brown. Add the freekeh and mix with a wooden spoon until well combined with the onion and spices. Continue to cook, stirring occasionally, until lightly toasted and you can smell its nutty aroma, another 6–8 minutes.

Pour in the broth (stock), give it one final stir, and bring to a boil. Reduce the heat, cover the pan, and simmer gently over low heat for 35–45 minutes. Check on the freekeh from time to time, giving it a good stir to make sure it is not sticking to the bottom, and add water as necessary. Taste and adjust seasoning (this will depend on the broth you are using), and if it still has too strong a bite, add some more water and continue to cook over low heat until it is fully cooked. You neither want the freekeh too soft like rice, nor do you want to feel you are biting into hard, uncooked grains. The consistency of cooked pearl barley is ideal. Once ready, remove from the heat and allow to sit for up to 15 minutes before serving.

While the freekeh is simmering, fry the pine nuts, then drain and set aside. Heat the olive oil in the same pan over high heat until hot but not smoking. Add the meat, sprinkle with the spice mix and salt and cook, stirring frequently, for 10–15 minutes, or until any released water evaporates and the meat starts to brown. Remove the pan from the heat and set aside, covered, until you are ready to serve the freekeh.

To serve, pour the freekeh into a large serving platter and fluff up with a fork. Top with the meat and pine nuts and serve immediately.

Variation: In place of the fried meat, you could top the freekeh with either roast lamb cutlets (2–4 per person) or roast chicken pieces (1 leg or 1 breast per person) or simply shredded chicken.

LENTIL AND BULGUR PILAF

مجدرة برغل

Preparation time: 10 minutes
Cooking time: 45–60 minutes
Serves 4–6

1 cup (8 oz/225 g) whole lentils, picked
    over and rinsed (see Note)
½ cup (4 fl oz/120 ml) olive oil
3 onions, finely diced
1 teaspoon salt
½ teaspoon ground cumin
1 cup (6 oz/175 g) coarse bulgur

For the crispy onion topping
vegetable oil, for frying
1 large onion, cut into thin half-moons
1 teaspoon cornstarch (cornflour)

When you look at the simple ingredients list, you might be sceptical of the end result, but the combination of toasted onions, bulgur, lentils, and good quality olive oil is actually divine. Eaten with Palestinian Salad (page 104) and some plain yogurt, this is a wholesome and nutrient-dense meal. However, because of the ingredients, it's considered a peasant dish that no one would serve at special occasions. It's a shame, because this dish is truly an unsung hero.

Put the lentils and 4 cups (1¾ pints/1 liter) water into a pan over high heat and bring to a boil. Reduce the heat and simmer for 15–30 minutes, or until almost done but still with a bite. The exact time will depend on the variety, but generally cook the lentils for 5 minutes less than stated on the package.

Meanwhile, heat the olive oil in a skillet (frying pan) over medium-high heat. Add the onions and sauté for 15–20 minutes, stirring regularly, until they turn a deep golden brown and start to crisp. Onions can very quickly go from deep brown to burnt, so keep an eye out as you stir and remove them from the heat before they burn. It is very important to cook them to this point though, because that is what will give the pilaf its distinctive dark color and flavor.

Pour the onions and their oil over the lentils in the pan, add the salt and cumin and give them all a good stir. Add the bulgur, bring back to a boil, then reduce the heat to its lowest setting and simmer, covered, for 10–15 minutes. Check on the pilaf from time to time; if the bulgur and lentils are still not fully cooked but the water has evaporated, top up with water and continue to cook until done.

This dish is quite forgiving and there is no right or wrong texture. Some people prefer it fluffy like a pilaf, while others prefer it denser, like sticky rice. I like mine somewhere in the middle and that's what you get with the specified quantity of water here. When done, place a dish towel or paper towels under the lid and let sit for 15 minutes before serving.

In the meantime, prepare the topping. Heat the oil in a small, deep skillet. Sprinkle the sliced onion with the cornstarch (cornflour) and toss to combine. Add to the hot oil and fry until crisp and dark golden brown. Remove with a slotted spoon and drain on paper towels until dry and crispy.

Serve the pilaf topped with crispy onions.

Note: Traditionally we use brown lentils, but any variety (not split) such as green, French green, Puy, or beluga also works.

SPICED LAMB AND RICE PILAF

حشوه

Preparation time: 10 minutes + soaking
Cooking time: 45 minutes
Serves 6–8

2 tablespoons butter
2 tablespoons olive oil
1½ tablespoons Nine Spice Mix
    (page 24)
1 lb 8½ oz/700 g ground (minced)
    lamb or beef (see Note)
1 lb 2 oz/500 g jasmine (or any medium
    grain) rice, washed, soaked for
    15 minutes, and drained
4 cups (1¾ pints/1 liter) chicken, beef,
    or lamb broth (stock)
½ cup (2 oz/50 g) Toasted Pine Nuts
    (page 31)
1 cup (4 oz/120 g) Toasted Almonds
    (page 31)
salt

We call this dish *hashweh*, which actually means stuffing, because it's what we use to fill chicken, lamb, pigeon, and almost any other meat that we stuff (see page 193 for the picture). It is so delicious, however, that we often serve it on its own, and, if it's a special occasion, topped with shredded chicken or lamb. Either way, the warmth of the spices infusing the rice and meat along with the crisp nuts is a real treat. Almost always served with plain yogurt, I also love to have it with a side of Cabbage and Tomato Salad (page 108).

Heat the butter and olive oil over high heat in a heavy Dutch oven (casserole) or nonstick pan. Once the butter starts to sizzle, add the spice mix and fry until fragrant, about 1 minute. Add the meat and sauté for 10–15 minutes, or until browned. If the meat releases liquid, cook until the water evaporates (you will hear the oil sizzling again) and the meat browns.

Add the drained rice and toss to combine with the meat and coat in the oil. Pour in the broth (stock) and bring to a boil. Once boiling, reduce the heat, cover the pan, and let simmer until the rice is fully cooked, 15–20 minutes. Check on the rice from time to time—if the liquid evaporates before the rice is cooked, gradually add more water and continue cooking until it is done. You want the rice soft to the bite but not so overcooked that it all sticks together. As a test, when you remove from the heat, you should still be able to easily stir the rice with a spoon.

When the rice is almost done, taste and adjust seasoning, depending on how salty your broth is. Add the toasted pine nuts, give it one final stir, then remove from the heat and allow to sit, covered, for 10 minutes before serving.

To serve, fluff the rice up with a large fork, transfer to a serving platter and top with the toasted almonds.

Note: When I am in a rush, I use ground (minced) beef or lamb to make this dish, although I do prefer the texture when I buy my own piece of meat and dice it into very small cubes. Any cut of meat will do, but I generally buy flank if it's beef or a cut from the hind leg if it's lamb. To chop the meat into small cubes—no larger than a chickpea—it's easiest if you freeze it until almost fully frozen but still workable with a knife; you can then slice through it like you would a root vegetable.

LENTIL AND RICE PILAF

مجدرة رز

Preparation time: 10 minutes + soaking
Cooking time: 45–60 minutes
Serves 4–6

1 cup (8 oz/225 g) whole lentils, picked
    over and rinsed
1 cup (7 oz/200 g) rice, soaked for
    15 minutes and drained
2 teaspoons salt
½ teaspoon ground cumin
½ teaspoon Nine Spice Mix (page 24)
    (optional)
½ cup (4 fl oz/120 ml) olive oil
3 onions, finely diced

For the crispy onion topping
vegetable oil, for frying
1 large onion, cut into thin half-moons
1 teaspoon cornstarch (cornflour)

Rice and lentils are staple foods for many cultures. This dish, which combines them, is the staple pantry meal in Palestine as its ingredients are almost always to hand. In spite of its simplicity, and being considered a "poor man's dish" because it contains no meat, the combination of rice and lentils with crispy onions and spices produces a dish nothing short of marvelous. It is very similar to the bulgur variety (page 164) except that the onions are not fried to such a deep brown color.

Put the lentils into a pan with 6 cups (48 fl oz/1.5 liters) water, place over high heat, and bring to a boil. Reduce the heat, cover, and simmer for 15–30 minutes, or until the lentils are almost done but still have a bite. The exact time will depend on the variety of lentil you are using, but generally cook them for about 5 minutes less than stated on the package.

Add the rice, 1 teaspoon of the salt, and the spices to the lentils. Bring to a boil, then reduce the heat and simmer until the rice is fully cooked. If the water seems to have evaporated and the rice is still not done, gradually add more water. If the rice appears to have cooked but water remains visible, remove the lid and cook until all of the water is absorbed and the rice is fluffy.

Meanwhile, heat the olive oil in a skillet (frying pan) over medium-high heat. Add the onions and remaining salt and sauté for 12–15 minutes, stirring regularly, until a golden brown color and just starting to crisp around the edges.

Once the rice is done, pour the onions and their oil over the rice and lentils, give them one gentle stir, and place a dish towel or paper towels under the lid and cover. Remove from the heat and set aside for at least 10 minutes before serving to allow the flavors to settle in together.

In the meantime, prepare the crispy onion topping. Heat the vegetable oil in a small, deep skillet until hot. Sprinkle the onion slices with the cornstarch (cornflour) and toss to combine. Add to the hot oil and fry until crisp and a dark golden brown, again taking care to remove them before they cross the fine line between golden brown and burnt. Remove with a slotted spoon and drain on paper towels until dry and crispy.

Serve the pilaf topped with crispy onions.

FREEKEH, BEEF, AND VEGETABLES PIES

صرر أوزي بالفريكه

Preparation time: 30 minutes
Cooking time: 1 hour 30 minutes
Makes 8 (to serve 4–8)

1 tablespoon butter
2 tablespoons olive oil
1 large onion, finely diced
1 teaspoon salt
½ teaspoon Nine Spice Mix (page 24)
½ teaspoon ground cumin
7 oz/200 g ground (minced) beef or lamb
7 oz/200 g freekeh
3½ oz/100 g carrots, diced
3½ oz/100 g green peas
1 quantity Toasted Pine Nuts (page 31)
1 lb 2 oz/500 g bought all-butter puff
    pastry sheets
1 egg, lightly beaten with 1 tablespoon
    water

This dish is often made during special occasions because it looks very pretty and is easy to serve in individual portions. Sometimes, for an even more impressive presentation, it is made in a giant bowl as one large dome that is then cracked open at the table. Normally made with rice, I opted for freekeh in this recipe because that's how my mother makes it. To do with rice, just use cooked white rice and mix it with the fried meat, pine nuts, carrots, and peas.

Heat the butter and oil in a large pan over medium heat. Add the onion, salt, and spices, reduce the heat, and cook for 6–8 minutes, stirring occasionally, until the onions have softened and started to brown.

Increase the heat to high and add the ground (minced) beef. Break up any lumps with a wooden spoon and cook for 10–12 minutes, or until browned. If your beef releases water, you may need to cook a little longer until the water has evaporated and the beef has browned. Reduce the heat, add the freekeh, and mix until combined. Continue to cook, stirring occasionally, until lightly toasted, about 6 minutes.

Pour in 18 fl oz/500 ml water, give it one final stir, and bring to a boil. Reduce the heat, cover the pan, and simmer gently over low heat for 35–45 minutes. Taste the freekeh, if it still has too strong a bite, add some more water and continue to cook over low heat until it is fully cooked.

Meanwhile, bring a small pan of salted water to a boil. Add the carrots and cook for 3–4 minutes before adding the peas and cooking for another 3 minutes. Drain and rinse under cold water to stop the vegetables from cooking any further.

When the freekeh is done, transfer to a large platter or tray and allow to cool for about 10 minutes. Add the peas, carrots, and toasted pine nuts and mix until combined.

Preheat the oven to 400°F/200°C/Gas Mark 6. Roll out your puff pastry as thinly as possible and cut the pastry into roughly 6-inch/15-cm squares. Press one of the squares into a small bowl, fill the bowl with 3–5 tablespoons of the freekeh mixture and bring the edges of the pastry together to close it on the stuffing. Flip the bowl over and you will have a lovely circle-shaped parcel with the stuffing inside. Transfer to a baking sheet and repeat with the remaining pastry squares and filling.

Brush the pies with the egg then bake for 20 minutes, or until the pastry is a light golden brown. Serve immediately.

BAKED KUBBEH PIE

صينية كبه

Preparation time: 30 minutes
Cooking time: 1 hour
Serves 6–8

For the kubbeh dough
1½ cups (9 oz/280 g) very fine bulgur
    wheat
1 small onion, quartered
1 teaspoon salt
½ teaspoon Nine Spice Mix (page 24)
½ teaspoon ground cumin
9 oz/250 g lean goat, lamb, or beef meat,
    twice ground (minced) through a fine
    mincer
olive oil, for brushing

For the stuffing
1 quantity Toasted Pine Nuts (page 31)
½ cup (2 oz/50 g) coarsely chopped
    walnuts, lightly toasted
1 quantity Lamb with Onion and Spices
    (page 30)

Fried kubbeh is delicious but requires time and effort to make—and then it still has to be fried. So on those occasions when you want to make kubbeh but do not have the patience, this baked version is a an equally delicious alternative.

To make the dough, put the bulgur into a large bowl and cover with cold water. Allow to soak for 15 minutes, then drain, squeezing out as much excess water as you can.

Put the onion, salt, and spices with 1 tablespoon of cold water into the bowl of a food processor and process until finely ground (minced). Add the meat and pulse until combined. Add the soaked bulgur and process until the mixture resembles a smooth and pliable dough. Knead briefly with your hands to smooth out and evenly combine. Refrigerate for at least 1 hour, and up to overnight.

Meanwhile, prepare the stuffing by combining the pine nuts, walnuts, and lamb with onion and spices.

Preheat the oven to 400°F/200°C/Gas Mark 6 and grease a shallow 28cm round or 12 × 8-inch/30 × 20-cm rectangular ovenproof dish with olive oil. Keep a bowl of water nearby to wet your hands while you shape the kubbeh.

Divide the dough mixture into 2 equal halves. Spread one half of the mixture evenly in the bottom of the baking dish, wetting your hands as you go to ensure an even and smooth finish. Spoon the stuffing over the dough and gently press in with your hands. To spread the top layer of kubbeh, tear off a handful of the dough and flatten out with your hands to a similar thickness as the bottom layer. Place the flattened piece on top. Tear off another portion and repeat, slightly overlapping it with the first. Continue, wetting your hands as you go, until the top layer is covered, then smooth out.

With the tip of a sharp knife, score the top layer to form a geometric pattern. If using a rectangular dish, the most customary is a diamond pattern, which can be achieved by doing criss-crossing diagonal lines. If using a round dish, you can divide the circle into quarters or eighths and then do a diamond pattern within each triangle. Once you have created your pattern, cut all the way through the kubbeh along the lines that you want each serving sizes to be.

At this point, it can be baked or it can be frozen for up to 3 months. To cook, brush generously with olive oil and bake, uncovered, for 35–45 minutes, until dark golden brown. Check it once or twice and if it seems dry, brush with olive oil. Allow to cool for 10 minutes before slicing and serving.

FATTEH: BREAKING BREAD

It's hard to say that *fatteh* is Palestinian because it's eaten across the entire Levant region. While some variations of it are typical to Palestine—like Gazan Fatteh (page 176)—*fatteh* itself refers to a preparation method and is seen everywhere from Syria to Lebanon to Jordan and even Egypt.

The word *fatteh* is derived from an old Arabic verb meaning "to break bread into morsels and steep in some kind of liquid or sauce". Whether it's bread torn apart and thrown into lentil soup, or paper-thin bread topped with rice and meat, the act of soaking torn bread in a cooked meal is known as *fatt* in Arabic, and hence the ensuing dish is a *fatteh*.

If one is to look back at its origins, this method of eating probably hails back to historic times when rice and other grains were not as readily available as wheat, so bread was one of the surest ways to include carbohydrates in a diet—and this was an easy way to do it.

Nowadays, though, when people talk about *fatteh* it is generally in reference to dishes made of some kind of bread that is topped with a warm cooked meal and then dressed with a cool sauce that can be tahini-, yogurt-, or lemon-based. The breads can vary from paper-thin flatbreads to crispy fried or baked pita croutons, while the meals and toppings can vary from vegetables to beans and meats.

The following three recipes are some of the most traditional ones Palestinians prepare. The ingredients lists might seem long at first, but a closer look reveals they are actually very simple dishes to put together and ones you can always count on for a contrast of soft and crunchy, warm and cool; not to mention an absolutely satisfying flavor that begs you to help yourself to more.

Right
A stack of pita bread in
Jerusalem.

CHICKPEAS AND LAMB ON TOASTED PITA WITH TAHINI SAUCE

فتة حمص

Preparation time: 15 minutes
Cooking time: 1 hour 15 minutes
Serves 6–8

3 large, thin Lebanese pita breads
　　(about 9 oz/250 g)
2 x 14-oz/400-g) cans chickpeas
1 teaspoon ground cumin

For the yoghurt and tahini sauce
1 cup (8 oz/225 g) tahini
1 large clove garlic, crushed
1 teaspoon salt
1 cup (8 oz/225 g) yogurt
4 tablespoons freshly squeezed
　　lemon juice

For the lemon dressing
1 large clove garlic, finely diced
1 green chilli, finely diced
2 tablespoons freshly squeezed
　　lemon juice
2 tablespoons olive oil

For the meat
1 tablespoon butter or ghee
1 quantity Toasted Pine Nuts (page 31)
1 lb 2 oz/500 g lamb leg meat
　　or beef sirloin/fillet, cut into
　　½-inch/1-cm cubes
1 teaspoon Nine Spice Mix (page 24)

To serve
－ 2 tablespoons finely chopped
　　flat-leaf parsley
－ red chilli flakes or pomegranate
　　seeds (optional)

This is the quintessential Palestinian brunch dish. Humble ingredients like chickpeas and tahini are transformed into something magical when combined with toasted bread and topped with succulent small pieces of fried lamb or beef and pine nuts. As much as we love to use bread to mop up our hummus, in this particular dish we toast the bread and put it at the bottom, then eat it with a spoon. For a vegetarian version, just use pine nuts for the topping.

Preheat the oven to 350°F/180°C/Gas Mark 4. Cut the pita breads into ¾-inch/2-cm squares and put on a baking sheet. Bake in the oven for about 15 minutes, or until the squares are dry and crisp and starting to darken in color, moving around with a wooden spoon from time to time. (This step can be done a couple of days in advance.)

Put the tahini, garlic, salt, yogurt, and lemon juice into a large bowl and stir to combine; the sauce will be thick and sticky. Remove about ½–¾ cup of the chickpea canning liquid and gradually mix with the tahini. You want a consistency similar to maple syrup: thick but pourable.

Prepare the lemon dressing by whisking all the ingredients together in a small bowl; set aside.

Start on the meat. Prepare the Toasted Pine Nuts in a large skillet (frying pan). Remove the pine nuts and set aside, reserving the oil in the pan. Add the ghee to the pan, and once sizzling tip in the meat, sprinkle with the Nine Spice Mix, and cook over medium-high heat, stirring occasionally, for about 10 minutes until all liquid released by the meat evaporates and the pieces are nicely browned.

While the meat is cooking, put the chickpeas and cumin into a pan and cover with water. Bring to a boil then simmer on very low heat, keeping them warm, until the meat is done.

To assemble the dish, spread out the bread in a large, deep serving platter and spoon half the dressing over the top. Setting aside about 2 tablespoons of the chickpeas for garnish, use a ladle to scoop the remaining hot chickpeas, along with some broth, and spread over the bread. You want the bread to soak up the liquid but not become mushy, so add just enough water, about ½ cup (4 fl oz/120 ml).

Pour the tahini and yogurt mixture over the chickpeas. Top with the meat and pine nuts, and garnish with the reserved chickpeas, parsley, and chilli flakes or pomegranate seeds. Drizzle over the remaining dressing and serve straight away.

GAZAN FATTEH

فته غزاويه

Preparation time: 10 minutes
Cooking time: 2 hours 30 minutes
Serves 6–8

3 large, thin Lebanese pita breads
    (about 9 oz/250 g)
2 tablespoons olive oil
1 lb 2 oz/500 g rice, soaked for
    15 minutes and drained
1 quantity Toasted Pine Nuts (page 31)

For the broth (stock)
4 tablespoons olive oil (optional)
4½ lb/2 kg bone-in meat pieces such
    as lamb shanks, cross-cut veal
    shanks, lamb leg or shoulder steaks,
    or 1 whole chicken
3 mastic pieces, crushed with a pinch
    of salt (optional)
2 bay leaves
2 tablespoons salt
1 tablespoon Nine Spice Mix (page 24)
1 onion
1 carrot

For the chilli garlic sauce
4–6 large cloves garlic
2–4 green chillies or jalapeño peppers
    (membrane and seeds removed
    for less heat)
½ cup (4 fl oz/120 ml) freshly squeezed
    lemon juice
salt

This particular take on fatteh is uniquely Palestinian, from Gaza to be exact, in which the yogurt sauce is completely replaced with a chilli, garlic, and lemon sauce. I learned of it from my mother's old neighbour, Oula, a native of Gaza who also taught me how to make Gazan Tomato Salsa (page 113).

Preheat the oven to 350°F/180°C/Gas Mark 4. Bake the pita squares in the oven until crisp and starting to brown, about 15 minutes. Remove and set aside. (This can be done a couple of days in advance.)

To prepare the broth (stock), heat the oil in a large stockpot over medium-high heat until hot, then add the meat and sear until nicely browned, about 6–8 minutes on each side. If using a whole chicken, skip the searing step. Add 8 cups (3½ pints/2 liters) water and bring to a boil, skimming away the scum that rises to the surface. Add the crushed mastic, bay leaves, salt, Nine Spice Mix, onion, and carrot. Reduce the heat, and simmer, covered, for 1–2 hours, depending on meat cut, until tender (30–50 minutes in a pressure cooker).

Meanwhile, place the garlic and chillies in a mini food processor and process until finely chopped. Transfer to a bowl, sprinkle with salt, and pour in the lemon juice. Stir to combine then set sauce aside.

Once the broth is done, remove the meat and set aside, topped with ¼ cup of the broth and covered with aluminum foil to keep warm. Strain the remaining broth, discarding the onion and bay leaves, and set aside.

For the rice, heat 2 tablespoons olive oil in a Dutch oven (casserole) over medium-high heat. Add the rice and toss for 1–2 minutes to coat evenly. Pour in 2½ cups (1 pint/600 ml) of the broth and bring to a boil. Reduce to a simmer, cover, and cook until done, about 20 minutes. Remove from the heat and allow to sit for 10–15 minutes before serving.

To assemble the dish, arrange the toasted bread in a large deep serving platter. Drizzle about 3 tablespoons of the chilli garlic sauce over the bread. Measure 7 fl oz/200 ml of the strained broth and spoon over the toasted bread. Fluff up the cooked rice with a fork and spoon it over the toasted bread. Top with the cooked meat, (if using a whole chicken, allow to cool slightly then remove whole pieces of meat from the breast and thighs, discarding the bones, skin, and wings). Spoon another 3 tablespoons of the chilli garlic sauce on top and sprinkle with the toasted pine nuts.

Serve immediately with the remaining chilli garlic sauce and broth on the side for people to spoon more over their plates.

EGGPLANT (AUBERGINE) FATTEH

فتة باذنجان

Preparation time: 15 minutes + salting
Cooking time: 1 hour 30 minutes
Serves 4–6

3 large, thin Lebanese pita breads
 (about 9 oz/250 g)
2¼ lb/1 kg eggplants (aubergines)
salt
vegetable oil, for frying
1 quantity Lamb with Onion and Spices
 (page 30)
2¼ lb/1 kg tomatoes, coarsely chopped,
 or substitute with 2 x 14oz / 400g
 tins of crushed tomatoes
½ teaspoon tomato paste (purée)
1 tablespoon pomegranate molasses
 (optional)

For the yogurt sauce
1 lb 2 oz/500 g plain yogurt
¼ cup (2 oz/50 g) tahini
4 tablespoons freshly squeezed
 lemon juice
1 large clove garlic
½ teaspoon salt

To garnish
½ quantity Toasted Pine Nuts (page 31)
½ quantity Toasted Almonds (page 31)
1 small bunch flat-leaf parsley or mint,
 finely chopped
red chilli flakes or pomegranate seeds
 (optional)

Originally made with small eggplants (aubergines), which have been cored, stuffed, fried, then cooked in a tomato sauce, I opt for an easier alternative that uses fried eggplant and cooks the meat and tomato sauce separately. On top of being easier, I've found this method also allows the flavors to combine really well with a taste of each element in every bite.

Preheat the oven to 350°F/180°C/Gas Mark 4. Cut the pita breads into ¾-inch/2-cm squares and put on a baking sheet. Bake in the oven for about 15 minutes, or until the squares are completely dry and crisp and starting to darken in color, moving the bread around from time to time. Remove and set aside. (This step can be done a couple of days in advance.)

Slice each eggplant (aubergine) in half lengthwise, then in half lengthwise again, then cut each strip into cubes. Put the eggplants into a large colander, sprinkle generously with salt, and let stand for about 1 hour.

To fry the eggplants, heat the vegetable oil in a deep fryer or heavy Dutch oven (casserole) to 350°F/180°C, or until a morsel of bread immediately rises to the surface when dropped in. Pat the eggplants dry with paper towels. Working in batches, fry the eggplants until golden brown; remove with a slotted spoon and drain on paper towels.

Meanwhile, in a large skillet (frying pan), prepare the toasted pine nuts and almonds; remove from the pan and drain on paper towels. Use the same pan to prepare the Lamb with Onion and Spices. When done, add the chopped tomatoes and tomato paste (purée) and pomegranate molasses, if using. Bring to a boil, then reduce the heat and simmer until the tomatoes are cooked and the sauce has darkened in color, about 30 minutes. When done, remove from the heat and set aside.

Prepare the yogurt sauce by combining all the ingredients together and mixing well.

This dish can be served on one large platter or on individual plates. To assemble, place the bread at the bottom of a serving platter. Top with the eggplants, leaving a border so the bread is still visible. Top the eggplants with the piping hot sauce. Pour the yogurt on top of the sauce and sprinkle with the toasted nuts, parsley, and chilli flakes or pomegranate seeds, if using. If serving individually, then divide equally between plates and assemble as above. Serve immediately to retain the crunchiness of the bread.

CELEBRATION DISHES

I remember watching with curiosity as, slowly, Teta Fatima poured water into a tray. Her hands were going round in circles, a subtle dance, as she hummed to herself. She was making *maftool*: an image that has been etched in my mind since childhood. I also remember wondering what she was doing and thinking it was magic that turned bulgur and flour into beautiful little pearls, similar to couscous but larger and more flavorful. The more water she added, the more flour, the more she rolled, the larger the pile grew until there was a mountain of golden brown pearls. Her brother was coming from the United States that week, after more than twenty years of absence, and nothing short of a feast would do.

And what a glorious feast it was when platter after platter piled high with food made their way to the tables in the garden, under a canopy of pecan trees. Rays of sun seeped through the leaves and glowed on platters of *maftool* topped with golden-crisp baby chickens and bowls of butternut and onion stew (page 196). Alongside those platters sat Flipped Over Chicken and Vegetable Rice (page 198). I can recall the aromatic garlic from the *shushbarak* dumplings (page 204) floating in a sea of white yogurt as my mother carried serving bowls to tables dotted with small plates of olives, pickles, spreads, and fresh vegetables.

I was a child at the time, no more than ten, and with so many children running around, we were all instructed not to interrupt the feast. So we gathered round a straw mat in the kitchen and ate together, enjoying the rich, delicious food.

Eating together always felt like a festive occasion in my family, and having grown up in an interfaith household, there really was no shortage of holidays to celebrate. Whenever I have the chance to recreate those wonderful and simple years, I do so wholeheartedly. This chapter is about those recipes we most often enjoyed during holidays and special occasions: everything from weddings, graduations, and birthdays to the arrival of out-of-town guests or the coming together of the wider family.

The reason these particular dishes are used during gatherings is because it is easy to make them in large portions, and with big families, this practical consideration becomes quite important. In addition, almost all of these recipes can be served alone with only simple accompaniments like yogurt, olives, and fresh vegetables, making entertaining simple yet abundantly generous.

However, these dishes are by no means reserved for holidays alone. I often find myself making many of them on a regular basis at home. They may require a bit more work, but the flavors are so delicious, and continue to be so the following day, meaning they are truly worth the effort.

CUMIN-SPICED RICE AND FISH

صياديه

Preparation time: 15 minutes + soaking
Cooking time: 1 hour 45 minutes
Serves 6–8

For the broth (stock)
2¼ lb/1 kg fish heads, bones, and
    trimmings (avoid very oily fish
    like salmon or trout)
2 bay leaves
1 tablespoon salt
1 tablespoon allspice berries
1 tablespoon coriander seeds
1 teaspoon cumin seeds
1 teaspoon black peppercorns

For the rice
½ cup (4 fl oz/120 ml) olive oil
4 onions, finely chopped
½ teaspoon salt
1 teaspoon ground cumin
1 teaspoon ground coriander
1 teaspoon Nine Spice Mix (page 24)
1 lb 2 oz/500 g jasmine or basmati rice,
    washed, soaked, and drained

For the fish
1 tablespoon olive oil
1 tablespoon lemon juice
1½ teaspoons cumin
1½ teaspoons ground coriander
1 teaspoon Nine Spice Mix (page 24)
1 teaspoon salt
2¼ lb/1 kg white fish fillets, such as sea
    bass, sea bream, turbot, or halibut
1 cup (4 oz/120 g) all-purpose (plain)
    flour
2 tablespoons fine semolina (optional)
vegetable oil, for frying

To serve
— Parsley or Cilantro (Coriander)
    Tahini Spread (page 76), to serve
— 1 quantity Toasted Pine Nuts
    (page 31)

This is a real fisherman's dish. The base of it is a good broth (stock) made with fish heads, tails, and bones. Traditionally, it was made in coastal cities like Haifa, Akka and Yaffa, where you could buy the day's catch then use the bones for broth, and the fillets for the rest of the dish. Serve it with a side of Parsley or Cilantro (Coriander) Tahini Spread (page 76).

To make the broth (stock), rinse the fish bones of any blood. Put the fish bones into a large stockpot and add enough water to cover, about 6 cups (2½ pints/1.5 liters). Bring to a boil, skimming any scum that rises to the surface, then add the remaining ingredients and reduce the heat to a simmer. Continue to simmer, covered, for 30–40 minutes, then strain, discarding the fish trimmings and spices.

Meanwhile, marinade the fish by adding the olive oil, lemon, spices, and salt to a dish and tossing the fish fillets in them to coat. Refrigerate until ready to use.

While the broth is simmering, start the rice. Put the olive oil into a medium pot over high heat, add the onions and sauté for 15–20 minutes, stirring regularly, until crispy and brown. Once the broth is ready, add 4 cups (1¾ pints/1 liter) to the onions followed by the salt and spices. Bring to a boil and then simmer for 5 minutes. Taste and adjust the seasoning.

Add the rice to the broth and onions and stir to combine. Boil, covered, for 3–4 minutes, then reduce the heat and simmer for 15–20 minutes, or until the rice is done. Check halfway through cooking, and if the water has already evaporated, add a few more tablespoons of broth and continue to cook. Once the rice is done, place a dish towel under the lid, and set aside while you fry the fillets.

Pour enough oil into a large skillet (frying pan) to cover the bottom of the pan and place over medium-high heat. Combine the flour and semolina and spread out on a large, flat work surface. When the oil is hot, take one fish fillet at a time, dip into the flour mixture and coat evenly on both sides. Shake to remove any excess flour, then place in the hot oil, skin side down. Depending on the thickness of your fillets, you will need to fry them in batches for 2–5 minutes on each side, flipping once during cooking. Remove from the pan and drain on paper towels and keep warm; repeat until all the fish fillets are fried.

To serve, place the rice in a large serving platter, top with the fish fillets and sprinkle with the toasted nuts. Serve with Parsley or Cilantro (Coriander) Tahini Spread, loosened with 1 tablespoon of water and 1 tablespoon of lemon juice.

MAHASHI:
WE STUFF EVERYTHING

Arabs in general—and Palestinians in particular—love to stuff our food. We stuff everything from vegetables like carrots, cucumbers, eggplants (aubergines), zucchini (courgettes), tomatoes, potatoes, bell peppers, onions, cabbage, and grape leaves to meats like whole chicken, lamb necks, lamb variety meats (offal), lamb ribs, and even an entire lamb. The stuffing itself can vary as can its flavoring, but in general, it is either a mixture of rice and meat (page 188), a spiced ground (minced) meat, onion, and pine nut stuffing called *hosseh* (page 30), or a vegetarian stuffing of bulgur, tomatoes, and herbs (see tabuleh recipe, page 98).

The word *mahashi* is generally used to refer to vegetables that are stuffed regardless of the cooking method and sauce. In order to stuff these vegetables, they need to be cored first. There is a special tool for coring them, similar to a zucchini (courgette) corer but longer and narrower, which can now easily be found online or in Middle Eastern food stores.

As for the cooking method and sauces, just like the stuffing, there is a lot of variation. Cucumber, for example, is given more flavor by being cooked in a tamarind sauce, while the traditional squash is cooked in either a tomato sauce or a yogurt sauce. There is no limit to the combinations and cooking methods, but the recipes in this book are some of the most traditional ones and should help give you ideas if you decide to experiment with different meats, vegetables, stuffings, and flavors.

STUFFED POTATOES
IN TOMATO SAUCE

بطاطا محشيه

Preparation time: 1 hour 30 minutes
Cooking time: 45–50 minutes
Serves 6–8

3¼ lb/1.5 kg potatoes (about 8 medium
    or 12 small)
1 quantity Toasted Pine Nuts (page 31)
1 quantity Lamb with Onion and Spices
    (page 30)
vegetable oil, for frying

For the sauce
2 tablespoons olive oil
8–10 cloves garlic, crushed
1 lb 8½ oz/700 g sieved tomatoes
    (passata)
1 teaspoon salt
¼ teaspoon Nine Spice Mix (page 24)

To serve
— Vermicelli Rice (page 32)
— plain yogurt

This is a rustic dish that can be made with very simple ingredients that are almost always at hand. The potatoes—normally a side to meats—take center-stage in this recipe and their flavor is amplified from the spicy stuffing and rich tomato sauce. A substantial and warming meal, this is the perfect thing to eat on a cold winter's day when you are very hungry and in need of both comfort and energy.

Peel the potatoes and core them by inserting the corer until it almost reaches the bottom, then twisting and pulling out the core. Repeat this a few times, scraping the sides, until the potato has been hollowed and is roughly ¼ inch/5 mm thick all the way around. Wash the potatoes from the inside to ensure all the core has come out and set upside down in a colander to dry.

Mix the toasted pine nuts and Lamb with Onion and Spices and use this mixture to stuff the potatoes. Any leftover stuffing can be added to the sauce later.

Pour enough vegetable oil into a large skillet (frying pan) to reach about ¾ inch/2 cm up the sides. When the oil is hot, place the stuffed potatoes into the oil, taking care because the oil may splutter. Fry for 10 minutes, turning over once halfway through, until a nice golden brown on both sides. Remove from the oil and drain on paper towels. Continue until all the potatoes are fried.

To prepare the sauce, heat the olive oil in large pot or shallow Dutch oven (casserole) and add the crushed garlic. Cook for 2–3 minutes, or until fragrant but not colored. Pour in the passata, 2 cups (18 fl oz/500 ml) water, the salt, and Nine Spice Mix and any leftover stuffing.

Place the potatoes in the tomato sauce, cover, and bring to a boil. Reduce the heat and simmer for 30–40 minutes, or until the potatoes are cooked through. If the sauce starts to thicken too much before the potatoes are done, gradually add more water and continue to cook. Taste and adjust the seasoning to your liking before serving.

To serve, place vermicelli rice in individual bowls, top with a stuffed potato, and ladle tomato sauce over the top.

STUFFED VEGETABLES
IN TOMATO SAUCE

محشي بندوره

This is my ultimate comfort food. The vegetables you use and the tomato sauce you make vary from one person to the next, although for me, the zucchini (courgettes) are a must. I also prefer to use fresh tomatoes that I purée at home, but you can easily substitute with Italian sieved tomatoes (passata) if you prefer or even broth (stock) and tomato paste (purée). Not only is it delicious on the day you cook it, but on the second and third day as well.

Preparation time: 1 hour 30 minutes
Cooking time: 1 hour
Serves 6–8

For the vegetables and sauce
5½ lb/2.5 kg (about 25–30) white zucchini (courgettes), baby eggplants (aubergines), or cucuzza squash (see Note)
1 lb 7 oz/650 g ripe tomatoes, pureed in a blender (or use tomato passata)
4 cups (1¾ pints/1 liter) chicken broth (stock), homemade (page 34) or store-bought, or use water
1 tablespoon salt
½ teaspoon Nine Spice Mix (page 24)
2–4 tablespoons tomato paste (purée) (optional)

For the stuffing
1 lb 2 oz/500 g short or medium grain rice
4 tablespoons olive oil or melted butter (or a combination of both)
1 tablespoon Nine Spice Mix (page 24)
1 tablespoon salt
2 teaspoons tomato paste (purée)
1 lb 2 oz/500 g ground (minced) lamb or beef

Remove the stems from the vegetables and core them by inserting the corer until it almost reaches the bottom then twisting and pulling out the core. Repeat this a few times, scraping until hollowed, the sides roughly ⅛ inch/3 mm.

Meanwhile, prepare the rice and meat stuffing by combining the rice, olive oil, Nine Spice Mix, salt, and tomato paste (purée) in a large bowl. Add the lamb and mix with your hands, breaking any clumps, until everything is well mixed.

Stuff the vegetables until they are a little more than three-quarters full, or with about ½ inch/1 cm room at the top. Do not push the stuffing too forcefully inside or overstuff the vegetables, as that will prevent the rice from cooking. You can tap the bottom of your vegetables on the work surface to help the stuffing drop further down while you stuff.

Arrange the vegetables in a large pot and pour over the puréed tomatoes, broth (stock), salt, and Nine Spice Mix. Bring to a boil over high heat and boil vigorously for about 10 minutes. Reduce the heat to low and simmer until done, about 1–1½ hours. When they are ready the skin should give way easily when pierced with the tip of a knife.

Halfway through cooking, taste the broth and adjust the seasoning. Taste for the tomato as well—depending on how flavorful the tomatoes are you may need to add some tomato paste. In that case, just remove a little liquid from the pot into a bowl, mix in the paste and return to the pot. If you are using passata, you can skip this step.

Remove from the heat and strain the tomato broth into a serving bowl. Arrange the vegetables in a serving platter and serve with the bowl of tomato sauce to allow people to pour as much sauce as they like on to their individual plates.

Note: If you want to use a combination of seasonal vegetables in this recipe, make sure to pick ones similar in size so they cook evenly. This recipe is based on vegetables all about 4 inches/10 cm in length and not too thick.

STUFFED GRAPE LEAVES

ورق دوالي

Preparation time: 1 hour 30 minutes
Cooking time: 2 hours 30 minutes
Serves 6–8

For the stuffing
1 lb 2 oz/500 g short or medium
    grain rice
4 tablespoons olive oil or melted butter
    (or a combination of both)
1 tablespoon Nine Spice Mix (page 24)
1 tablespoon salt
1 lb 2 oz/500 g ground (minced) lamb
    or beef
1 teaspoon tomato paste (purée)

For the grape leaves
1 lb 2 oz/500 g vine leaves (see Note)
3 tablespoons olive oil
12 lamb cutlets, 6 beef short ribs, or
    25 chicken wings, or any other
    flavorful cut of meat you prefer
    (optional)
3 tomatoes, sliced into rounds
4 cups (1¾ pints/1 liter) beef, lamb,
    or chicken broth (stock) or water
2 tablespoons tomato paste (purée)
1 tablespoon salt
1 teaspoon Nine Spice Mix (page 24)
1 tablespoon lemon juice, or to taste
    (only if using jarred vine leaves)

There's not a single Palestinian family that doesn't make this dish several times throughout the year. For our family, it has been present at every happy event in our lives, from holidays, graduations, weddings, birthdays, and everything in between. I also make it for family dinners when I have time.

Prepare the stuffing by combining the rice, olive oil, Nine Spice Mix, tomato paste (purée), and salt in a large bowl. Add the meat and mix with your hands, until everything is well incorporated.

Lay out as many of the leaves as will fit on a work surface. The vein side should be up and the stem end closer to you. Depending on the size of leaf, spoon about 1 tablespoon of the stuffing above the stem of each leaf. With your fingers, stretch the stuffing into a thin line with enough of the leaf showing on each side so you can fold over. Fold the sides over the stuffing then, from the bottom, roll the leaf away from you. Roll securely so it doesn't come apart but not so tightly the rice doesn't cook. Repeat with the rest of the leaves.

If you are using meat, heat the oil in a large pot or Dutch oven (casserole) over medium heat until hot but not smoking. Add the meat and sear on all sides until browned. Remove the pot from the heat and place the tomato slices between the meat to fully cover the bottom of the pot. If you are not using meat, simply line the bottom with sliced tomatoes.

Arrange the rolled leaves on top of the meat and the tomatoes, in either concentric circles or rows.

In a separate bowl or pot, combine the broth (stock) or water with the tomato paste, salt, and Nine Spice Mix. If you are using meat to line the bottom of the pot, water alone will yield a fantastic flavor. If you are not using meat, use broth, as it will enhance the flavor. Pour over the grape leaves and top with an inverted plate slightly smaller than the diameter of the pot; this prevents the leaves from moving when they come to a boil. Bring to a boil, then reduce the heat to low and simmer for 2–2½ hours until cooked and almost no liquid remains.

If you have used the jarred variety of leaves, add the lemon juice 5 minutes before removing from the heat.

To serve, remove the lid and the plate from the pot. Place an inverted serving platter over the pot then flip the pot over and lift to reveal the vine leaves and browned meat.

Note: If you use jarred grape leaves, soak them in warm water for 15 minutes, then rinse well to remove any brine.

STUFFED CABBAGE ROLLS

ملفوف

Preparation time: 1 hour 30 minutes
Cooking time: 1 hour
Serves 4–6

1 Middle Eastern green cabbage,
    roughly 4½ lb/2 kg (see Notes)
8–10 cloves garlic, unpeeled
2 cups (18 fl oz/500 ml) chicken, lamb,
    or beef broth (stock)
salt

For the stuffing
9 oz/250 g short grain rice, rinsed,
    soaked for 15 minutes, and drained
3 tablespoons olive oil or melted butter
1 teaspoon salt
1 teaspoon Nine Spice Mix (page 24)
½ teaspoon ground cumin
9 oz/250 g ground (minced) lamb or beef

To serve
½ cup (4 fl oz/120 ml) lemon juice
1 teaspoon red chilli flakes
plain yogurt

My mother only makes this dish in the winter because that's cabbage season in Palestine and the plants then are watered only with rain, giving them the best taste. Abroad, I can't afford to be as picky, so as long as I find a good green cabbage, I buy it and *malfoof* is on the menu. "Good" green cabbage means it feels light when you pick it—not dense—and that's exactly what you need to be able to take the leaves apart. If you can't find Middle Eastern or green cabbage, savoy and sweetheart are possible alternatives. Some people add lemon and crushed garlic at the end of cooking, but I prefer to cook it with the whole cloves of garlic and serve lemon juice mixed with chilli flakes alongside it for the best of both worlds.

Find a large pot that is wide enough to hold the entire cabbage and half-fill with water. Sprinkle in some salt and bring to a boil.

With the tip of a sharp knife, make a circular incision at an angle around the core of the cabbage until it loosens up and you can pull out the core entirely. Once the water in the pot is boiling, carefully drop the entire cabbage into the pot and boil for about 5 minutes. As the leaves start to soften, use metal tongs to pull out one leaf at a time and set aside on a large platter or tray. Once you are left with the cabbage heart, you can take it out entirely and set aside with the leaves to cool, and later on remove its leaves.

Meanwhile, prepare the stuffing by combining the rice, olive oil or butter, salt, Nine Spice Mix, and cumin in a large bowl. Add the meat and mix with your hands, breaking up any lumps of meat, until everything is well incorporated.

To prepare the leaves for stuffing, set each one on a cutting (chopping) board and remove the tough stalk in the middle, leaving you with two halves. If each half is very large, you can cut in half again. You want each piece to be roughly the size of your palm with a somewhat regular shape.

Place about 1 teaspoon of the stuffing at the bottom edge of each leaf and spread lengthwise, leaving at least ¾ inch/2 cm empty at each side. Tightly roll each leaf up without folding over the edges. If the edges are not neat once rolled, use a knife to slightly trim them, making sure to leave some empty space on each side so the rice has room to expand during cooking without escaping from the leaves.

Place any leftover leaves and stalks in the bottom of a large pot (if you prefer to have a few leaves stick to the bottom for that crispy, browned flavor, place the leaves directly in the pot). Arrange the parcels, seam side down, snugly in the pot and tuck the unpeeled cloves of garlic in between them as you go along.

Pour the broth (stock) over the cabbage leaves and place a plate on top to prevent them from moving around while cooking. Taste the broth and, if not salty enough, adjust the seasoning. Cover the pot with a lid and bring to a boil over high heat, then reduce the heat and simmer for about 1 hour, or until the stuffing is fully cooked, the leaves are very tender, and the liquid is almost entirely evaporated. Check on the leaves from time to time to make sure the liquid has not completely evaporated; if it has and the leaves are not fully cooked, gradually add more and continue to cook until done.

When the parcels are done, remove from the heat and allow to sit for 10 minutes before flipping over: place a large inverted serving platter over the pot and, with one hand over the platter and another under the pot, flip the pot over and set the platter down. Slowly lift up the pot, allowing the leaves to settle down into the platter.

Serve with lemon juice mixed with chilli flakes to be spooned over the leaves and a side of yogurt. Leftovers can be stored in the refrigerator for 2 days and frozen for several weeks.

Notes: It's also possible to microwave the cabbage. Put the cabbage into a large shallow bowl and microwave on high for 5–7 minutes. Take out and peel off as many leaves as possible. Once you reach the center or leaves that have not softened enough, return the rest of the cabbage to the microwave for another 5 minutes.

Another alternative is to freeze the entire cabbage overnight, remove the following morning, and allow to defrost, at which point the leaves will have softened enough to be removed individually. This method is by far the easiest if you have a large freezer. The downside, however, is that some of the leaves will become brown around the edges.

RICE-STUFFED CHICKEN

دجاج محشي

Preparation time: 30 minutes + soaking
Cooking time: 2 hours
Serves 4

3 tablespoons olive oil, plus extra
    for drizzling
1 tablespoon salt
1 tablespoon Nine Spice Mix (page 24)
1 teaspoon paprika (optional)
1 whole chicken (3–5 lb/1.8–2.5 kg)
large needle and thread

For the stuffing
1 tablespoon ghee or butter
1 tablespoon olive oil
11 oz/ 300 g ground (minced) lamb
    or beef
1 teaspoon Nine Spice Mix (page 24)
9 oz/250g jasmine (or any medium
    grain) rice, washed, soaked for
    15 minutes, and drained
1 teaspoon salt
½ cup (2 oz/50 g) Toasted Pine Nuts
    and Almonds (page 31)

This was unequivocally, and by far, my favorite meal growing up. It was the first dish my grandmother made me when I returned home after my first year in university, and it continues to be the first one my mother makes when I return for a visit. Perfectly spiced and crisp chicken encasing a rich stuffing is comfort food at its best. It's so perfect, in fact, that all it needs are some fresh tomatoes and green olives on the side—simple, delicious, and so satisfying.

Combine the olive oil, salt, and spices in a bowl and mix well. Rub the chicken with it, making sure to rub inside the cavity, outside and under skin. Refrigerate until ready to use.

Start on the stuffing: heat the ghee or butter and olive oil over high heat in a large heavy Dutch oven (casserole) or nonstick pot. Once the butter sizzles, add the meat and Nine Spice Mix and sauté for 5 minutes until browned. If it releases liquid, cook until the meat evaporates and browns.

Add the rice and toss to combine with the meat and coat in the oil. Pour in 2 cups (18 fl oz/500 ml) water, add the salt, and bring to a boil. Once boiling, reduce the heat, cover, and simmer for 10–12 minutes until the rice is al dente (it will continue to cook in the oven inside the chicken). If the liquid evaporates before the rice is ready, add more water and continue cooking. If the rice is ready but there's too much liquid, uncover and cook over high heat until it evaporates.

When done, transfer the rice immediately to a large platter, add the toasted pine nuts and fluff up with a fork. Cool for at least 30 minutes before stuffing the chicken.

Spoon as much stuffing as possible into the chicken, then reserve the rest to reheat and serve alongside the chicken. Seal the cavity shut by sewing the skin between the thighs with a needle and thread, or tying the drumsticks together.

Preheat the oven to 400°F/200°C/Gas Mark 6. Remove any stuffing from the outside of the chicken, drizzle with olive oil and place on a rack within a roasting pan with about 4 tablespoons of water. If you do not have a pan with a rack, place the chicken directly in the pan but do not add water. Cover with aluminum foil and place in the oven.

Roast for 30 minutes, then reduce the heat to 350°F/180°C/ Gas Mark 5 and cook for 1–1½ hours, or until the chicken is cooked and the juices run clear. Uncover and continue to roast until the skin has crisped, between 5 and 25 minutes.

Remove from the oven and allow to rest before carving. Serve each portion of chicken with the stuffing.

Right
Rice-stuffed chicken on *hashweh*
(recipe page 166)

LAMB-STUFFED VEGETABLES IN LEMON GARLIC SAUCE

شيخ المحشي

Preparation time: 1 hour 30 minutes
Cooking time: 1 hour
Serves 6–8

about 20 (3¼ lb/1.5 kg) medium-small
Italian white zucchini (courgettes)
1 quantity Lamb with Onion and Spices
(page 30)
1 quantity Toasted Pine Nuts (page 31)
vegetable oil, for frying

For the sauce
2 tablespoons olive oil
8–10 cloves garlic, finely chopped
2 cups (18 fl oz/500 ml) chicken, lamb,
    or beef broth (stock)
¼ teaspoon Nine Spice Mix (optional,
    page 24)
1 teaspoon cornstarch (cornflour)
2–4 tablespoons lemon juice
salt

To serve
— Vermicelli Rice (page 32)
— Plain yogurt

This dish, which translates from the Arabic as "the king of stuffed vegetables", was so named because the vegetables were stuffed exclusively with meat, unlike their counterparts, which are stuffed with a mixture of meat and rice. Popular across the Levant, this dish normally calls for small white zucchini (courgettes) or *kusa* to be stuffed with a meat and onion mixture, shallow-fried, then cooked in either a tomato or yogurt sauce. The recipe here is typically Palestinian, cooking the zucchini in a lemon and garlic flavored broth.

Core the zucchini (courgettes) as on page 184 but a little thicker than normal, roughly ¼ inch/5 mm all the way around. Mix together with the Lamb with Onion and Spices and toasted pine nuts and use this mixture to stuff the zucchini.

Pour enough vegetable oil into a large skillet (frying pan) to reach about ¾ inch/2 cm up the sides. When the oil is hot, place the stuffed zucchini into the pan, taking care because the oil may splutter. Fry for 4–6 minutes, turning over once halfway through until a nice golden brown on both sides. Remove from the oil and drain on paper towels. Continue, until all the zucchini are fried.

Alternatively, preheat the broiler (grill). Brush the zucchini with olive oil all around and broil (grill) for 10–15 minutes, turning once halfway through, until browned all over.

Preheat the oven to 400°F/200°C/Gas Mark 6 while you prepare the sauce.

Heat the olive oil in a pot and add about 1–2 teaspoons of the chopped garlic. Cook until fragrant but not colored, about 2 minutes. Pour in the broth (stock) and, if you have used store-bought broth, season with salt and Nine Spice Mix. Bring to a boil. Put the cornstarch (cornflour) into a small bowl and add 2–3 tablespoons of the broth to it. Mix well and return the mixture back to the broth. Mix well and simmer for another minute. Add the lemon juice and remove from the heat.

Arrange the fried zucchini in a round or rectangular ovenproof dish that is large enough to fit them in a single layer. Pour the broth over the zucchini, sprinkle with the remaining garlic and drizzle with olive oil. Bake in the oven for about 15 minutes, or until the broth is bubbling and the garlic a golden brown. Remove from the oven and serve with vermicelli rice and yogurt.

WHEAT BERRY STEW

هريسه بلحمه

Preparation time: 5 minutes
Cooking time: 5–6 hours
Serves 8–10

2 tablespoons olive oil
1 small chicken (2¼–2½ lb/1.1–1.3 kg),
    cut into 4 pieces
1 lb 2 oz/500 g stewing beef, cut
    into large cubes
1 oxtail tip (optional)
1 large onion, quartered
1½ teaspoons salt
1 teaspoon Nine Spice Mix (page 24)
4 pieces mastic
14 oz/400 g wheat berries
ground cinnamon

To serve
— ground cinnamon
— toasted nuts

This dish, along with Spiced Meat and Rice Pilaf (page 166), were the hallmark foods of my Teta Asma's Christmas. Heartwarming and soul soothing, this is the perfect dish to make in the depths of winter. It does take a long time to cook in order to break down the wheat berries and achieve the porridge-like consistency (unless you use a pressure cooker), but it freezes very well so is worth the effort.

Heat the olive oil in a large heavy stockpot or pressure cooker until hot but not smoking. Put the chicken skin side down into the pot and brown for 1–2 minutes, then add the stewing beef and oxtail tip, if using, and toss to sear on all sides, about 5 minutes. Add the onion, salt, Nine Spice Mix, and mastic, give it one more toss to combine. Pour in 5 pints/3 liters water. Bring the water to a boil, removing the foam and scum from the surface with a slotted spoon, then reduce the heat and simmer for 60–80 minutes (25 minutes in a pressure cooker), or until the chicken is fully cooked.

Meanwhile, soak the wheat berries in plenty of cold water. When the broth (stock) is done, remove the chicken and set aside on a plate to cool. Strain the broth, discarding the oxtail and onion, and return the beef and broth to the pot.

Drain the wheat berries, add to the pot, and bring to a boil, then reduce the heat slightly, bringing to a vigorous simmer. Cook for about 2 hours (1 hour in pressure cooker), stirring occasionally until the wheat has softened and fluffed up.

Meanwhile, shred the chicken into very thin strips and discard the bone and skin. When the wheat berries have been cooking for their 2 hours, add the chicken, stir to combine and cook for a further 2 hours (1 hour in pressure cooker), stirring frequently to prevent it from sticking to the bottom of the pot. Unless you are using a pressure cooker you will likely need to add water throughout as it evaporates more quickly, and it is better to err on the side of more water than too little as the wheat berries will eventually absorb it all. If you can see the wheat berries and meat through the bubbling liquid, then you need to add more water.

After the 4 hours (2 hours in pressure cooker) uncover the pot or pressure cooker and continue to cook and stir until the meat falls apart, the wheat berries begin to break down, and the dish takes on a thick, porridge-like consistency; this could takes anything from 15–45 minutes. Much of this will depend on the grain, the size of the cuts, and the pot.

When ready to serve, ladle into bowls. Allow it to cool for a minute then sprinkle with cinnamon and toasted nuts.

CHICKEN, ONION, AND SUMAC FLATBREADS

مسخن

Preparation time: 30 minutes
Cooking time: 1 hour
Serves 8

For the chicken
8 skin-on, bone-in chicken legs or
    breasts
3 tablespoons olive oil
1 teaspoon Nine Spice Mix (page 24)
1 teaspoon sumac
½ teaspoon salt

For the flatbreads
¾ cup (6 fl oz/175 ml) olive oil
8 onions, coarsely diced
1 tablespoon salt
1–2 tablespoons sumac
1 tablespoon ground cumin
2 teaspoons Nine Spice Mix (page 24)
8 Taboon Breads (page 42), 8 inches/
    20 cm in diameter (see Note)

To serve
— 4 tablespoons sumac
— 1 quantity Toasted Pine Nuts
    (page 31)
— olives

If there is one dish that is exclusively Palestinian, it's *msakhan*. The key to *msakhan* is simple, good ingredients, cooked well. For me, and even more so my brother, this dish is associated with Teta Fatmeh. So much so in fact, that one summer, when my brother was two years old and we went with some friends to a restaurant in Jericho, he threw a tantrum when he saw the food arriving, crying that he only wanted "Teta Fatima's *msakhan*". While neither of us throws tantrums over *msakhan* anymore, we still associate this dish with her.

Preheat the oven to 375°F/190°C/Gas Mark 5.

Put the chicken into a large roasting pan and top with the olive oil, spices, and salt. Give it a good rub with your hands, making sure to get some of the marinade under the skin, then arrange the pieces skin side up and place in the oven while you prepare the onions. The chicken will take about 1 hour in the oven to fully cook.

Meanwhile, put the olive oil, onions, salt, and spices into a large skillet (frying pan) over low heat. Cook for 30–40 minutes, stirring occasionally, until the onions have softened and cooked completely. If the onions seem dry or do not release water during cooking, add in a few tablespoons of water. When done remove from heat and set aside.

Check on the chicken, and if done, remove from the oven and allow to rest for 15 minutes, loosely covered in aluminum foil. Pour any juices in the roasting pan over the onion mixture and toss to combine.

Preheat the broiler (grill). To assemble, dip the edges of each bread in the oil on the surface of the onion mixture then lay flat on an baking sheet. Place enough onion mixture on each bread to cover it completely but leave a border around the edge (similar to a pizza). Sprinkle with sumac and toasted pine nuts. Continue, until all the breads are completed.

Taking one or two flatbreads at a time, put on an oven rack and place under the broiler for 2–5 minutes to brown the edges and the onions. Remove, top each flatbread with a piece of chicken, and serve.

Note: Taboon bread is best for this dish, but if you do not want to make it at home, you can substitute with a sturdy store-bought flatbread, like naan or Greek pita bread.

MAFTOOL WITH BUTTERNUT, CHICKPEA, AND CHICKEN STEW

مفتول

Maftool—gorgeous caviar-size pearls made of whole wheat—is one of the most distinctively Palestinian dishes you will find. The word *maftool* means "rolled" and refers to the way flour is rolled around small bulgur grains to arrive at these pearls. In Galilee, people tend to make them larger and call them *moghrabieh*, while in central and southern Palestine they are made as small as caviar and called *maftool*.

First make the broth (stock). Put the chicken into a large stockpot and cover with 8 cups (3½ pints/2 liters) water. Bring to a boil on high heat, skimming away scum from the surface, then add the onion, salt, spices, bay leaf and tomato paste, if using, and reduce the heat to a simmer. Cook until the chickens are done but not falling apart, about 1 hour. When done, remove the chicken pieces and set aside, covered in aluminum foil to keep warm.

To prepare the stew, heat the olive oil in a pot over medium heat and add the sliced onions. Sauté for about 5 minutes until softened and golden brown at the edges. Add the squash, toss to combine, and cook for a further 2–3 minutes. Using a fine-mesh strainer, pour in 4 cups (1¾ pints/1 liter) of your broth into the pot, then add the chickpeas and allow everything to simmer until the squash is cooked and the flavors have all melded together, about 15 minutes.

Meanwhile, heat the olive oil and butter in a pot with a tight-fitting lid over medium heat. Add the *maftool*, tossing to coat, and stir to toast lightly, about 5 minutes. Using a fine-mesh strainer, pour 2 cups (18 fl oz/500 ml) of your broth into the pot, cover, and bring to a simmer. Once the *maftool* has absorbed about half the liquid, turn off the heat and allow to sit for 15 minutes. This method, which is halfway between the absorption and steaming methods, produces the best texture for the *maftool*: fully cooked but still fluffy.

To assemble, preheat the broiler (grill). Drizzle the chicken with olive oil, salt, and black pepper and place under the broiler, skin side up, for 3–5 minutes or until the skin is a crispy golden brown. Meanwhile, tip the *maftool* into a large serving platter and ladle some of the stew over it. Top with the chicken and serve with bowls of the stew on the side.

Note: *Maftool* is becoming widely available in supermarkets and online, but if you can't find it, use *moghrabieh*, fregola sarda or giant couscous.

Preparation time: 30 minutes
Cooking time: 2 hours
Serves 4

For the broth (stock)
2¼ lb/1 kg chicken joints (about 4 bone-in breasts or 4 legs, or two of each)
1 whole onion
1 tablespoon salt
2 teaspoons Nine Spice Mix (page 24)
2 teaspoons ground caraway
2 teaspoons ground cumin
1 bay leaf
½ teaspoon tomato paste (purée; optional, just for color)

For the stew
2 tablespoons olive oil
1 onion, sliced into half-moons
½ butternut squash, diced
1 x 14-oz/400-g can chickpeas, rinsed and drained

For the maftool
1 tablespoon olive oil
1 tablespoon butter
1 lb 2 oz/500 g *maftool* (see Note)

FLIPPED OVER CHICKEN
AND VEGETABLE RICE

مقلوبه

Maqlubeh means "flipped over" and refers to the way the pot is flipped after being cooked to reveal a cake-shaped dish of rice, meat, and vegetables. There are as many variations of *maqlubeh* as there are Palestinian families, and this particular one is my Teta Fatima's. You could also use bone-in lamb cuts (preferably from the shoulder) in place of the chicken, for example.

Preparation time: 15 minutes + soaking
Cooking time: 2 hours
Serves 8

For the rice
1 quantity Spiced Cooking Broth (Stock) using 4 chicken legs or 4 bone-in breasts (page 34)
vegetable oil, for frying
2 eggplants (aubergines) (about 2 ¼ lb/1 kg) sliced into ¾ inch/2-cm rounds
1 head of cauliflower, broken into florets
1 tablespoon olive oil, plus extra for drizzling
1 lb 10 oz/750 g jasmine rice (or any other long grain rice), rinsed, soaked for 15 minutes, and drained
1 tablespoon turmeric
1 tablespoon Nine Spice Mix (page 24)
1 tablespoon salt, or to taste

For the chicken
olive oil, for drizzling
salt
freshly ground black pepper

To serve
— 1 quantity Toasted Almonds (page 31)
— Palestinian Salad (page 104)
— yogurt

Prepare the broth (stock) according to the recipe, and when done, remove the chicken pieces and place, skin side up, on an oven roasting tray. Strain the broth and reserve.

Pour enough vegetable oil into a large skillet (frying pan) to reach about ¾ inch/2 cm up the sides. When the oil is hot, fry the eggplants (aubergines) and cauliflower until a nice golden brown all over, about 5–10 minutes, then drain on kitchen paper. For an easier but less traditional option, you could brush the vegetables with oil and broil in the oven.

Add 1 tablespoon of olive oil, the turmeric, spices, and salt to the rice and toss until fully coated.

To assemble the dish, drizzle some olive oil in a large nonstick casserole to coat the bottom. Sprinkle just enough rice to cover the bottom of the pot. Arrange the fried vegetables over the rice and top with remaining rice. If your pot is small, you may need to repeat the layers.

Place the pot over medium-high heat and ladle the fresh broth on top until it reaches approximately ¾ inch/2 cm above the rice. Set a plate on top of the rice to help maintain the shape during cooking. Bring to a boil and cook for 15 minutes, then reduce the heat and simmer until done, about 15–20 minutes.

Remove from the heat and set aside, covered, to rest for 10–15 minutes.

Meanwhile, preheat the oven broiler (grill). Brush the chicken with olive oil and sprinkle with salt and pepper. Broil for 5–7 minutes or until the skin is a nice golden brown color.

To serve, remove the lid and place a large inverted serving platter over the pot of rice. Using both hands, flip the pot over, and slowly lift it to reveal a beautiful cake-shaped rice dish. Top with the broiled chicken, sprinkle with toasted almonds and serve with Palestinian Salad and yogurt.

KUBBEH TARTARE

كبه نيه

Preparation time: 1 hour
Serves 4-6

9 oz/250g lean goat, lamb, or beef meat,
    completely cleaned of any fat or
    gristle and cut into cubes
9 oz/250g very fine bulgur wheat
1 teaspoon salt
1 onion, quartered
¼ firmly packed cup (1 oz/25 g) fresh
    herb leaves (any combination of mint,
    marjoram, basil, and thyme)
2 tablespoons red bell pepper paste
    (found in Middle Eastern and
    Turkish grocery stores, if unavailable
    substitute with 1 teaspoon
    of tomato paste (purée) mixed
    with 1 tablespoon of paprika and
    1 tablespoon of water)
1 teaspoon lemon zest
½ teaspoon Nine Spice Mix (page 24)
½ teaspoon ground cumin
olive oil, for brushing

To serve
— 1 quantity Lamb with Onion and
    Spices (page 30)
— fresh vegetables, such as scallions
    (spring onions), radishes, mint
    leaves, green chillies, tomatoes,
    lettuce
— bread (optional)

This is the quintessential festive dish in the Galilee. No wedding, holiday, or gathering is complete without a plate of this deep-orange, smooth tartare served alongside Lamb with Onion and Spices (page 30) and fresh vegetables. Traditionally, the meat was ground with a giant wooden pestle and stone mortar, the sound of which signaled a village in celebration. You need the freshest meat possible for this recipe so source it from a trusted butcher and grind (mince) it at home. You could also freeze it for a couple of days and partially defrost in the refrigerator before grinding. Supermarket or pre-ground meat are absolutely not an option for this dish so if you don't have a powerful food processor or meat grinder at home, then pre-order the meat from your butcher and ask him to grind it twice through a meat grinder the very first thing in the morning on sparkling clean blades.

Arrange the meat cubes on a plate and freeze while you start on the rest of the dish.

Put the bulgur in a large bowl, wash with water then pour out most of the water. Any remaining water will be absorbed by the bulgur. Sprinkle with the salt and set aside for about 15 minutes.

Knead the bulgur very well with your hands until softened. Taste, and if the bulgur still has a bite, add 1 tablespoon cold water at a time and continue to knead (this should take 10–15 minutes). Set aside.

Put the onion, herbs, red pepper paste, lemon zest, and spices in the bowl of a food processor and process to a very smooth paste. If necessary, add one tablespoon cold water at a time to achieve a paste. At this point, remove the meat from the freezer and add to the food processor with 1–2 ice cubes and process to a fine paste.

Pour the meat mixture over the softened bulgur and mix with your hands for a couple of minutes until fully combined. Have a bowl of ice-cold water to dip your hands into as you knead to avoid heating the raw meat.

When combined, transfer to a serving platter and flatten into a slightly raised dome. Wet your palms with iced water if necessary to shape. Drizzle with olive oil and use the back of a small spoon to make indentations in any design you like.

To serve, spoon desired portion into plate, flatten out with the back of a spoon and top with the Lamb with Onion and Spices mixture. Enjoy alongside fresh vegetables and bread, if desired.

LAMB, GARLIC, AND CHICKPEA PILAF

قدره

Qidreh, which literally means "pot" in Arabic, is almost never cooked at home. This hallmark dish of Hebron is prepped at home but then sent to the neighborhood oven where a special copper pot and wood-fired oven are used to cook it. Traditionally made with lamb on the bone, it's actually quite easy to make at home with smaller pieces of stewing lamb and cook it in the oven in a cast-iron Dutch oven (casserole) for an almost identical taste. Serve it with a side of plain yogurt to contrast with the rich rice and meat.

Preparation time: 15 minutes + soaking
Cooking time: 2 hours 30 minutes
Serves 6–8

For the broth (stock)
3 tablespoons olive oil
2–3 pieces mastic
2 bay leaves
1 tablespoon Nine Spice Mix (page 24)
½ teaspoon turmeric
1 lb 5 oz/600 g boneless shoulder of
    lamb, cut into 2-inch/5-cm cubes,
    or 5 lb 7 oz/ 2.5 kg bone-in stewing
    cuts of lamb or beef
1 whole onion
1 tablespoon salt

For the rice
2 tablespoons olive oil
2 tablespoons butter
1 large onion, sliced into half-moons
15–18 whole cloves garlic
1 teaspoon ground cumin
1 teaspoon Nine Spice Mix (page 24)
1 teaspoon salt
1 teaspoon turmeric
1 lb 2 oz/500 g rice (jasmine or medium
    grain), washed and drained
1 x 14-oz/400-g can chickpeas, rinsed
    and drained

To serve
— Toasted Pine Nuts and Almonds
    (page 31)
— plain yogurt

To make the broth (stock), heat the olive oil in a large stockpot until hot but not smoking. Add the mastic, bay leaves, Nine Spice Mix, and turmeric and stir until fragrant, about 1 minute. Add the lamb and sear on all sides, about 3 minutes. Add the whole onion, tossing to coat in the spices, then add 8 cups (3½ pints/2 liters) water and the salt. Bring to a boil, skimming the foam from the surface, then simmer for 60–80 minutes (20 minutes in a pressure cooker) until the meat is tender. Remove from the heat, strain the broth, and set the meat aside.

Preheat the oven to 325°F/160°C/Gas Mark 3. Heat the oil and butter in a cast-iron pot. Once the butter has melted, reduce the heat to low, add the onion and cook for 10–15 minutes, stirring occasionally, until softened and golden, then add the garlic and sauté for 2–3 minutes. Sprinkle in the spices and stir for another minute, then add the rice and toss to coat evenly. Add the chickpeas and give one final toss to combine all the ingredients.

Pour 4 cups (1¾ pints/1 liter) of the prepared broth over the rice mixture and increase the heat to high. As soon as the broth starts to boil, remove from the heat, arrange the meat on top of the rice, cover the pot, and place in the oven for 1 hour until the rice has fully cooked and the meat has browned nicely.

Remove from the oven and let sit for 5 minutes before sprinkling with toasted nuts and serving with fresh yogurt.

Note: Traditionally, when served at large gatherings, the pieces of meat are removed, the pot is inverted onto a large serving platter, then the pieces of meat rearranged on top and sprinkled with the almonds. However, for a small family gathering it looks just as beautiful served from the pot, especially if you are using a nice Dutch oven (casserole).

LAMB DUMPLINGS IN YOGURT SAUCE

ششبرك

Preparation time: 1 hour 30 minutes
Cooking time: 1 hour
Serves 6–8

4 ½ cups (1 lb 2 oz/500 g all-purpose
    (plain) flour
1 teaspoon salt
4 tablespoons vegetable oil
1 quantity Lamb with Onion and Spices,
    without nuts (page 30)
1 quantity Cooked Yogurt Sauce
    (page 29)

To serve
— 2 tablespoons crushed dried mint
    (optional)
— Toasted Pine Nuts (page 31)

A friend was once invited to Hebron to eat "cats' ears". He politely declined, appalled that people were eating cats. It was only after several such affronts the he finally found out he was being invited to eat *shushbarak*, dumplings folded to resemble a cat's ear, hence the name "*denein qtat*" used in some areas of Palestine. At its heart, this dish is quite simple; it just requires some patience.

Put the flour and salt into a large bowl and mix together. Add the oil and work with your hands until well incorporated. Pour in 1 cup (8 fl oz/250 ml) water; mix through with your fingers. Gradually add more and more water and knead until the dough comes together. If the mixture feels tough, leave for 5 minutes then come back and knead again. Repeat once or twice until you have a soft but fairly robust ball of dough. Divide into 2 balls and rest, covered, for 30 minutes.

On a floured surface, roll one of the balls to roughly ⅛ inch/ 3 mm thick. Using a 2½-inch/6-cm round cookie cutter or inverted glass, cut as many circles as you can out of the dough. Gather up the scraps, knead into a ball, and set aside.

To stuff the dumplings, place about ½ teaspoon of the lamb mixture into the middle of each circle and fold over in half. Take the ends of the half circle and attach together to form a hat shape. Once all the circles are filled, roll out the leftover pastry and repeat the process until the stuffing is finished.

Preheat the oven to 350°F/180°C/Gas Mark 4. Place the dumplings on baking sheets and bake in the oven in batches for 15–20 minutes until a very light golden color (you are just drying them out). At this point, the dumplings can be cooled and then frozen for later use or cooked the same day.

To cook, prepare the yogurt sauce and bring to a boil. Add 4 cups (1¾ pints/1 liter) water and bring back to a boil. Place the dumplings in the sauce and simmer until soft, 20–30 minutes. If they are still chewy, continue to cook for 10 minutes. Ladle into bowls and top with pine nuts and mint.

Note: This dish uses a lot of water in the sauce because no matter how much you add, it always thickens as it cools. Start out with the amount the recipe calls for but be prepared to add more. When you do, taste and adjust the seasoning.

Variation: Instead of the dumplings, use kubbeh (page 90) but instead of frying, bake them in a 400°F/200°C/Gas Mark 6 oven for 10–15 minutes then cook in the yogurt sauce for 5 minutes before serving.

LAMB AND YOGURT RICE STEW

منسف

Preparation time: 15 minutes + soaking
Cooking time: 1 hour 30 minutes
Serves 4–6

For the broth (stock)
2 tablespoons olive oil
4–6 lamb shanks (3½ lb/1.5 kg in total)
1 whole onion
5 pieces mastic
15 allspice berries
4 cloves
4 cardamom pods
3 bay leaves
1 piece mace
1 cinnamon stick
1 teaspoon salt

For the rice
14 oz/400 g rice (jasmine or short grain)
1 quantity Cooked Yogurt Sauce
    (page 29) (see Note)
½ cup (2 oz/50 g) Toasted Pine Nuts
    (page 31)
1 cup (4 oz/120 g) Toasted Almonds
    (page 31)
1 tablespoon butter or ghee
2 tablespoons olive oil
½ teaspoon salt
¼ teaspoon turmeric
2 large paper-thin *shrak* breads, or good
    quality Indian rotis, Mexican flour
    tortillas or thin Lebanese pita bread

Food is one of the ways Palestinians show respect and appreciation to others. In many parts of the country, if you want to truly honor a guest, nothing does it so quite as well as a giant plate of *mansaf*. This is especially true in Taybeh, my husband's hometown. The first time my parents visited my husband's family, there was a plate of tangy and rich *mansaf* piled on top of paper-thin shrak bread, topped with lamb shanks, and sprinkled with pine nuts and almonds.

Heat the oil in a large stockpot over medium-high heat. Add the lamb shanks and sear on all sides. When the shanks are nicely browned on all sides, add 6 cups (2½ pints/1.5 liters) water and bring to a boil, skimming away the scum from the surface. Once you have skimmed all the foam from the surface, add the onion, spices, and salt. Reduce the heat, and simmer for 1½–2 hours (40–50 minutes in a pressure cooker), or until the meat is tender but not falling off the bone.

Meanwhile, rinse the rice under running water until the water runs clear. Soak for 15–30 minutes, drain, and set aside. While the rice is soaking, prepare the yogurt sauce, fry the almonds and pine nuts, then set everything aside.

When the shanks are done, strain the broth (stock) through a fine-mesh strainer, discarding the onion and spices. Mix the broth with the yogurt sauce, add the lamb, and cook for another 15–30 minutes. The strength of flavor will depend on whether you have used *kishek* for your yogurt sauce; it should be quite salty and sour, so taste and adjust salt.

Meanwhile, continue with the rice by melting the butter and oil in a pan over high heat. Add the drained rice, tossing to fully coat in the oil, and pour in 2½ cups (18 fl oz/ 550 ml) water, the salt, and turmeric and bring to a boil. Let it simmer for 2–5 minutes, give it one more stir, then place a dish towel over the pan, close the lid tightly, and remove from the heat. Let it sit for about 15 minutes.

To assemble, tear up the bread and arrange in a large, round stainless steel or ceramic platter. Spread the rice over the bread and top with the shanks. Pour some of the yogurt sauce on top, enough to soak through the rice and bread. Sprinkle with the toasted almonds and pine nuts. Pour the remaining sauce into a bowl and serve with the rice.

Note: Mansaf is traditionally made with *kishek* or *jameed* (page 29) but without garlic. The taste is so distinctive it really is worth hunting down. If you do find it, skip the fried garlic in the sauce. If you cannot find it, then keep the garlic in to enhance and improve the flavor of the yogurt.

DESSERTS AND SWEET TREATS

Whenever someone asks if she wants dessert, my mother repeats a saying that roughly translates to "There's room in my stomach, no matter what I eat, that can only be filled with something sweet." Clearly, she never says no to dessert, and frankly, neither do I.

I've always had a sweet tooth, but I convince myself that it's okay because Arab sweets—unlike many Western desserts of creamy cakes, tarts, and puddings—tend to rely on nuts, dried fruits, seeds, and spices. Of course I neglect to remind myself they are all sweetened with sugar or sugar syrup.

While I often enjoy some of the lighter desserts like Fenugreek Semolina Cake (page 220) and Aniseed Cookies (page 224) for breakfast or as an afternoon snack, on a day-to-day basis, indulge in the more substantial desserts is not the norm. In fact, most family meals are rounded off only with seasonal fruits or nuts and desserts are left mostly for when you have a larger gathering of people or a more special occasion. The exciting exception to this rule is the Arab world's "dessert season": the month of Ramadan. During this time, the streets explode with vendors selling all kinds of sweet treats, but most notably *atayif* (see Sweet Cheese Turnovers, page 222). For almost thirty days, families enjoy decadent desserts every night after the breaking-of-the-fast dinner, everything from *knafeh* (see Shredded Phyllo (filo) and Cheese Pie, page 214) to Baklawa (page 216 and even desserts that are difficult to find throughout the year—like syrup-dunked fried dough balls— which pop up in bakeries everywhere.

Luckily, you do not have to wait from one year to the next to enjoy these desserts, since most can easily be replicated at home. Nonetheless, one of the beautiful things about Palestinian desserts is that many of them are tied to specific events, seasons, or holidays. Caraway Pudding (page 228) for instance, is made for the birth of a new baby, Palestinian Holiday Cakes (page 230) for Eid al-Fitr, and Holiday Date and Nut Cakes (page 212) for Easter, to name just a few.

Of course people do not always follow these traditions, but there is something special about looking forward to certain times of the year because of the foods associated with them, or knowing what occasion you are celebrating by the food and its surrounding atmosphere. After all, these traditions tie us together as proud Palestinians, across religions, continents, and time, ensuring the end of any meal is as notable as its start.

Left
Street-side fresh-juice vendor
in Jerusalem's Old City.

TOASTED BREAD PUDDING
WITH CREAM AND PISTACHIOS

عيش السرايا

Preparation time: 15-20 minutes
Cooking time: 5-10 minutes
Makes one 9-inch/23-cm round cake

For the base
vegetable oil, for greasing
5 oz/150 g ready-prepared toasted
    bread, such as melba toast
1¼ cups (9 oz/250 g) superfine
    (caster) sugar
1 teaspoon lemon juice
1 oz/25g butter
1 tablespoon orange blossom water

For the topping
9 oz/250 g mascarpone cheese (or use
    ricotta for a lighter version)
½ cup (4 fl oz/125ml) heavy (double)
    cream
1 teaspoon orange blossom water
1 cup (4 oz/120 g) unsalted pistachios,
    coarsely ground
preserved lemon blossom flowers,
    raspberries, strawberries, or
    pomegranate seeds (optional)

The name of this dish means "bread of the royal palaces" and a royal dessert it is indeed. A vestige of the Ottoman rule over Palestine (*saraya* is a Turkish word), this luxurious dessert is actually very easy to make. Toasted bread is soaked in flavored sugar syrup then topped with cream and pistachios. While it sounds very simple, the flavors are anything but.

Lightly grease (use a paper towel dipped in vegetable oil) a 9-inch/23-cm round springform pan and set aside.

Put the toast into a large bowl and crush with your hands into small bite-size pieces. Alternatively, pulse to a very coarse crumb in a food processor. Set aside.

Put the sugar, 1¼ cups (10 fl oz/300 ml) water, and lemon juice into a small, heavy pan, place over medium-high heat, and bring to a boil. Reduce the heat and simmer for 3–4 minutes until slightly thickened. Remove from the heat, add the butter and orange blossom water, and stir until the butter is melted.

Pour the syrup over the toast, mixing very well with a spoon, until all the liquid is absorbed. Transfer to the greased pan, smoothing out into an even layer, and set aside to cool.

Meanwhile, in the bowl of a freestanding mixer fitted with the whisk or paddle attachment, whip the mascarpone, heavy (double) cream, and orange blossom water together on medium-high speed until smooth and creamy with stiff peaks, about 1 minute. Avoid overmixing.

Evenly spread out the cream mixture over the bread base, smoothing it out with the back of a spoon. Sprinkle the pistachios over the cake. Refrigerate for a couple of hours before serving, until the cream is set.

To serve, remove the cake from the springform pan and place on a cake platter (do not attempt to remove the springform pan base). If using, top with preserved blossom flowers, raspberries, strawberries or some pomegranate seeds for color.

HOLIDAY DATE AND NUT CAKES

كعك ومعمول

Preparation time: 2 hours + resting
Cooking time: 5–10 minutes
Makes about 30

For the pastry
2¼ lb/1 kg fine semolina
1 lb 2 oz/500 g butter, at room
  temperature
¼ cup (2 fl oz/60 ml) vegetable oil
2¼ cups (9 oz/250 g) all-purpose
  (plain) flour
1 teaspoon salt
½ teaspoon mastic ground with
  ½ teaspoon sugar (optional)
½ teaspoon ground mahlab (optional)
1 teaspoon active dry (fast-action) yeast
2 tablespoons sugar
4 tablespoons rosewater
4 tablespoons orange blossom water

For the filling (option 1)
2¼ lb/1 kg date paste
2 teaspoons ground cinnamon
¼ teaspoon ground nutmeg and cloves

For the filling (option 2)
2¼ lb/1 kg coarsely chopped walnuts
  or pistachios (or use a combination
  of both)
1 cup (7 oz/200 g) granulated sugar
2 tablespoons orange blossom water
2 tablespoons rosewater
4 tablespoons melted butter
1 teaspoon ground cinnamon

To serve
— confectioners' (icing) sugar,
  for dusting

With a Muslim mother and a Christian father I got to celebrate twice as many holidays as most people: this meant double the gifts, double the days off from school, and more importantly, to a foodie like me, double the amount of time we had *ka'ak wa ma'amoul* at home. These bite-size stuffed semolina cakes are synonymous with the holidays for both Christians and Muslims in Palestine. They may be labour intensive, but they last for weeks and so are worth the effort.

Place the semolina, butter, and oil in a large bowl and work with your hands until fully combined and the mixture resembles wet sand, at least 10–15 minutes. Cover with plastic wrap (clingfilm) and leave overnight.

The next day, add the flour, salt, mastic, and mahlab to the semolina and gently rub with your hands. Add the yeast, sugar, rosewater, and orange blossom water and mix to combine. Start to add water, a tablespoon at a time, and knead gently (do not overmix, or your *ma'amoul* will be too tough) until you can take a clump of dough and it holds together without crumbling. Cover and leave to rest for 15–30 minutes.

Meanwhile, if using the date filling, put all the ingredients into a bowl and knead together until combined, then shape into grape-sized balls. If using the nut filling, combine all the ingredients together and set aside.

To make the date cakes, take a walnut-size piece of dough, flatten slightly, and place a date ball inside. Make sure the date is fully enclosed by the dough and roll into a ball. Slightly flatten with your palm and with the round tip of a wooden spoon, make a hole in the middle of the cake. Use a metal pincher or cake mold to decorate.

To make the nut cakes, take a similar size piece of dough and use your thumb to create an indentation. Fill with about 1 teaspoon of the nut mixture. Close carefully, form into a dome or oblong shape, and use a cake mold or metal pincher to decorate.

Preheat the oven to 400°F/200°C/Gas Mark 6 and line a couple of baking sheets with parchment. Place the cakes on the lined baking sheet and bake until the bottom edges are a very light golden brown, 5–10 minutes. Remove and cool completely.

Transfer to an airtight container. They keep for 7–10 days at room temperature or in the freezer for 3 months. Dust with confectioners' (icing) sugar before serving.

SHREDDED PHYLLO (FILO) AND CHEESE PIE

كنافه

Preparation time: 20 minutes
Cooking time: 30 minutes
Serves 6–8

6 oz/180 g ghee, melted (or use butter),
    plus extra for greasing
14 oz/400 g dry/low moisture mozzarella
    (not fresh buffalo mozzarella)
9 oz/250 g ricotta cheese
1 lb 450 g shredded phyllo (filo) pastry
    (see Note)
1 quantity Flavored Sugar Syrup
    (page 35), cooled to room
    temperature
4–6 tablespoons ground pistachios

Believed to have originated in the Palestinian town of
Nablus, it is quite uncommon to make *knafeh* at home in
Palestine nowadays because it is so readily available at
bakeries. Not only that, but it's available in multiple varieties
like *na'ameh* (fine), *khishneh* (coarse), or *malfoofeh* (rolled)
and with various stuffings, including pistachios, cream,
cheese, or walnuts. This recipe was handed down from my
father's uncle to my uncle's wife, and now finally to me.
It's a very simple dessert where the ingredients really shine,
so use the very best that you can find.

Preheat the oven to 400°F/200°C/Gas Mark 6. Generously
grease an 11-inch/28-cm round baking dish, or a 12 ×
8-inch/30 × 20-cm rectangular one, with ghee or butter.

To prepare the cheese stuffing, grate the mozzarella into a
large bowl or slice it into thin pieces. Add the ricotta cheese
and mix well to combine. Refrigerate until ready to use.

Place the shredded phyllo (filo) pastry in a food processor
and process until the shreds are roughly ¾ inch/2 cm in
length. Alternatively, if using frozen pastry, you could also
crush and shred them apart with your fingers. Transfer to
a large bowl and pour over the melted ghee. Work with your
hands until the pastry has fully absorbed the ghee.

Transfer half the dough to the greased baking dish, pressing
it tightly with your hands to cover the bottom. Spread the
cheese mixture evenly over the pastry. The easiest way to
do this without the bottom layer of pastry coming loose
is to drop spoonfuls of the filling evenly over the pastry, then
lightly press with the back of a wet spoon or a damp hand.

Spread the remaining pastry evenly on top of the cheese
filling, making sure to fully cover the cheese, then firmly
pat down with your hands.

Bake in the oven for 25–35 minutes, or until the cheese
has melted and the crust is a golden brown.

Remove from the oven, allow to cool for 5 minutes, then flip
over onto a serving platter. Immediately drizzle with enough
sugar syrup to soak the cake. Sprinkle over the pistachios
and serve with extra sugar syrup on the side.

Note: Shredded filo pastry, or *kataifi*, can be found in
the frozen section at any Middle Eastern, and even
Mediterranean, grocery store. Around Ramadan, it is also
common to find it fresh; it can then be frozen for later use.
It is much easier to shred the dough if partially frozen.

BAKLAWA

بقلاوه

Preparation time: 1 hour
Cooking time: 15-20 minutes
Makes 40 pieces

2 cups (7 oz/200 g) ground pistachios,
    plus extra for sprinkling
3/4 cup (6oz / 180g) granulated sugar
1 tablespoon rosewater
5 oz/150 g ghee or butter, melted
40 phyllo (filo) pastry sheets, about
    6 × 8 inches/15 × 20cm (you will
    probably have to cut larger sheets
    down to this size)
½ quantity Flavored Sugar Syrup
    (page 35), at room temperature

Despite the prevalence of the Middle East's most famous dessert, it's actually quite hard to find one that tastes good. There's either too much syrup or not enough, poor quality butter or nuts, too burnt, not cooked enough—the list goes on. Making it at home can seem like too much trouble though, so people often just buy it. All this changed for me when I was in the United States for a wedding and I saw my mother-in-law take out several packages of phyllo (filo) pastry and whip up a large tray of the cutest spiral-shaped baklawas in thirty minutes. Although not traditional, this recipe, adapted from hers, is so easy, fresh, and delicious that I now regularly make this once finicky dessert at home.

Preheat the oven to 350°F/180°C/Gas Mark 4 and line a baking sheet with parchment.

Combine the ground pistachios, sugar, and rosewater in a bowl.

Place the phyllo (filo) sheets on your work surface and cover with a damp dish towel to avoid drying. Working with just one sheet at a time, remove a sheet of phyllo and brush with the melted ghee. Spoon about 1 teaspoon of the pistachio mixture across the short edge of the phyllo sheet. Roll the sheet into a cigar shape, brushing with the melted ghee as you roll, then roll the cigar into a snail shape, taking care not to rip the pastry. Brush the rolled baklawa all over with more melted ghee and place onto the lined baking sheet.

Continue until all sheets are rolled. Brush all the rolled pieces with the melted ghee one more time then bake in the oven for 15–20 minutes, or until the baklawas are a light golden brown.

Remove from the oven and pour the sugar syrup over the baklawas. Alternatively, let the baklawa cool down to room temperature and pour freshly made warm syrup over. Sprinkle each piece with very finely ground pistachios and transfer to a serving platter.

Variation: In place of the pistachios, you can use other nuts, such as walnuts, almonds, cashews, or hazelnuts. If using walnuts, add 1 teaspoon ground cinnamon to the stuffing.

FRAGRANT MILK PUDDING
WITH PISTACHIOS

مهلبيه

Preparation time: 2 minutes
Cooking time: 10 minutes
Serves 10–12

4 cups (1¾ pints/1 liter) whole (full-fat)
  milk
1 cup (8 fl oz/250 ml) heavy (double)
  cream
¾ cup (4 oz/120 g) granulated sugar
¾ cup (3 oz/80 g) cornstarch (cornflour)
3–4 pieces mastic

To serve
— coarsely ground pistachios
— desiccated coconut
— flaked almonds
— pomegranate seeds

Mhalabiyeh is basically a Palestinian version of panna cotta, but lighter and easier to make. Mastic is the most traditional flavor for this dessert, but you can replace it with 1 teaspoon of rosewater or orange blossom water or ½ teaspoon of each, just before removing from the heat. As for the toppings, the possibilities are endless: whole nuts, desiccated coconut, crushed or ground pistachios, and syrups or jams such as rose or pomegranates are all good options. If you plan on serving it with jam or syrup, reduce the sugar in the recipe to ½ cup (4 oz/120 g) since the topping will be sweet as well.

Put three-quarters of the milk, the cream, and the sugar into a large, heavy pan and place over medium heat until it just begins to simmer.

In the meantime, mix the remaining milk and cornstarch (cornflour) in a small bowl or measuring pitcher (jug) until fully dissolved. With a pestle and mortar, grind the mastic pieces with a pinch of sugar, then add to the milk and cornstarch mixture.

When the milk and cream are on the verge of coming to a boil, pour in the milk and cornstarch mixture, whisking continuously until the mixture thickens, about 2 minutes.

Remove from the heat and pour into very small dessert bowls or glass tumblers or mini jars. Refrigerate for at least 4 hours and preferably overnight.

Garnish with your chosen toppings and serve.

FENUGREEK SEMOLINA CAKE

صينية حلبه

Preparation time: 45 minutes + resting
Cooking time: 20–30 minutes
Makes one 11-inch (28-cm) cake

tahini or butter, for greasing
2 tablespoons fenugreek seeds
2 cups (11 oz/300 g) semolina
½ cup (2¾ oz/60 g) all-purpose
    (plain) flour
4 tablespoons olive oil
4 tablespoons vegetable oil
1 tablespoon granulated sugar
1 tablespoon nigella seeds
1 tablespoon ground anise seeds
1 teaspoon baking powder
1 teaspoon active dry (fast-action) yeast
½ teaspoon ground cinnamon
½ teaspoon salt
¼ teaspoon turmeric
20–30 pine nuts or blanched almonds
1 quantity Flavored Sugar Syrup
    (page 35), cooled to room
    temperature

This is one of the most typical Palestinian desserts, but localized to the center and south of the country. The fenugreek lends it a distinct "love it or hate it" flavor. The cake is soaked in syrup after baking and must then stand for a few hours, and preferably overnight, before serving. This recipe yields a cake of medium thickness, but some people prefer it thinner and crunchier, in which case you can adjust by using a larger cake pan. This moist rich cake is one of my favorite desserts, at its best when enjoyed with a strong cup of Cardamom Coffee (page 235).

Put the fenugreek seeds into a medium pan with 2 cups (16 fl oz/475 ml) water and place over high heat. Bring to a boil, then reduce the heat and simmer for 20–25 minutes, or until the seeds are tender and plump. Strain the seeds, reserving the cooking water.

Meanwhile, put all the remaining ingredients, except for the pine nuts and sugar syrup, into a large bowl and mix until well combined and resembling wet sand in texture.

Add the strained fenugreek seeds and 1 cup (8 fl oz/250 ml) of the fenugreek cooking water. Mix well with your hand or a wooden spoon and, if necessary, gradually add more water. you want a soft dough—not so loose it can be poured like cake batter but not so stiff it can be kneaded liked bread.

Wet your palms and use them to spread the batter into the greased dish and smooth out the surface. With a sharp knife, score the cake with diagonal lines in one direction, then in the opposite direction, to form a diamond pattern. Place a pine nut or blanched almond in the center of each diamond. Set aside, covered with a tea towel, to rest and rise for 1 hour.

Meanwhile, preheat the oven to 400°F/200°C/Gas Mark 6 and grease an 11-inch/28-cm round metal or glass cake pan with either tahini or butter (or use an 8 × 12 inch/20 × 30 cm rectangular cake pan) and set aside.

Bake the cake until a dark golden brown, about 20–30 minutes. Remove from the oven and pour over the cooled syrup while the cake is still warm. Cool completely before serving, for several hours, or overnight. If you attempt to cut the cake before it has cooled, the pieces will crumble.

Once cooled, cut out individual portions from the cake tin and serve. The remaining cake pieces in the tin will keep, covered in aluminum foil or clingfilm, at room temperature for up to 5 days or in the refrigerator for up to 2 weeks.

SWEET WALNUT OR CHEESE TURNOVERS

قطايف

Preparation time: 30 minutes + resting
Cooking time: 15 minutes
Makes about 10 large or 20 small
turnovers

For the batter
1 cup (4 oz/120 g) all-purpose (plain)
flour
1½ cups (12 fl oz/350 ml) water
2 tablespoons semolina
1 tablespoon sugar
1 teaspoon active dry (fast-action) yeast
1 teaspoon baking powder
¼ teaspoon salt

For the walnut stuffing
9 oz/250 g lightly toasted walnuts,
coarsely ground
½ teaspoon cinnamon

For the cheese stuffing
9 oz/250 g cheese, coarsely chopped
or grated (if unavailable, substitute
with equal portions of mozzarella
and ricotta)
2 pieces mastic, ground into a powder
(optional)
¼ teaspoon rosewater or orange
blossom water

For the mini atayif stuffing
9 oz/250 g ricotta
2 tablespoons heavy (double) cream
¼ teaspoon rosewater or orange
blossom water
1 oz/25 g pistachios, coarsely ground,
to garnish

softened butter, for brushing
1 quantity Flavored Sugar Syrup (page
35), cooled to room temperature,
to serve

For Christians and Muslims alike back home, *atayif* is synonymous with the month of Ramadan. It is only during this month that bakeries make the pastry for these turnovers, and the lines go out into the street the first week as people wait their turn to buy the pancakes before returning home to stuff them. The pancakes are cooked only on one side and can be large or small: the large ones are normally stuffed with nuts or cheese, baked, then drenched in sugar syrup. The small ones are simply stuffed with a creamy filling, only half closed, then dipped in pistachio and drizzled with thick sugar syrup. Either way the batter is quite simple to make, so do try it at home, regardless of month and season.

Put all the batter ingredients into a blender or food processor and process until smooth. The batter should be quite loose, similar to pouring cream in consistency. Set aside in a pouring or mixing pitcher (jug), or keep it in the blender if it has a pouring spout, for about 30 minutes to allow the yeast to activate.

Prepare your chosen stuffing. The quantities above assume you are only choosing one kind. For the walnut or cheese, mix the ingredients together in a small bowl until combined. For the mini atayif, mix all the ingredients except the pistachios, and set the latter aside for garnish.

When you are ready to cook, place a large nonstick pan over medium heat until hot. Mix the batter once more to ensure it is smooth and start pouring it into the pan—for the large *atayif,* pour about 4–5 tablespoons of the batter and for the small ones about 1 tablespoon, fitting as many circles as you can into the pan. Small bubbles should start to appear around the edges of each circle and quickly spread all over the surface. Once the entire surface is covered in bubbles and you no longer see wet batter, the *atayif* are ready, about 2 minutes, depending on size. The pancakes are cooked only on one side, so do not turn them over during cooking. When done, transfer them to a tray lined with a dish towel and cover with another dish towel while you make the rest of the pancakes. Stuff them as soon as possible to prevent them from drying out.

To make the large walnut or cheese atayif
Preheat the oven to 400°F/200°C/Gas Mark 6 and line a large baking sheet with parchment.

Place about 1 tablespoon of either the nut or cheese filling on the "bubble" side of the pancake and fold the circle over so it forms a half-moon. Seal the edges by pressing them between your thumb and index finger. Make sure you do not overstuff them as this may cause them to open or crack during cooking.

Place the stuffed pancakes on the lined baking sheet and generously brush with the softened butter on both sides. Bake in the oven for 10–15 minutes, or until crispy and golden brown—keep an eye out to avoid burning them.

Remove from the oven and immediately plunge into the cooled sugar syrup; quickly remove with a slotted spoon and transfer to your serving platter.

To make the mini atayif
To stuff the mini atayif, first fold over each small circle into a half-moon, "bubble" side on the inside, and with your thumb and index finger close the edges together halfway. Using a teaspoon, fill the remaining opening with the ricotta cheese, then dip it into the ground pistachios.

Arrange the mini *atayif* on a serving platter and serve with a bowl of cooled flavored sugar syrup. Drizzle the syrup over each one as you serve them on individual plates.

Note: If you find when frying the pancakes that they are not getting covered in bubbles, it's possible that your batter is too thick or that you have used expired baking powder. Add a tablespoon of water to the batter at a time until it reaches pouring consistency and try again. If that doesn't work, you may need to start again with fresh baking powder.

ANISEED COOKIES

معكرونه

Preparation time: 1 hour 30 minutes
Cooking time: 20-30 minutes
Makes 65

4½ cups (1 lb 2 oz/500 g) all-purpose
    (plain) flour
¾ cup (5 ½ oz/150 g) caster
    (superfine) sugar
¾ cup (3 oz/90 g) unhulled sesame
    seeds, toasted (see Note)
4 tablespoons ground aniseed
1 tablespoon nigella seeds
2 teaspoons baking powder
3½ oz/100 g softened butter
1 cup (8 fl oz/250 ml) olive oil (or use
    half olive oil and half vegetable oil)

Whenever one has guests back home, the meal doesn't end until you have been served coffee or tea with a small sweet treat. These tiny cookies, which are very common in the Galilee region, are a fantastic option as they are light and last for weeks once made. They are the perfect sweet to have as an after-meal treat, as well as with an afternoon pick-me-up coffee, or even as a first morning bite—my father did not properly wake up until he had a few of these with his Cardamom Coffee (page 235) in the morning.

Preheat the oven to 350°F/180°C/Gas Mark 4 and line 2 baking sheets with parchment.

Put the flour, sugar, sesame seeds, aniseed, nigella seeds, and baking powder into a large bowl and mix until well combined.

Add the softened butter and olive oil and mix until combined (the mixture will be quite stiff and crumbly). Slowly add a tablespoon of water at a time until the dough comes together. Depending on the flour you are using and the climate, you may need to use a little less or a little more than ½ cup (4 fl oz/120 ml) water.

Pull off small portions of dough, about the size and shape of a Medjool date. With your finger, flatten each piece on an inverted colander or fine grater to create a pattern, then roll over so the sides touch and the pattern is on top. Continue until all the dough is used up, placing the finished cookies on the lined baking sheet. You may need to do this in batches.

Bake in the oven for 20–25 minutes, or until the cookies are a deep golden brown. Remove from the oven and transfer to a wire rack until completely cooled, then store in an airtight container at room temperature.

Note: To toast the sesame seeds, put into in a large skillet (frying pan) over medium-low heat and stir for 7–10 minutes until golden brown, then set aside on a large tray to cool.

OTTOMAN SEMOLINA COOKIES

هريسه تركيه

Preparation time: 30 minutes
Cooking time: 20–25 minutes
Makes about 30

4 oz/125 g butter, softened
½ cup (2½ oz/60 g) confectioners'
   (icing) sugar
1 egg
2¼ cups (9 oz/250 g) all-purpose
   (plain) flour
2 tablespoons finely ground almonds
   (or use cashews or hazelnuts)
1 teaspoon baking powder
1 teaspoon pure vanilla extract
4 tablespoons finely ground pistachios
½ quantity Flavored Sugar Syrup
   (page 35)

The first time I had these was on a family vacation in Turkey as a child. We all fell in love with them so the chef at the hotel gave my mother the recipe, and we have continued to make it ever since. At home, we call it "Turkish *hareeseh*" because it's very similar to the Palestinian *hareeseh* (semolina cake, recipe opposite) but with a different texture and flavor. Admittedly not Palestinian, you cannot deny the Ottoman influence on the cuisine of the entire Levant region, and since it has been enjoyed by my family for decades, it deserves its place amongst these recipes.

Preheat the oven to 350°F/180°C/Gas Mark 4 and line a baking sheet with parchment.

Put the butter and confectioners' (icing) sugar into the bowl of a freestanding mixer fitted with the paddle attachment. Beat together on medium-low speed until evenly combined, about 1 minute. Add the egg and beat again until combined, then add the flour, ground almonds, baking powder, and vanilla and beat until the dough starts to come together, about 2 minutes. With your hands, remove the dough and gently knead into a ball.

Divide the dough into 30 small balls the size of a walnut and place on the lined baking sheet, leaving some room between them. Flatten the top of each one slightly with your hand, then bake for 20–25 minutes, or until a light golden brown.

Meanwhile, prepare the sugar syrup. The syrup will be used warm in this recipe, so there is no need to cool it down.

Remove the cookies from the oven and, with a small ladle, pour warm syrup over each cookie a couple of times. Immediately sprinkle the ground pistachios over each cookie so they stick to them as the syrup cools down.

Once cooled, the cookies can be stored at room temperature, covered in plastic wrap (clingfilm), for up to 5 days.

SEMOLINA CAKE

هريسه

Preparation time: 15 minutes + resting
Cooking time: 30 minutes
Makes one 11-inch/28-cm round cake

butter or tahini, for greasing the pan
2 cups (12 oz/350 g) semolina
1 x 14-oz/400-g can condensed milk
½ cup water
4 tablespoons tahini
4 tablespoons vegetable oil
1½ teaspoons baking powder
pinch of salt
⅓ cup (1¼ oz/40 g) blanched almond
    halves or pistachios
1 quantity Flavored Sugar Syrup (page
    35), cooled to room temperature

To serve
— Greek yogurt (see Note)
— crushed pistachios

Every culture has their own version of a semolina cake; it also happens to be one of the most popular desserts in the Middle East. So popular, in fact, that you'll find it in almost every bakery next to the daily bread and pastries. Different countries call it by different names (*basbousa* in Egypt, *nammoura* in Lebanon), but in Palestine it's called *hareeseh*. It is essentially baked semolina drenched in a rosewater and orange blossom syrup. The exact recipe varies from one person to the next, but after years of experimenting, this one is the most delicious I have come across—the perfect balance of rich and sweet yet light and fluffy.

Brush an 11-inch/28-cm round cake pan (or 8 × 12-inch/20 × 30-cm cake pan) with tahini or butter and set aside.

Put all the ingredients, except for the almond halves and sugar syrup, into a large bowl and mix well with a spoon until combined. The batter will be slightly runny and sticky. Pour into the prepared pan and, with wet palms, smooth out the top. Cover with plastic wrap (clingfilm) and set aside for at least 1 hour, and up to several hours, until the batter solidifies slightly and is easier to handle.

When ready to bake, preheat the oven to 350°F/180°C/Gas Mark 4.

With a pointed knife dipped in water, score diamond shapes in the top of the batter (you can do this by cutting lines diagonally in one direction then the opposite direction), or any other pattern you prefer. Press one almond half into each diamond shape. Bake in the oven for 20–30 minutes, or until the top is a dark golden brown.

Remove from the oven and pour the cooled syrup over the hot cake. Allow to sit for a few hours before cutting and serving, otherwise you risk the cake crumbling and falling apart. The cake will keep, covered with plastic wrap (clingfilm), for several days at room temperature.

The cake can be eaten on its own for a simple treat, but for a more impressive presentation, spoon some Greek yogurt onto a plate, top with a slice of the cake, and sprinkle generously with pistachios.

Note: This method of serving with Greek yogurt and crushed pistachio is not traditional, but I find the tang from the yogurt is a great way to break through the sweetness of this dessert, while the nuts add another element to the texture.

CARAWAY PUDDING

مغلي كراويه

Preparation time: 5 minutes
Cooking time: 15 minutes
Serves 8–12

½ cup (3 oz/80 g) finely ground rice
    or rice flour (see Note)
½ cup (3½ oz/100 g) granulated sugar
1 tablespoon ground caraway seeds
¾ teaspoon ground cinnamon

To serve
— coconut flakes
— slivered pistachios
— flaked almonds, lightly toasted

One of the oldest recorded desserts in the Levant, this pudding is normally made and served after the birth of a child. The origins of this tradition herald back to the benefits of the caraway and cinnamon, as both have antioxidant and digestive properties. Served warm in the winter months and cold in the summer, you most definitely do not need to give birth to enjoy this delicious pudding. The toppings are most commonly coconut flakes, pistachios, and almonds but this comes down to preference—you could also use sultanas, walnuts, or pine nuts.

Put all the pudding ingredients into a heavy pot with 4 cups (1¾ pints/1 liter) water and place over medium heat. Stir for 10–15 minutes until the mixture boils and is thickened. Make sure you stir continuously to avoid it sticking to the bottom of the pot.

Ladle the pudding into small dessert bowls or cups. If not serving immediately, place in the refrigerator to cool.

To serve, sprinkle each bowl with the coconut, pistachios, and almonds.

Note: Rice flour is most commonly found in Middle Eastern or Asian grocery stores. To achieve the correct texture, though, it is preferable to grind your own rice at home as store-bought rice flour tends to be extremely fine, even though both taste the same. If you cannot find it or do not want to grind your own at home, you can substitute with an equal quantitiy of fine semolina for a similar taste.

WHEAT BERRY PUDDING

برياره / سنونيه

Preparation time: 5 minutes
Cooking time: 1–2 hours
Serves 6–8

For the pudding
9 oz/250 g wheat berries, soaked in
warm water for 1 hour and drained
1 cup (200 g/7 oz) granulated sugar
1½ tablespoons ground aniseed
1 tablespoon ground fennel
1 tablespoon ground cinnamon
¼ teaspoon grated nutmeg

For the toppings (optional)
golden raisins (sultanas)
toasted walnuts
toasted sesame seeds
toasted flaked almonds
pistachios
pomegranate seeds

This pudding is usually made on one of two occasions and its name varies accordingly. The first is for Saint Barbara's Day, a holiday observed among Middle Eastern Christians, in which case it is called *burbara*. The second occasion is when a baby's first tooth appears, and it is then called *snooniyeh*. When made on this occasion it is usually covered in plenty of colorful candies (sweets) to symbolize the baby's ability to now bite into such candies. A delicious pudding with a sweet significance, it is worth indulging in, regardless of the occasion.

Put the wheat berries and 4 cups (3½ pints/2 liters) water into a large stockpot and place over high heat. Bring to a boil, skimming away any foam from the surface, then reduce the heat and simmer, partially covered with a lid, for about 1½ hours until fully cooked.

Add the sugar and spices and simmer for a further 15 minutes. Ladle into small dessert bowls, sprinkle with any or all of the toppings, and serve warm.

Note: The pudding can be stored in the refrigerator for up to 1 week, but it will start to solidify the longer it sits. To serve, reheat on the stove, slowly adding enough water to bring it back to the desired consistency and sweeten to taste.

SPICED PALESTINIAN
HOLIDAY CAKES

كعك عيد فلسطيني

Preparation time: 1 hour 30 minutes
 + resting
Cooking time: 10–15 minutes
Makes 30–35

For the pastry
1½ cups (9 oz/250 g) semolina
2¼ cups (9 oz/250 g) all-purpose
 (plain) flour
4 oz/125g softened butter
½ cup (4 fl oz/120 ml) vegetable oil
1 tablespoon nigella seeds
1 tablespoon ground aniseed
1 tablespoon ground fennel seeds
1 teaspoon baking powder
¼ teaspoon salt
1 teaspoon active dry (fast-action) yeast
1 teaspoon granulated sugar
1 cup (8 fl oz/250 ml) warm water

For the filling
1 lb 2 oz/500 g date paste (page 212)
1 teaspoon ground cinnamon
pinch each of grated nutmeg and
 ground cloves (optional)

Date-stuffed cakes are synonymous with the holidays in the Middle East for both Christians and Muslims. The Holiday Date and Nut Cakes on page 212 are widespread across the whole region, whereas these are typically Palestinian, made with a mixture of flour and semolina and spiced with anise and fennel seeds. This is my Teta Fatima's recipe.

Put the semolina, flour, butter, and oil into a large bowl and work with your hands until fully combined and the mixture resembles wet sand. Cover with plastic wrap (clingfilm) and leave for several hours or overnight.

The next day, add the nigella seeds, aniseed, fennel seeds, baking powder, and salt to the semolina mixture and gently rub together with your hands.

In a separate bowl, dissolve the yeast and sugar in ½ cup (4 fl oz/120 ml) of warm water then add to the semolina mixture. Knead gently, gradually adding remaining water as necessary, until you can take a clump of dough in your fingers and it holds together without crumbling. Cover with plastic wrap and leave to rest.

Meanwhile, prepare the filling. Combine the dates and spices, knead slightly until evenly incorporated, then tear off pieces the size of a walnut and roll each into a rope about 4 inches/10 cm long.

To make the date cakes, take a walnut-size piece of dough, keeping the rest of the dough covered to prevent it from drying out, and roll into a thin sausage shape. Using the tips of your fingers, gently press to flatten it. Take one of the date strings and place on top, cutting off as much as necessary from it to fit the dough. Enclose the dough around the date filling and roll it into a slightly longer sausage shape, about 6 inches/15 cm. Take one end and place it slightly overlapping the other to form a ring shape. With the end of a thin object (like a chopstick), press down to make two holes where the ends overlap to ensure they are firmly attached and won't come apart during baking.

Preheat the oven to 400°F/200°C/Gas Mark 6 and line baking sheets with parchment.

Place the cakes on the lined baking sheets and bake until a light golden brown, about 10–12 minutes. Cool for at least 15 minutes before transferring to a wire rack to cool, then transfer to an airtight container. They will keep for 2–3 weeks at room temperature or 3 months in the freezer.

DRINKS, PRESERVES, AND CONDIMENTS

Before refrigerators and supermarkets, we lived off nature and what the earth provided. If the land gave us olives, we made oil with some and pickled the rest. If the trees gave us fruit, we made jams and juices to last the whole year. If the mountains bloomed with za'atar in the spring, we collected and dried it to last until the next season. You took what you were given, enjoyed it in season, and found a way to preserve the rest until the next time it came around.

I have long felt similarly about our cooking. We make certain recipes in each season of the year, but we also seem to make different recipes in each season of our lives. One of my fears growing up and a question I always asked my mother was "when I don't live with you anymore, how can I keep eating this food?" Childhood fears are funny. They seem so big to us when we are young, but we outgrow them with age. This particular worry though, continued to nag at me even as I matured. Living abroad, there were many dishes prepared by my mother and grandmother that I was only able to enjoy once a year. Others I replicated but they did not taste the same. My worry felt even more real once I had children and realized they would likely be raised in a different country. This made me wonder: how would they understand our culture if they didn't know its food?

So I started organizing and saving these recipes in order to preserve our past, but also to build a future for my children in which they would always know the comfort of true Palestinian home cooking. And out of this, *The Palestinian Table* was born.

This concluding chapter includes many of the staple items we often made in season and stored from one year to the next, as well as drinks we enjoyed in different seasons. As you go through these recipes, I hope they help you to build a bridge to a past that Palestinians are deeply connected to and invite you into the warm, generous culture that Palestinians are proud to share with you.

<u>Left</u>
Traditional coffee pots and mills in Jerusalem's Old City.

CARDAMOM COFFEE

قهوه عربيه

Preparation time: 1 minute
Cooking time: 7–10 minutes
Serves 4–6

2–3 teaspoons sugar (optional)
6 level teaspoons finely ground Arabica
    coffee beans
¼ teaspoon finely ground cardamom

Nothing spells home to me more than the sight of my mother or aunt standing at the stove over a *breeq* of water, waiting for the right moment to stir in the coffee then lifting and stirring, lifting and stirring, until the coffee boils without overflowing—a very delicate dance. The hallmark Middle Eastern drink, coffee plays a central role in our culture and is served at every important event, gathering, and social call or meal. The way it's made, the beans used, how much sugar, and how much cardamom varies from location to location and from family to family. In essence, however, it is an unfiltered boiled coffee flavored with cardamom, sometimes sweetened, and served in very small cups called *fenjan*. Even when sweetened, the coffee retains a bitter flavor, which is why it is almost always served alongside a sweet treat.

Put the sugar, if using, and 1½ cups (12 fl oz/250 ml) water into an Arabic coffee pot (this is easily found in Middle Eastern grocery stores, but if you cannot find one, you can use a Turkish *cezve* which is easily available online). Place over medium-high heat.

When the water is very hot but not yet boiling, remove the pot from the heat, add the coffee and cardamom, and return to the stove. Reduce the heat and stir until the coffee boils. Continue to boil and stir until the froth dissipates. Some people like this froth so they remove the coffee from the heat after 1–2 boils. To ensure the coffee does not boil over, every time you see the coffee rising to the top, lift the pot up from the stove and stir until it goes back down. Repeat this process until it boils.

Remove from the heat and let stand for at least 5 minutes until the coffee grounds have settled to the bottom. Pour into small cups and serve immediately.

CINNAMON TEA

مغلي

Preparation time: 5 minutes
Cooking time: 30-60 minutes
Serves 6-8

8-10 cinnamon sticks, lightly crushed
1 tablespoon ground cinnamon
1 teaspoon anise seed (optional)
1 teaspoon ground ginger or a 2-inch/
    5-cm piece fresh ginger, sliced
    (optional)
sugar, to taste
any combination of toasted and coarsely
    chopped walnuts, almonds, and pine
    nuts, to serve

A spiced and warming tea, *maghlee* is most often made after the birth of a child and served to both the new mother and all her guests. This tradition is common in the Middle East, but if you look into its roots, you'll discover that cinnamon actually has many medical benefits. It has a variety of antioxidant and anti-inflammatory properties as well as medicinal benefits like lowering cholesterol and blood pressure. Traditionally, this drink is served to guests in teacups with plates of lightly toasted nuts. You sweeten to your liking and you add whatever nuts you fancy.

Put the spices and ginger into a pan with 6 cups (2½ pints/1.5 liters) water and bring to a boil over medium-high heat. Reduce the heat and simmer for 30-60 minutes. The longer you wait, the stronger the tea.

Remove from the heat and allow to sit for at least 15 minutes until the spices settle at the bottom. Using a strainer, pour into teacups and sweeten to taste. Serve alongside toasted and coarsely chopped nuts to be sprinkled over the tea.

Tip: Whatever nuts you use, make sure they are coarsely chopped so it is easy to drink them with the tea without the need for a spoon. This way you get the flavor of both the cinnamon and the crunchy nuts in each sip.

BEDOUIN TEA

شاي بدوي

Preparation time: 2 minutes
Cooking time: 12 minutes
Serves 4-6

4 cups (1¾ pints/1 liter) water
4-6 cardamom pods
1 cinnamon stick
3 tablespoons good-quality black
    loose-leaf tea
6 sprigs dried sage
sugar, to taste

My father's sister first introduced me to this tea. She picked it up from the Bedouin women who supplied her with fresh milk and yogurt from the goats on her farm. Bedouins are the desert dwellers of the Middle East and are famous for their hospitality. Serving coffee or tea to any visitor that crosses their path is an age-old custom. Their tea was originally made from a herb called *maramia*—a plant from the sage family. To replicate this at home, we mix black tea with sage, cardamom, and cinnamon.

Pour 4 cups (1¾ pints/1 liter) water into a medium tea kettle and place over high heat. When the water starts to simmer, add the cardamom and cinnamon and let boil for 5 minutes.

Add the tea and sage and let boil for another 1-2 minutes. Remove from the heat, and steep for 3-5 minutes. To serve, pour the tea through a strainer into cups and sweeten to taste with sugar.

MINT OR SAGE TEA

شاي بالنعناع أو الميراميه

Preparation time: 5 minutes
Cooking time: 2 minutes
Serves 4

3 tablespoons good-quality black
    loose-leaf tea
6 sprigs fresh mint or 6 sprigs dried
    sage leaves
sugar, to taste

Teta Fatima always made her tea according to the season.
In the spring and summer she livened it up with mint; in the
fall (autumn) and winter she warmed it up with sage.
To this day, I find these two teas taste best "in season". With
the mint version, it's important to add the mint after the
tea has steeped to achieve that deep amber color. The sage
version tastes best when using dried, not fresh, leaves,
which can be found in any Middle Eastern grocery stores
as they are slightly different from the fresh leaves available
from supermarkets. Both teas taste best when served
sweet. If using teabags instead of loose-leaf tea, use 1 tea
bag per serving.

Pour 4 cups (1¾ pints/1 liter) water into a medium tea kettle
and place over high heat. When the water starts to simmer,
add the tea and let boil for 1–2 minutes.

Remove from the heat, add the mint or sage leaves and let
steep for another 3–5 minutes. To serve, pour the tea
through a strainer into cups and sweeten with sugar to taste.

ROSE SYRUP LEMONADE

عصير لمون وورد

Preparation time: 3 minutes
Serves 1

few fresh mint leaves
sprinkle of sugar
2 tablespoons freshly squeezed lemon
    juice
2–3 tablespoons rose syrup, homemade
    (page 240) or store-bought
1½ cups (12 fl oz/350 ml) chilled still
    or sparkling water

In the middle of a hot day, nothing is more refreshing than
this rose lemonade with fresh mint. While it sounds intricate,
it's actually a very quick and easy drink to prepare. You
can use other flavored syrups as well, such as pomegranate,
mulberry, or lavender, but I find rose to be the perfect
partner for lemons. It's also the most traditional one we use
at home. You can use the Rose Syrup recipe (page 240),
or any good quality store-bought pure rose syrup.

Put the mint leaves into a tall tumbler glass and sprinkle
with sugar. Using a muddler or a long spoon, press down
lightly on the leaves and give a few gentle twists to release
the oils and aroma.

Pour the lemon juice over the mint and mix. Add the rose
syrup then pour in the cold water. Give a very gentle stir with
a spoon and adjust the sweetness with more syrup if you
need to.

Variation: Try using pomegranate syrup and flavor it with
a teaspoon of orange blossom water instead of the mint.

POMEGRANATE MOLASSES

دبس رمان

Preparation time: 2 minutes
Cooking time: 1-2 hours
Makes about ½ pint/300 ml

4 cups (1¾ pints/1 liter) fresh
    pomegranate juice (see Note)
¼-⅓ cup (2-2½ oz/50-65 g) sugar
    (optional)
1 tablespoon freshly squeezed lemon
    juice (optional)

If you were to talk to my mother in the late summer, she would tell you she can't bear pomegranates. The reason? My father spends every single afternoon picking pomegranates from our tree, meticulously peeling and seeding them so that not a single seed is squashed, and then juicing them to making cordial, syrup, and molasses. Our kitchen becomes a factory, my father's shirts become irreparably stained, and my mother no longer owns her kitchen. Soon after, however, she gives out much of the season's bounty in molasses and juice to all our family and friends, proudly tells them how her husband did it all, and all the weariness is forgotten. While you can buy this in stores, I highly recommend you make your own—only then can you really know what has gone into it.

Pour the pomegranate juice into a pan and place over medium heat. If you are using freshly squeezed pomegranate juice, then all you need to do is bring to a boil, reduce the heat and simmer, stirring occasionally, until you reach a light syrup consistency. If you are using a store-bought variety of pomegranate juice, add the sugar and lemon juice to the pan and cook until the sugar has dissolved, then reduce the heat and simmer as above. You want it to reduce to about a quarter of the original amount, or to coat the back of a spoon but not be too thick, as it will thicken more when it cools. This can take anywhere between 1–2 hours.

Once the desired consistency is reached, remove from the heat, allow to cool in the pan, then transfer to a glass bottle or jar. Cool completely before storing in the refrigerator.

Note: At home, we use different varieties of pomegranate for different purposes, but for molasses, we use a specific kind that is deep red in color and has a fine balance of sweet and sour. We juice it, then simply boil it down until it reduces to a thick syrup. Since I cannot always find the same variety of pomegranates abroad, and that method is extremely time-consuming, I tend to use the fresh juice of any kind I find and adjust the flavor with sugar and lemon as I reduce it. If you do not have the patience (or desire) to squeeze your own pomegranates, then I recommend using a really good-quality fresh pomegranate juice, made from 100 percent pomegranate juice, not concentrate.

ROSE SYRUP

شراب ورد

Preparation time: 15 minutes + soaking
Makes about 2 cups (16 fl oz/475 ml)

2 cups tightly packed rose petals (see
   Note)
1 teaspoon food-grade citric acid
2 cups (16 fl oz/475 ml) boiling water
2 cups (16 oz/450 g) superfine
   (caster) sugar

Arab desserts are often perfumed with rosewater, but this strong syrup recipe takes things to another level. You can make this syrup and use it as a base for lemonade (page 237), as a topping for Fragrant Milk Pudding (page 218), drizzle it over ice cream, flavor whipped cream with it, or simply use it as a cordial with sparkling water.

Check your rose petals for any insects or dirt (if they are dirty you can wash them, but preferably use clean petals that don't need washing) then put into a large pitcher (jug) and sprinkle with the citric acid. Pour the boiling water over the petals and stir well to combine. Set aside for 1–2 hours.

Place a fine colander over a large bowl and pour in the rose mixture. Using your hands squeeze as much liquid out of the rose petals as possible then discard them. Gradually add the sugar to the liquid, stirring after each addition until dissolved. Pour into sterilized glass bottles and store in the refrigerator for up to a year.

Note: The type of rose typically used is *Rosa damascena*, an incredibly delicate and fragrant rose that comes in all shades of pink and red. You will be able to tell these roses apart simply by their smell, which is extremely strong and fragrant. Ensure you always use roses that have never been sprayed with any kind of pesticide or chemical.

TRADITIONAL PICKLES

مكابيس

Preparation time: 20 minutes
Makes 1 x 3½ pint/2-liter jar

8-10 turnips
2 beets (beetroot)
8 tablespoons coarse sea salt

You'd be hard-pressed to find a Palestinian family that doesn't have some kind of pickle at home—a plate of pickles is standard fare at almost every meal. Depending on the season, we would pickle turnips, cucumbers, eggplants (aubergines), chillies, or green tomatoes. The method we use is very simple: for every cup of water (8 fl oz/250 ml), use 1 tablespoon of coarse sea salt. We do not use vinegar because that prohibits the beneficial probiotic activity, so we simply use salt and water and leave it a little longer to develop the acidic flavor. The recipe below is for pickled turnips but see the variations below for other vegetable and flavor options.

Cut the turnips in half then slice into ½ inch/1 cm semicircles and set aside. Peel and chop the beets (beetroot) into medium cubes.

In a large mixing pitcher (jug), make a brine by combining 8 cups (3½ pints/2 liters) water with the coarse sea salt. Allow to sit, stirring from time to time, until the salt is fully dissolved.

In the meantime, tightly arrange the turnips and beets in a sterilized jar with an airtight lid. If you don't have one large 3½-pint/2-liter jar, arrange the vegetables equally between two sterilized jars. Pour the brine over the vegetables until fully covered. Close the lid and allow to sit at room temperature for about 1 week. Once opened, pickles can be left at room temperature for a couple of weeks or refrigerated for several months.

Variations

Cucumbers: Pick the smallest and firmest Persian cucumbers you can find (if unavailable, use Kirby cucumbers and leave whole or quarter lengthwise) and add 2–3 unpeeled cloves garlic cloves, 1 green chilli (if you like heat), and a few grape leaves, if available, to increase the sour flavor.

Green Tomatoes: Quarter the tomatoes three-quarters of the way, so they remain intact but can be pulled apart once pickled. Add a green chilli if you like heat.

Green Poblanos or Chillies: Slice down the middle for a quarter of the way to allow brine to enter, then flavor with a few cloves garlic.

DRIED FIG AND WALNUT PRESERVE

قطين معقود

Preparation time: 15 minutes
Cooking time: 15-20 minutes
Makes about 2¼ lb/1 kg

1½ cups (11 oz/300 g) granulated sugar
1 teaspoon freshly squeezed lemon juice
1 lb 2 oz/500 g dried figs, cut into
    quarters
1 tablespoon ground aniseed
½ cup (2½ oz/65 g) coarsely chopped
    walnuts, lightly toasted
½ cup 2½ oz/65 g) unhulled sesame
    seeds, toasted

In the cold winter months, this was the dessert my Teta Asma would always make. The aniseed flavors running through the figs, along with the crunch of sesame and walnuts made for a very rich and warming treat. This preserve can be eaten slightly warm the first day and then stored for several weeks in the refrigerator and eaten as a jam on bread, or even as a topping for milk-based desserts.

Put the sugar, lemon juice, and 1½ cups (12 fl oz/350 ml) water into a large pan and place over high heat. Bring to a boil, stirring occasionally, until the sugar has dissolved. Reduce the heat, add the dried figs and aniseed, and cook, stirring from time to time for 10–15 minutes, or until most of the syrup has been absorbed. Do not wait for all the syrup to be absorbed, as the mixture will thicken once chilled.

Add the walnuts and sesame seeds, give it one final stir, and remove from the heat. Cool before serving or storing in the refrigerator. Once cooled, place in a large jar or covered container in the refrigerator where it will keep for several weeks. If you want to keep it for longer, then place in sterilized jars where it will keep for several months in the refrigerator.

ZA'ATAR

زعتر

Preparation time: 15 minutes + cooling
Makes about 9 oz/250 g

2 cups (1½ oz/45 g) dried za'atar leaves,
  firmly packed (see Note)
1½ cups (6 oz/180 g) unhulled roasted
  sesame seeds
1 tablespoon sumac
1 teaspoon salt

When I was a child, every spring my family would take trips to the mountains surrounding Jerusalem and pick za'atar leaves in the wild. We'd use some in salads and bread, then dry the rest for use throughout the year. The za'atar condiment is made from these dried leaves which are ground and mixed with sesame seeds and sumac.

Place the za'atar leaves and only one-third of the sesame seeds in a powerful food processor and grind to a fine powder. Transfer to a large mixing bowl, add the remaining sesame seeds, sumac, and salt and whisk until combined.

Transfer to an airtight container and store at room temperature where it will keep for several months.

Note: As the exact za'atar plant is difficult to find outside the Middle East, a mixture of dried oregano, marjoram, and thyme leaves is the best substitute. For the freshest and best flavor, it is preferable that you dry your own.

DUQQA

دقه

Preparation time: 15 minutes + salting
Makes about 1 lb 2 oz/450 g

1½ cups (6 oz/180 g) unhulled
sesame seeds
1 cup (5½ oz/160 g) whole wheat berries
(whole or unhulled)
2 tablespoons coriander seeds
2 tablespoons cumin seeds
2 tablespoons dill seeds
2 tablespoons sumac
2 teaspoons salt
1 teaspoon hot chilli powder (optional)

Similar to za'atar, duqqa is also a condiment eaten with olive oil and bread or used to spice other foods. It originated in Egypt but is now famously made in Gaza in a different and uniquely Palestinian way.

Dry roast the sesame seeds in a large skillet (frying pan) over medium-low heat, stirring regularly, for 7–10 minutes, or until golden brown. Set aside on a large tray to cool.

Meanwhile, place the whole wheat berries in the same pan and roast for about 15 minutes, stirring regularly, until a dark golden brown. Set aside on a separate platter to cool.

Add the coriander, cumin, and dill seeds to the same pan and roast, stirring frequently, until fragrant, about 3 minutes. Pour over the roasted wheat then make sure you leave to cool completely.

Once cooled, place one-third of the toasted sesame seeds along with the roasted wheat, spices, sumac, salt, and chilli powder, if using, into a spice grinder and grind to a powder. Pour into a large bowl, add the remaining sesame seeds, and mix well with a spoon until combined. This will keep in an airtight container at room temperature for several months.

THE PALESTINIAN PANTRY

المونة

The Palestinian pantry is very rich including everything from beans, pulses, olives, oil, jams, and spices to condiments, preserved vegetables, dried herbs, pickles, and sauces. It can healthily sustain a family for weeks, if not months, without a single external item. Needless to say, it is quite vast, so the list below is not comprehensive. Rather, it is a description of the items that may be less common, or whose culinary use may be less familiar to a non-native.

Left
Wooden trays used to carry bread, bagels or pastries across Jerusalem's Old City.

ALL SPICE / PIMENTO

This is the dominant spice used in Palestinian cuisine. It is often combined with other spices to lend distinct flavors to dishes, but by and large, it is the central spice used in our cooking.

ANISEED

The small seeds of a flowering plant, this spice has a very distinct fennel and licorice-like flavor. In Palestinian food, it is used mostly in desserts or as a tea to soothe a stomach upset.

BULGUR WHEAT

The staple Palestinian grain, this is essentially cracked dried wheat. It comes in varying coarseness from very coarse (used for salads and *mjadara*) to medium (used for *tabuleh* or pilafs) to extremely fine (used mostly for *kubbeh*). It also comes in whole grain / dark variety although there is hardly any difference in flavor to the standard white variety.

CARDAMOM

Arabic coffee is notably flavored with this spice, but is also used in conjunction with pimento and several other spices to flavor many Palestinian savoury dishes.

CUMIN

A spice with very earthy, smoky flavors, it is used mostly in Palestinian dishes that contain onions as it is believed to counteract their gas-inducing properties.

DUQQA

A condiment of Egyptian origin, it is now made in Gaza in a uniquely Palestinian way and consists of ground toasted wheat kernels combined with ground coriander, cumin, and dill seeds and some sumac, chilli, salt, and toasted sesame seeds. It used in much the same way as za'atar.

FREEKEH

Another staple grain, freekeh is made of wheat stalks harvested while green, then roasted in fields over open fire to lend them a smoky flavor. The ensuing grains are then shucked and cracked resulting in freekeh or "cracked wheat". It's used in much the same way as rice, although nutritionally superior, and is readily available in supermarkets.

GRAPE LEAVES	The leaves of grapes harvested in Palestine are quite different from the variety found in jars. They tend to be softer and more flavorful and are often used fresh off the vine. To preserve them for out of season cooking, we either freeze them or vacuum pack them. Outside the Middle East, grape leaves are available year round in jars with brine. To use, always soak in hot water for 15 minutes to remove the brine flavor.
JIBNEH BAIDA	Literally meaning "white cheese", this is the Levantine equivalent of halloumi cheese. It is a hard white cheese with a salty taste, oftentimes with a slight mastic flavor, and is usually boiled before eating.
KNAFEH DOUGH	This comes in both a fine and coarse variety. The basis of the fine one (*na'ameh*) is semolina while the coarse one (*khishneh*) is made from a watery dough shaped into long thin noodle threads. Outside the Middle East, the coarse one, called shredded phyllo (filo) or *kataifi* dough, is much easier to come across and the variety used in these recipes.
MAFTOOL	Dubbed "Palestinian couscous," *maftool* is essentially whole-wheat flour rolled around grains of bulgur to produce nutty tasting caviar-like beads of pasta. Although versatile, it is most commonly cooked by steaming and enjoyed alongside a chickpea stew. Traditionally rolled at home and used fresh, dried *maftool* is now readily available in many grocery stores.
MASTIC	This is the resin obtained from the Pistacia tree and is used to flavor certain dishes in the Middle East, especially desserts. The teardrop-like resins (0.5–2cm) are often crushed with sugar or salt before using. When cooking meats, it is common to use one or two pieces to prevent any unpleasant meaty stench from arising.
MLUKHIYEH	An extremely nutritious green leaf rich in iron, vitamins, and fiber, *mlukhiyeh* is very common across the Middle East where its leaves are cooked into a soup or stew. The leaves, which impart a glutinous consistency when cooked, can be found fresh in the summer and dried or frozen year-round in any Middle Eastern grocery store.
NIGELLA SEEDS	Native to the Levant, nigella seeds look like black sesame seeds but taste completely different. These pungent seeds are often used to flavor things like cheese, dough, and desserts. At one point believed to be a panacea to all ailments, their Arabic name is *habbat-al-baraka* or seed of grace.

ORANGE BLOSSOM WATER	Produced by distilling the flowers of the bitter orange, orange blossom water originated in the Middle East where it is still used to lend a subtly sweet aroma to syrups and pastries. A few drops are often used with boiling water to soothe an upset stomach.
PINE NUTS	The edible seeds of the pine tree, these little gems are widely used across the Middle East to garnish and add texture to dishes, both savoury and sweet. European varieties are considered superior to Asian ones, both in shape and flavor, but they are substantially more expensive. Depending on availability, both kinds are used interchangeably in our cuisine.
POMEGRANATE MOLASSES	The best pomegranate molasses is made by reducing the juice of good quality pomegranates (juicy pulp with sharp yet sweet flavor) to a thick syrup consistency. It is not as common in the Palestinian kitchen as it is in its Lebanese, Syrian, and Iranian counterparts, but it is still used to impart a deeper flavor to some Palestinian dishes.
ROSEWATER	Produced by distilling the leaves of fragrant roses, rosewater is used in much the same way as orange blossom water to flavor syrups and desserts. When buying, ensure you choose a variety that is the real distilled water of roses and not rose flavored water.
SUMAC	Made by grinding the dried berries of a shrub native to the Middle East, sumac is a dark red to purple spice used to impart a sour flavor to dishes. When purchasing, ensure you buy from a trusted brand and read the ingredients list because oftentimes it includes salt, flavorings, and colorings, which will greatly detract from the overall quality of the dish.
TAHINI	A paste made from grinding toasted sesame seeds, tahini is used widely in Palestinian cuisine for both salads and cooked foods. Is is also the primary component of hummus and *halaweh* (halva) and can even be eaten on its own as a sandwich spread. In cooking, it is often diluted slightly with yogurt and lemon to lighten its earthy and dense flavor. The flavor of any dish containing tahini will come down to the quality of the tahini, so buy the best you can find.
ZA'ATAR	This can refer to the plant or to the condiment made from its leaves. Za'atar is the Arabic name given to a plant that grows in the Levant and closely resembles oregano or wild thyme. Even across the Levant, the species of za'atar vary from one country to the next. The condiment is made by crushing the dried leaves of the plant and mixing them with sumac, salt and toasted sesame seeds.

ACKNOWLEDGEMENTS

Though the words in this book are mine, the recipes and stories within belong to all Palestinians across the globe, and I am grateful to all those who helped me capture the essence of Palestinian family, food, and culture in such a beautiful way. I am also grateful to you, dear readers, for your interest in my country and its food. May the recipes within keep you satisfied and the stories throughout give you hope.

Above all, I want to thank my parents without whom these pages would not be in your hands. Mama, you are the unsung hero of this book. For painstakingly testing every recipe with me, for overseeing the photoshoot, and for standing by my side, I thank you with all my heart. But for teaching me how to cook, how to live and love life, for inspiring and pushing me, and for believing in me when I doubted myself, I can never thank you enough. Baba, not only did you teach me the value of good ingredients and the importance of precision in all I do, but you gave me the wings to *see* the world and do all I have done, without which I would not have been able share our culture with others. You have both given me such a strong foundation and appreciation of family, which makes being away from you the hardest thing I deal with every day, but through my cooking, I carry you and our family in my heart wherever I am in the world.

Najib, I'm back in the kitchen! Thank you for believing in this dream and putting up with all my recipe testing, and for being the best brother and *khalo* in the world.

Teta Fatima, Teta Asma (bless her soul), and Teta Salma (bless her soul), you were the main inspiration for this book. You made sure your families were the best fed regardless of the circumstances and I hope I have done our families, our food, and our country justice with this book.

A special thank you to the people in my life whose voices are heard throughout this book and who taught me about good food and its importance to our culture. Auntie Juju, Amto Lamees, Amo Shawqi (bless his soul), Auntie Nadia, Maha and Iman, Khalto Alice, and Khalo Yousef: this book is as much yours as it is mine.

A very big thank you to my friends and family: Vickie Alvo, Hannah Venables, Sudarshan Venu, Khalto Noha and Amo Dawood, Vinita Chhay, Katie and Sruthi, Denise Fernandes, Katya and Ilya, Ratna and Zack, Mai and Jon, Sudeep and Shivani, Lucy Jay Kennedy, and Dianne Jacobs. Your encouragement, support, and friendship, and in many cases your willingness to let me overfeed you, are appreciated beyond words.

Writing may be a solitary endeavor, but publishing a book is a mass effort and I am grateful to the people who tirelessly worked to bring this book to life. Jon Elek, how did I get so lucky? Thank you for taking me on and supporting this idea against the odds. Ellie Smith, I can't possibly express my gratitude in one sentence: thank you for everything. Eve O'Sullivan, you are the most amazing editor and I have loved every minute of working with you. Emilia Terragni, without you, this book would not be here—so thank you for seeing this idea for what it could be. Dan Perez, for doing such a marvelous photo shoot in spite of the intense timing and long hours and for seeing the book through my eyes, I can't thank you enough.

Lastly but most importantly, my husband Aboud whose steadfast commitment to our family and culture has made this book possible. Thank you for sharing my dream, for pushing me to write this book every time I put it down, and for being my fiercest critic and my best friend. Yasmeen and Hala, my greatest loves, thank you for showing me what really matters in life and giving me the inspiration to tie our past to your future. I pray that you find your wings, but never forget your roots. To that end, this book is for you so you can carry our heritage, along with a piece of my heart and our home, wherever you go in the world.

INDEX

Exercise a high level of caution when following recipes involving any potential hazardous activity, including the use of high temperatures, open flames and when deep-frying. In particular, when deep-frying, add food carefully to avoid splashing, wear long sleeves and never leave the pan unattended.

Cooking times are for guidance only, as individual ovens vary. If using a fan (convection) oven, follow the manufacturer's instructions concerning oven temperatures.

Some recipes include raw or very lightly cooked eggs, meat, or fish and fermented products. These should be avoided by the elderly, infants, pregnant women, convalescents and anyone with an impaired immune system. Exercise caution when making fermented products, ensuring all equipment is spotlessly clean, and seek expert advice if in any doubt.

When no quantity is specified, for example of oils, salts, and herbs used for finishing dishes or for deep-frying, quantities are discretionary and flexible.

All herbs, shoots, flowers and leaves should be picked fresh from a clean source. Exercise caution when foraging for ingredients; any foraged ingredients should only be eaten if an expert has deemed them safe to eat.

The publisher would like to thank Hilary Bird, Kate Calder and Clare Sayer for their contributions to the book.

Phaidon Press Limited
Regent's Wharf
All Saints Street
London N1 9PA

Phaidon Press Inc.
65 Bleecker Street
New York, NY 10012

phaidon.com

First published 2017
© 2017 Phaidon Press Limited

ISBN 978 0 7148 7496 8

A CIP catalogue record for this book is available from the British Library and the Library of Congress.

Commissioning Editor: Ellie Smith
Senior Project Editor: Eve O'Sullivan
Production Controller: Matt Harvey

Designed by Hans Stofregen
Photographs by Dan Perez

Printed in China